THE VIEW FROM THE CREEK

THE VIEW FROM THE CREEK

NOTES FROM LAKE SUPERIOR'S OJIBWE COUNTRY

Howard Paap

NORTH STAR PRESS OF ST. CLOUD, INC.
Saint Cloud, Minnesota

Drawings: Robert Holton

Printed in the United States of America

Published by
North Star Press of St. Cloud, Inc.
St. Cloud, Minnesota

www.northstarpress.com

For a man who figured it out long ago.

My big brother –

Marshall Victor Paap

Other Books Published by the Author

Raspberry River

TABLE OF CONTENTS

PART IV

PART V

FOREWORD

For the past fifty years I have been spending time beside Lake Superior in far northern Wisconsin. This collection of short essays says something about my experience. At first visits were sporadic, but in time they became more regular and longer in duration. Now, for nearly a decade, I have been residing here full-time, rarely feeling the urge to leave even for short periods. I have found my home and here is where I choose to stay.

These short pieces speak to my attachment to this place, and the effect it has on me. They hold a tightly woven thread of truth that says my first awareness is of the land, and hopefully, they also show my determination to do well by it. I have no desires to change this place, to alter, or improve. It is enough just as it is. I simply hope to be allowed to partake of its wonder for a bit longer, and to write about the experience. My joy is in living on this land in this place, and to ponder that existence through writing. It is that simple. Hopefully, if I stay at it, in time I might finally get it right.

Most of my days are spent in the communities of Red Cliff and nearby Bayfield, Wisconsin. These essays offer commentary on experiences I have had in these locations, and all are influenced by my years of study of anthropology. The anthropological perspective has become part of my life. However, a longer and more important influence stems from the Ojibwe people of the community of Red Cliff. They continue to teach me how to understand this place.

All of these pieces were published in three northern Wisconsin newspapers: The Red Cliff News, The Lake Superior Sounder, and Ashland's The Daily Press. To editors and publishers, Bob Bear, Jared Glovsky, and Claire Duquette, I give my thanks for publishing them, and for their permission to re-republish them here.

It was Bob Bear who first encouraged me to contribute pieces to The Red Cliff News, and when agreeing to do so I used the name, Ben Thinken, as my nom de plume. Recognizing that many of the pieces were written at our family cabin beside a Red Cliff creek, I entitled my column The View from the Creek.

Later when writing for Jared and Norman Glovsky, Norm asked why I used a false name. By then I did not have a good answer so I dropped the pen name Ben Thinken. Whatever name is used, an author must face up to what he or she writes, so throughout those early years of hiding behind a pen name, and for all of the subsequent years, I must bear responsibility for these writings. Therefore, any errors, or other improprieties held in these pages are mine, and mine alone.

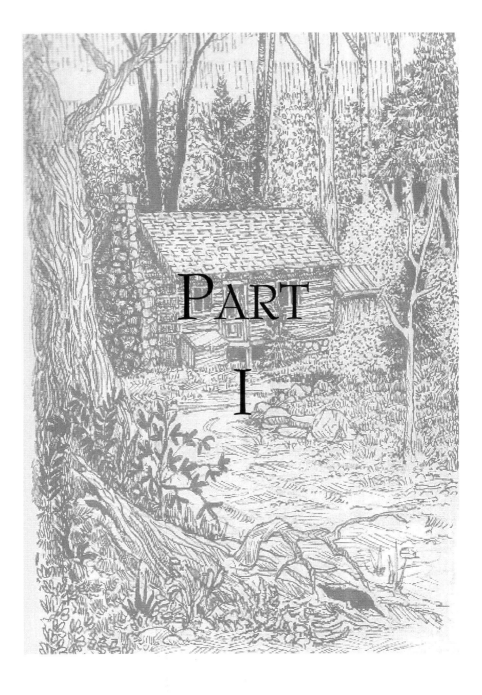

PART

I

PREFACE TO PART I

THE PIECES IN THIS INTRODUCTORY SECTION focus on the usual array of events and subjects found in the Red Cliff and Bayfield region throughout a typical year. For the past several decades Bayfield has become a tourist destination, and the buzz of summertime activity this causes is an overlay to the recurring deeper life rhythms of those who reside here all year long. We cannot escape the seasonal increase in the tempo of our lives brought by the tourist industry. This includes Red Cliff with its four seasons of recreational attractions. And of course one must acknowledge the activity brought by the reservation's casino.

Tourism has become a major part of life for Lake Superior country and that means from late June to early October visitors will be on our streets, in our coffee shops, and our communities' churches, but we must also recognize that the place we knew before the coming of the tourist industry is still here. These are the same waters, beaches, and forests that this area's residents of long ago knew even though there have been important changes. The tall white pines and ancient hardwoods have mostly given way to the woodsman's ax and saw, and today signs of humankind can be seen in almost every corner of the woods. Yet, the land, water, sky, and the non-human life forms of old remain. This is still Lake Superior country, and likely, in today's world things like the plants, animals, winds, sunrises, and winter's deep indifference are very similar to what they must have been hundreds, and possibly even thousands of years ago.

These essays attempt to reach out to that old reality that was this place in the distant past, to note important changes, and to speak to what life is like for those of us who choose to reside here year around. They tell of the seasonal cycle of our existence, and even though the fingers of the outside world occasionally reach into our days, we take the drumbeat of our lives from the strength of this place—natural features like the water, trees, cold winters and glorious springs, summers, and falls. This old and wonderful place is our home.

WALKING IN THE
RAIN IN APPLE TIME
October 1, 2002

Early this morning a friend from Michigan joined me on my daily walk, and it was an especially enjoyable outing for a number of reasons. Eddie has almost as many miles on his tires as I do, and we seem to have plenty to talk about, besides, it was raining, and the colored leaves were like bright dabs of paint, brushed onto life's canvas in exactly the right places. Just as importantly, my friend and I had not walked together for some time. On top of this, we took a five-mile jaunt out through Orchard Country—not my usual much shorter walk in town—so we had ample time to get into a good discussion. Then, upon reaching the top of our long ascent out of town we soon came upon fruit-laden apple trees and one of us remarked about the importance of next weekend. It is Apple Fest time, and it sets me to thinking.

For many folks in the Red Cliff and Bayfield area, Apple Fest Weekend is the culmination of the busy summer season. It is the last hurrah—the final big push to fill the cash register one more time before the shutdown with the onset of cold weather. For Jerry and Carol up at the ski hill, however, it signals the start of preparations for their busy season, but for many it is an ending, not a beginning. This morning as we walked past the orchards we saw empty apple crates piled in strategic places, waiting for pickers to fill them on Monday. After moving up Catholic Hill and the long ascending stretch that is Myers-Olson Road, we were passed by a few motor vehicles of employees driving out to their workstations at the orchard sheds, barns, and shops. Eddie and I agreed it is good to be retired, and off the clock. Now we watch other people go to work.

The rain was welcome, and with jackets, caps, and umbrellas, we enjoyed being out in it. It brought fading memories of years past, when as children, we sometimes ran out into a shower and excitedly squealed as we became drenched with warm summer rain. Unfortunately this morning we did not have our dogs with us. Rosie and Amigo are friends, would have loved to romp in the rain, but today the mutts were occupied with other things. They

4

have been our regular and welcome companions in the past when taking these periodic long walks, and today we missed them.

At Erickson's Orchards we stepped off the roadway to study the large new outdoor mural Bob Holton finished painting last week. It hangs affixed to the metal storage building in the farm's yard. This painting is one of Bob's crowning achievements and both Jim and Muriel Erickson are happy to have it. It is a great addition to their business, and another feather in the hat of the talented artist. How many of Bob's painting's adorn our area? Soon some-one might consider offering a summer tour for visitors, taking them from one of these colorful sites to another. As well as being a history lesson, it just could be a lucrative operation.

Inside the Country Store at Erickson's, we found Marian, Judy, Muriel, Jim and the others hard at work. They had no time for chatting and after a little nip of fresh cider we were on our way. Our usual friendly visits at Erickson's would have to wait for another morning. Today those folks had things to do and taking time to visit with two old fellows out on their walk was low on their list.

When we reached the end of Betzhold Road where it intersects with County I at the top of Cemetery Hill, we were at the point in the walk where we begin our descent back down into Bayfield. It is a welcome marker on that journey, one I always enjoy coming upon since there is a degree of pleas-ant poignancy when descending that hill. As we move along, the panorama of the scattered gravestones that cover that cemetery, like gray mushrooms after a spring rain, comes into view. I have been spending enough time beside our big lake that increasingly, more and more of the names on these stones are becoming familiar ones. Some of them are of friends.

This morning heavy fog still lingered among the stones when we passed through that burial ground, and together with the colored leaves, and the images of the rows of apple trees with their red, ripe fruit waiting for picking, we were silently told of the end of things. It is fall. We have had our busy summer and now must think of what is just ahead. Soon the apples will all be picked and sent on their way, and like them, the wonderful colors of those leaves will depart as well, and we will be faced with the starkness of what is bound to come.

Walking up Catholic Hill with a good friend, circling through Bayfield's Orchard Country, enjoying some of Jim Erickson's fresh-pressed cider with him, and coming down Cemetery Hill—how much better can a Sunday morning walk be? And all this on a rainy day in autumn. This morning I con-cluded it doesn't get much better than this.

BLUEBERRY ROAD

November 5, 2005

Yesterday I drove down Blueberry Road in Red Cliff and I was set to thinking. A road named Blueberry? It occurred to me that I really liked that name. Blueberry Road. Yes, I liked it from the beginning when I noticed it for the first time several years ago. Why not?

Maybe I was in one of those moods I slip into now and then, when I see nothing but good in the world. Today it might do all of us well to slip into such a mood more often. Wild blueberries are part of Red Cliff's past. Lake Superior's Ojibwe folks doubtless have been harvesting them for hundreds of years. I have been part of blueberry picking parties, and cherish their memories. All this came to mind yesterday as I moved along that dirt road. Yes, there is something pleasant about a road named Blueberry.

Most older Rez families, I suspect, have memories of picking Blues. There are stories of how someone would tell you, "Why, when you'd lift the branches there they were, hanging in big clumps. It was like a blue carpet."

I'm talking about wild blueberries, not the domesticated kind some local fruit growers now have. There is no comparison between the two. Sprinkling a few frozen wild blues onto a bowl of oatmeal in the deep of January can bring back fond memories. Wild blueberries are about more than the fruit itself.

I want to believe that the folks at Red Cliff who, several years ago, renamed some Rez roads were not trying to be "cute" like suburban land developers sometimes are. I hope those tribal leaders were, indeed, paying homage to the wild blueberry.

Many years ago I began noticing how land developers try to do what writers of good fiction do. They try to get us to suspend our disbelief. After leveling an old farmstead, and building dozens of townhouses to replace the orchards and fields that used to stand there, they sometimes give the new streets names like Mulberry Lane, Honeysuckle Drive, or Apple Creek Way. We are supposed to think about the quiet joy of mulberries, sweet honeysuckle, and picturesque creeks meandering through Grandma's apple orchard. We are asked to pretend we are in a pastoral setting instead of a heavy populated suburb with SUVs and minivans parked on antiseptic cement driveways.

You surely have noticed this. We moderns bulldoze nature out of the way then try to rebuild it after our own intentions. I guess we have been doing that ever since *Homo erectus* modified that first cave in the Orient and moved in a million or so years ago. It's done all the time with golf courses. Today, after we domesticate a countryside we try to bring back its pristine character, sometimes by giving it names that no longer ring true. The Mulberry Lanes and Apple Creek Ways of today's world are like cheap imitations made in China. Perhaps they exist because we want both worlds—the domesticated and the wild.

But, back to blueberries. For those of us who are not Ojibwe, it might be useful to spend a few moments and contemplate the name Blueberry Road. Such a simple name! So quiet and unobtrusive. Like a good friend, it does not shout for attention. It does not point at its cleverness. Wild blueberries usually exist out of harm's way, quietly by themselves, in a wooded or brushy place—a place isolated from humans. Perhaps it is as if they want to get away from us, or better yet, cause us to seek them out so we are forced to remember how nice it used to be before we changed so much of their world.

We search them out when the time is right and they allow us to lift their small branches and strip away their fruit. To do so we might have to actually get down to where they live, down on the earth itself. I find that I can do better when picking blues if I kneel next to the plant as if before a small altar. The photos from the blueberry-picking outing I was on this past summer show members of our party in such poses. We were kneeling in the forest, paying homage to something sacred.

In the Ojibwe language they go by the name *miinan*. (Pronounced "meenan" in English.) Said slowly and quietly, the old word rolls easily off the tongue, but sometimes when a certain young granddaughter of mine comes for a visit, it is said loudly, even demandingly, as this beautiful little person pads into the kitchen for a snack. "Miinan, minnan," she repeats, pointing up to the refrigerator's freezer where she knows a few plastic bags of frozen wild blueberries rest. These are portioned out as something very special. That little girl knows their worth. An honored pleasure of mine is to watch her seated at the dining table, newly bathed and dressed in clean pajamas at bedtime, quietly and pensively picking a frozen wild blueberry from a small serving of others in a white ceramic bowl, and slowly placing it into her mouth. Then, after letting it thaw a bit, she chews it just a little before swallowing. An Ojibwe child eating wild blueberries is a scene from long ago. It has never left these northern woods.

I hope you too, have a Blueberry Road in your life.

CHRISTMAS BOUTIQUES

December 9, 2007

It is a sunny and almost warm day on this hillside and signs of Christmas are all around. This is Saturday and our shops are open and bedecked with seasonal trimmings and many homes in Red Cliff and Bayfield are the same. In Bayfield the streets of our few downtown blocks are lined with automobiles and small trucks of one sort or another. People move around, some carrying plastic bags holding their new-bought treasures. This morning I see all this activity and it sets me to thinking.

This is the Christmas season and folks want to be with each other, to smile and say pleasant things. It is time to enjoy one another, so we get out of our caves and head downtown to see what is happening. Some of us go shopping. It's the American way.

Today two Christmas craft shows, or boutiques, were being held downtown. The Pavilion and the Bayfield Inn, right at the water's edge, were literally packed with vendors filling every open space. Nice gatherings, both were busy as folks streamed past the colorful tables of many wares offered for our perusal. Some were obviously handmade in the region, and some were just as clearly manufactured in distant places like New Jersey or the Republic of China. This morning all this domestic and imported Christmas finery mixed together to create a holiday air—a feeling of joy and goodness.

Boutique, the French word, has become part of our vocabulary but I recall when it was new and perhaps exotic. Forty or fifty years ago it was one of those uppity terms my family made fun of when we were tightly bound by our social class and the small community we resided in. Things really have changed since those times.

This morning I thought of how we surely are a society with a market exchange system. We buy and sell things, especially those most essential, like food, clothing, shelter, and health care, and many of us are still unconcerned with questions about where the things we buy are made. Give me the money and you get the goods. Money, that all-purpose medium of exchange, facilitates the movement of product. This morning money was moving from hand to hand as folks were buying and selling.

Perhaps only because I have been doing some reading on the history of our region lately was I moved to contemplate how life was lived here in Chequamegon Country before the coming of money. The reader does not have to look too hard to find writings that tell of those money-less days. Some of these accounts, from as late as the 1840s, speak to how the resident Ojibwe people were only then learning about money. Up until that time they exchanged through barter, sharing and gift giving. These three ancient means of economic exchange still go on for the Ojibwe, but it is noteworthy to consider how money has changed their world.

Yesterday at our local boutiques I was visited by a Dickensian image of British shopkeepers at this time of year. And I thought of what has been called "the shopkeeper's mentality" in which the margin of profit on a single item might be a mere few cents, but how in the long run can total into the hundreds or more. At the end of the day, the shopkeeper still counts her pennies. Each one is important.

And I thought of how when I was a kid it was deemed lucky to find a penny on the street or sidewalk. Such finds were few and perhaps because of their infrequency, they were readily remarked upon. Now, over these past few years, it is almost customary to find pennies as if they were tossed away. This past season when working in a Bayfield shop I was struck how twice, when handing change back to a customer, I was told, "Keep the coins. I don't want them in my pocket." In both cases the change amounted to over seventy-five cents, not a mere pittance to me. Are we so affluent that change is an encumbrance, and were my two customers signaling me that they were so wealthy that they no longer bothered with coins? Or, have we become so accustomed to handling plastic credit cards that real money is an anomaly—a nuisance? Are those TV commercials that try to make this point correct? Is cash passé?

This time of year, of course, is a warm and emotionally important season for us and finally, not because of money or plastic cards, and I do not mean to detract from that important fact. The Winter Solstice and Christmas bespeak of fellowship and a genuine coming together that is welcomed by most. It might be agreed that in December we humans take on a certain quiet glow, and that we seem to be quick to greet each other with warm smiles. Christmas boutiques can be filled with wonder, whether their items are locally made or in New Jersey. Yet what is more wonderful that a full cash box? A smiling shopkeeper can be a happy shopkeeper and a customer's willingness to part with their hard-earned cash is something to smile about. Money flows between outstretched hands this time of year. It's part of the season.

CABIN THERAPY

August 25, 2007

Our summer is quickly moving along and very soon it will make its colorful exit. I should not be wishing that the season hurry on its way since each day is a treasure and we old folks may not have many of them left, so we should do our darnedest to enjoy every one. But for some reason here in Red Cliff and Bayfield our summer has been inordinately busy, some days even bordering on what you might call hectic. I know I should not wish that summer would end, but lately its fast and full days set me to thinking.

Is it time to stuff a change of underwear and socks along with a little food into my old faded Duluth Pack and head out to the cabin? Nothing is noisy and hectic out there. The creek is so low that inquisitive kayakers cannot paddle in from the lake to explore, and no phones ring, no TV news readers show me the latest car bombing in Baghdad, and no letters to the editor or op-ed pieces get in my face. Besides, now that our long weather pattern of hot days has left, and cooler air is with us, a few days in the woods sounds pretty good. Most importantly, lately I have noticed that telling look in my bride's eye that says, "Dad, you haven't been to the cabin for a while." She must be noticing a hint of edginess in me.

That's what the Dog Days of August can cause: a quiet edginess. It's not that I am upset with anyone or anything, no, it's just that our summer has been too dry, too warm and lately it feels like too long. I am ready for fall.

Yesterday at the "doin's" under the big tent by the casino at Red Cliff I visited with my sister-in-law Patt for a few minutes and she, too, expressed dismay at how busy we all have been this summer. She lamented that the family hardly has had any get-togethers like we usually do, and I quickly agreed. She said she was actually looking forward to fall when we all could slow down a bit. I knew exactly what she was saying.

Ever since sometime after Memorial Day the downtown coffee shop that I frequent has been busy with customers. It is great to see those good people, and from time to time I enjoy the opportunity to converse a bit with some of them, but as nice as they are, I still miss the relative slower pace of winter in that place. Maybe I am only turf-tending, but so what? Long ago the writer, Robert Ardrey, told us we modern humans still carry a gene for what he called "the territorial imperative." Maybe I have come to see that coffee shop as my territory, and if that sort of urging is caused by my genes, there is little I can do about it.

I have not asked any other year-around residents if they feel like I do this time of year but I suspect some of them do. Surely those who have been putting regular shifts in at the local shops, B&B's, bars and eateries must be thinking of Labor Day and the slower pace it will bring. They cannot let their guard up yet because the real slow down does not come until after Apple Fest, but they must be looking forward to the lull that the month of September brings.

All season long I watched Bev and Dan run their candy, bakery and ice cream shop and they surely must be looking for a little down time. Those folks have been working hard all summer long. And there are others. You make it in summer or you don't last.

For the last few months it has been downright hard to find a parking space in our few downtown blocks. That's the way it has to be, given how a tourist destination works. Let our visitors have those spots. When I can, I walk downtown and leave the car in the garage. That long walk back up Manypenny Hill can be tough sometimes, especially with a sack of groceries, but it is good exercise. Still, I am looking forward to the time when there are plenty of parking spaces again. Enough already.

Yes, this week the cabin is on my mind. Today I can smell the sweet smoke from the wood fire and I can feel the heat from that little barrel stove. And the welcome soft glow of the oil lamps when I sit in my rocker and read or write is calling. Come on out, it says. Come and relax for a few days. Get things back in focus. Life does not need to be fast and filled with folks every day.

Sometimes when going downtown for the mail I sit on one of our sidewalk benches and just study our visitors. They look like the rest of us, but I imagine the busy towns and cities from whence they came. These folks are on vacation and have chosen to come here. They could have gone lots of other places, but they came here. I appreciate that, and wish them well, but, hey, it's late August and I'm a bit tired. It's time for fall.

13

CELEBRATION

November 2, 2007

W<small>E HAVE JUST GONE THROUGH</small> H<small>ALLOWEEN</small> and now might be thinking of our next celebration—Thanksgiving. Sometimes I think we live our lives moving from one celebration to another with hardly time for an idle thought between. I don't know, but it seems like we Americans spend more time, money and effort on celebrations than ever before. It surely sets me to thinking.

Earlier this week my bride and I passed a Red Cliff house with the most orange lights than I have ever seen on one building. They were strung along the eves, around the windows and doors and high on the gable end facing the street. Up near the peak they spelled out "Happy Halloween." It was neatly done and there was no doubt that whoever hung them did so with a determined skill. It was an orange house, and quite interesting.

Folks in these parts celebrate Halloween much more seriously than I ever did, but I think that could be said about the rest of our holidays, too. Nowadays it seems strings of colored lights and over-sized inflated plastic figures are made for every holiday imaginable. And some of us buy those things. Maybe that is the answer: if you make it they will buy it. And these customs can catch on. Lately, strings of electric lights and large plastic figures are popping up in more and more yards here in our Northland. Something's going on. Something has changed.

But, it is not just a matter of lights and inflatable yard figures. Holidays can call for dinners, luncheons, teas, boutiques, balls, and more. All these events call for celebration, so we are confronted with that transitive verb again.

What does celebrate mean? My dictionaries all say about the same thing: to celebrate is to honor or observe something publicly. In other words, to do it in a manner so others can see us. At such times we abstain from what we usually do—we leave our workplace and take a holiday.

Celebrations are social in the sense that when we decorate our houses and yards with lights and inflated figures, or when we put on our "good" clothes and join others at a tea or dinner, we are saying something to those around us, but sometimes I wonder if what we are saying is lost in the glitz and noise of our overstated expressions.

If I am right when suggesting we as a country have witnessed an increase in our propensity to celebrate than we must ask what has caused this? If anything, humans are rational and their behavior is typically purposeful, so there must be a reason for this change. We are not a nation of fools that carry out a perpetual party-time. No nation is. But rationality is always a cultural thing. That is, it is meaningful from a specific perspective: from a particular point of view with its own understandings and assumptions.

I have had friends declare to me that if anything, they were rational. It was clear that they took pride in this, but what I also understood them saying was that they were admitting to their being bound by their cultural assumptions. Reasoning is always done within a cultural context. Persons from different cultures can reason differently.

Well, this is getting a bit heavy and we had better get back to Halloween.

If, as I suspect, we are celebrating more it could mean we have more to celebrate. How could that be? Do we have more to celebrate than our forebears did? Or, might it just be that we have a greater need to celebrate than they did? Perhaps we have become so numbed by the impersonal and mundane nature of our work routines that we jump at the chance to break away and publicly express our hope for something beyond. In holiday celebrations we leave our social shackles behind as we rush to a place without bounds. That, I think, is what celebrations are finally about.

They are a reaching out as we attempt to escape the boundaries of our conventional space. They are times to retreat to a fantasy-like world, as at Halloween where people freely dispense candy to all comers, a world where we can hide our real identity behind costumes and masks as we try to break through to that wonderful place with a different set of rules.

Celebrations often have elements that involve all our senses. If they are really complex such events can be ceremonies where we are physically and mentally engaged. At these times we can lose ourselves. Some such events can include reversal rites in which individuals step out of their usual identity to become someone almost completely different. That is escape.

We need holidays with their celebratory character. And, to go even further, I like to imagine that life itself is a holiday during which we celebrate our existence. (I am using the terms, "holiday" and "celebrate," in a loaded manner here.) I can think of a few people whose lives are like that—always filled with an unabashed joy with just being here. Most of them are young-sters, and last week some of them came to my door with outstretched hands. I filled those little hands with candy.

Drawing 101

October 28, 2006

LAST WINTER I ENROLLED IN A CLASS ON DRAWING. Yes, drawing. You know, the simple matter of picking up a pencil and making lines on a sheet of paper. It is something most, and probably all of us have done since we were kids. Recently I completed a series of three such classes and this entire experience set me to thinking.

These were courses offered through our local vocational school and taught by an accomplished and well-schooled artist. Joan Porter is a professional painter residing here in Bayfield who maintains a studio and gallery on the old Lampaa Farm out on Myers-Olson Road just north of town. For the past few years she has been doing abstract pieces in oil, but throughout her career she has painted in many other styles and media. We are fortunate to have this high caliber artist in our midst. Ms. Porter claims that drawing is where painting begins.

The dozen or so of us who gathered together for that first class came with a wide variety of artistic experience. Like me, some of us struggled to recall our first attempts at drawing, but others had taken a good number of drawing classes in a variety of places. My memory did not bring images of any such classes I have ever taken. I had none in either high school or college, and as for grade school, while surely I did some drawing in those distant years, I do not remember being schooled in it.

Day care, preschool, and kindergarten were all unknowns to me. Instead, I began my schooling at the age of six, in 1942 in a one-room school in southern Wisconsin. In fact, I was the only person in first grade and I recall that an eighth-grade girl was often assigned to oversee my learning while our teacher was busy with the other grades. I remember drawing my favorite World War II fighter plane—the P-38 that Major Bong made famous—and I recall how occasionally one of those drawings would be tacked up on our single bulletin board.

Our one and only teacher had to teach all eight grades, covering all subjects. She excelled at this heavy load, but I cannot recall her ever teaching us how to draw. So, I told Ms. Porter that she was my first drawing teacher, ever.

Today I am struck by the fact that during my four years at Mattoon High School in northeastern Wisconsin, we did not have art classes. Could that be right? There were no foreign-language classes either, but we did have reading, writing and arithmetic—and basketball and baseball, but only for the boys. The girls took home economics, and of course, they could try out for cheerleading. Art classes must have been deemed unnecessary by the school boards that determined how the few dollars in our annual budgets were spent.

So when I came to her first drawing class, Ms. Porter had a good-sized task set before her. Luckily for me, she was a warm and friendly person and eager to teach. But a teacher can do only so much. At that first class meeting it did not take long before I was confronted with a huge blank sheet of paper. A blank sheet of paper is like a blank computer screen. Both sit there, waiting for you to do your thing. It can be intimidating.

But, on that first day I eventually put pencil to paper. We were told to start by drawing our hand. Yes, our hand. We students all struggled with this but at the end of the session when we taped our drawings up to the critiquing wall the ice had been broken. Some sketches were more accomplished than others but all were up there, and all were good. We were on our way.

At our first meeting we did contour drawing, and later worked with things like negative space and various shading techniques. The challenge of taking on a complex bouquet of flowers as a still life was done again and again, and in time we began to master it.

That first class met once a week at the local Lutheran Church for three hours on Wednesday afternoon. It was a nice setting, one that added to the casualness and openness of the class. Most of us knew each other before the class began, and the new persons soon were pulled into the group. Coffee and tea were available and someone usually brought something sweet to nibble on.

As the weeks sped by it became quite evident that our drawing skills were improving. In fact, some students were racing far ahead of me, producing what were very good pieces. I concluded that since it took me until my seventies before I was moved to attempt a drawing class that drawing was not something deep in my genes, and even though I was improving, I accepted the fact that drawing was not my strong suit. But, I persisted, and yesterday I enrolled in my fourth class.

It occurs to me that there is something almost magical about this business of drawing. I do not know where it will lead, but so far the trip has been very enjoyable. As long as Ms. Porter keeps offering these classes I will keep taking them.

E-MAILS FROM AFRICA

September 1, 2006

OVER THE PAST FEW WEEKS I HAVE RECEIVED a few emails from Africa. Some folks with official sounding titles professed to have special concerns for my future monetary standing and were willing to share huge amounts of money with me. Surely, I was set to thinking.

What is going on here? Is this something new, or just another example of the age-old Flimflam Man at work? Has that fellow who tried to sell my grandmother a special concoction of snake oil at the county fair back in 1899 gone global?

Perhaps some of us in the Midwest are hesitant to admit, that like plenty of other folks, we have fallen prey to these sorts of ancient scams. After all, isn't the Heartland supposed to be relatively safe from any foreign invasion? Aren't we Midwesterners the simple folks who live in that vast unknown fly-over space? How can it be that we have become vulnerable to these sorts of money schemes?

Deceit and deception are ancient habits of humans and are even said to be part of the repertoire of adaptive behaviors for some of the "lesser" primates. So we know that, like them, we of the "advanced" species also live by our wile as well as by our wit. But, there is something downright disquieting about regularly being hit upon by these global scam artists.

Last week when I mentioned this to a friend he brushed it off saying he gets emails from Africa all the time. He simply ignores them and by his manner intimated that I should start ignoring them, too. For a moment or two I was taken aback by what appeared to be his worldliness, and my suggested naiveté. Apparently he was quite familiar with—according to him—the trivial matter of receiving scam emails and I had better get with it because this is the way things are now.

Yet, when on this morning's walk over these steep Bayfield hills I could not help but ponder all this. Is this really the way it is now? Perhaps I am unwilling to admit that by subscribing to an email account that I have jumped into the morass of electrical nonsense that occurs in cyberspace. Have my name and number become part of that unending buzz?

Could it be that what I took for the wonderful music of Lake Superior breezes moving through the huge white pines before our Red Cliff cabin is really the unending noise of emails passing high above? I realize that according to our friend in the White House, my email must be scrutinized by federal agents lest it hold anything threatening to our national security, but must I expect to receive scam emails from Africa on a regular basis? Good lord! What has happened?

Last evening when I mentioned this to another friend and I asked him if this was something new, or just same-old, same-old, he responded by suggesting that we Americans have been bombarded with this sort of thing for years. He said that he receives "hundreds" of such email scams each month. Furthermore, he intimated that the last time my wife and I traveled to a "Third World" country and the street urchins descended upon us to beg, it was like getting scam email. In both instances we were the wealthy prey.

When in harness back in my teaching days some of my campus colleagues who taught law enforcement and criminology classes insisted that there really was a segment of our society that existed by preying upon we poor working stiffs and we would do well to keep our guard up. It was always difficult for me to accept this, feeling my paranoia was not yet severe enough to agree. It was too easy to say that some of my fellow humans who behaved in puzzling ways were simply no good. I refused to write them off, suggesting that the root causes for deviant behavior were more complicated than what my friends thought.

I still want to think that at base, humans are a loving species and really do not want to harm each other, but more and more I stand in awe of people like those Tibetan monks with their calm smiles who wrap themselves in silky flowing shawls as they wave their passive hands, spreading goodness all around. How do they do it? Haven't they checked their incoming email box lately?

There is the danger that if we continue to be bombarded with scam African emails we might start erecting walls along our borders, and who knows where that could lead? With such walls we might be left with only ourselves and I do not think we are up to that.

Well, these African emails surely are a test. Those folks sending them do not know that they are hitting on the wrong guy. I am only a simple pensioner, living on a pretty tight budget. But, maybe that is the point. Maybe they know that even though there is an image of wealthy Americans flying all over the world, in reality most of us here in the Heartland are doing battle with high taxes, high gasoline prices, and low incomes. Maybe they know about inflation, the national debt, and exorbitant costs for our ongoing wars. Maybe they really feel for us and just want to help out.

SOMETHING'S FISHY

September 14, 2007

A DAY OR TWO AGO ONE OF OUR REGIONAL NEWSPAPERS carried a short piece about a recent report from the Minnesota Pollution Control Agency regarding the state's lakes and rivers. It stated that the state's fishermen (and women) were advised "to limit eating fish from most Minnesota waterways." This sentence set me to thinking.

What have we done to our lakes, rivers and streams? And why are we not thoroughly upset about this situation? It seems to me that when we are told to stop eating fish from some waters, and to limit our consumption from most, that something drastic needs to be done. Yet, it is as if we have not heard the message. What is going on?

Many years ago when I first learned of fish advisories for Lake Superior I was naive enough to think the persons issuing them had made a mistake. Lake Superior? How could Gitchigami be so polluted with toxins that we were to reduce our consumption of its fishes, and if we were pregnant, or thinking of becoming so, to not eat any at all? As a youngster living in southern Wisconsin I learned that Lake Superior was not only our biggest freshwater lake, but that it was our purest. There was a pristine, even mystical character to Superior—it was unlike any other body of water. It was special. How could Lake Superior be polluted? Surely there had been an error.

This past spring I found myself studying a color-coded map of the lakes in northern Wisconsin highlighting those open for Ojibwe ceded-lands spearing. I was numbed by the amount of lakes given a color indicating that they were so full of pollutants that it was not recommended to eat any fish from their waters.

Some of these pollutants supposedly fall from the sky, coming from distant lands, even as far away as Asia. Others are more local in origin, coming from nearby sources, perhaps to include some of our front lawns. But, for me, the specific source of these toxins is not really the point. Instead, it is the realization that our culture has brought this pollution about. Could it be that our very way of life is at fault here?

Some friends pay me little heed when I mention this. They tell me of folks who supposedly have eaten a lot of fish from our Midwestern waters all their lives, and these people lived to be very old. They claim some of these oldsters ate fish "every day" and that the fish did no harm. Other friends are more circumspect. They suggest that discretion is in order. They say we should contemplate these advisories and take appropriate action.

Then, some friends laugh and say they eat hardly any fish anymore and that when they go fishing they do the "catch and release" thing. They just want to catch the fish, not eat them.

As I understand it for some waters the public is advised not to eat the bigger—meaning older—fish because these are more laden with PCBs, heavy metals, and what not. Long ago I learned that a fisherman should try to catch the biggest fish, but now it seems our notion that bigger is better does not apply any more. Today, bigger might mean more harmful. Now we are told to downsize our catch, and apparently, we should feel good if the fish we catch are not big. Things are getting confusing.

So far, to my knowledge at least, all this fish and water advisory talk has been about we humans. What about the fish? How are they faring now that they live in polluted waters? And what about the other forms of life that eat fish? What about the eagles, otters, mink, and the rest? How do we tell them what we have done to their waters?

And how about the water itself, and all the tiny forms of life that help make it what it is? What would water say if it could talk?

Well, I might be getting a bit nonsensical about this. After all, except for a few of those alarmist organizations that send their workers around telling us the sky is falling, few of us seem upset with this advisory thing. We still rise in the morning, do our bathroom ablutions, and soon join the gang down in the coffee shop. We complain about, or applaud, our local and national leaders, give the market page a glance, check how the Brewers and Packers are doing, peek at the weather report, and go on with our daily business. Nobody really cares for that person who always is speaking to the down side of life. We love optimists. A happy face is a welcome face.

Yet, I have been thinking about my way of life and the path I have walked all these years. Are things I have done long ago implicated in the unfortunate condition of our waters today? Is some of the carbon from the exhaust of my hot 1954 Mercury Monterey still in Wisconsin's lakes and streams?

And I wonder about things like industries and economies. I wonder about whitefish livers and Friday night fish fries, and how our long round of fall harvest dinners will begin soon and whether or not they will include fish.

Football Fanatics

January 19, 2007

ONCE AGAIN, LAST WEEKEND WE WITNESSED the way some fans of the National Football League act at the televised games. The painted faces, the striking headgear—and more—are certainly eye-catching. But, this is just the way they look—to attempt to describe their behavior would be another thing. Over these last several years these sports fans certainly set me to thinking.

Is it just I, or are some really weird things going on in these sports arenas? I don't know, but what causes some of these fans to do what they do? Their antics seem unlike anything that has ever gone on at sports events, but maybe I just have not been paying attention. Should I be more accepting of all this, or has something blown right by me?

Some years ago when streaking was popular I applauded it. At the time streaking seemed like an appropriate response to a very staid social conventionality that seemed to have a stranglehold on our society. Once, at a school I worked at, some students who were Vietnam War veterans streaked one of our major campus-wide events. A local television news station was alerted beforehand and it sent a crew of camerapersons out to cover it. Then, at a son's high school soccer game a student in the buff ran across the field before discreetly disappearing behind a fence. Those of us in the bleachers cheered. It was great. But the fans we see on TV at the NFL games are something else. There is something about them that speaks of much more than football.

Our professional football games have become carnivals. They are exuberant, sometimes riotous, and always filled with merrymaking. They are like Mardi gras. They are times when we can join a crowd of shouting fellow humans and act in ways we might never do during the rest of the week.

Students of carnival say such a setting is a time when many rules of personal conduct are put aside as the outrageous becomes the vogue. In some South American cities during carnival the central square becomes a place for all sorts of hi-ginks, some of which are illegal at other times of the year. Some that might be considered immoral, if not downright sinful, are staged right

25

next to the town's temple where the priesthood can observe, or even take a more active part. This coming together of opposites adds to the festiveness of the event. It is a ceremonial time when many rules are broken. Any of a community's members can come forth and step out of the social norms that restrain them through the rest of the year. It is a time to cross over the boundaries that otherwise hold us in place.

Sometimes when I see those painted bodies on TV I think that we are witnessing the emergence of a new American institution: the Sporting Event Jester. This is the individual who decorates his, or her, face—sometimes it is more than the face—with team colors while wearing some outlandish garb, and presents their new self to society. Such exhibitionism is not only colorful —it is applauded.

These antics counter the action going on down on the field and sometimes if the game is a particularly uneventful one, they might be more interesting than the game itself.

Several years ago a friend and I attended a Vikings game in the Minneapolis dome. After I settled into my seat I watched the entire field of action —not just the show down on the plastic grass. It was old-fashioned pageantry. Every minute of our time was filled with that show. There were professional cheerleaders, electronic flashing signboards, roving mascots, loud shouting vendors, amplified music, and much more that was carefully choreographed to hold our constant attention. It was full-time, unending entertainment from the start to the finish. We fans had no time to think—and I began to feel manipulated. Today's fans with the painted faces carry on that ethic of raw, ersatz entertainment.

In this time of rampant corporate privatization with millionaire athletes switching teams every few years it might be difficult for a fan to feel loyal to the local team. Maybe, in some feat of wizardry these folks with the painted faces are switching their allegiance from the overpaid team to some mystical sense of community that ultimately ignores the action down on the field in favor of the action in the crowd. Here is where the real players are, anyway. After all, the crowd is the community. The players down on the field are the hired foot soldiers that might be wearing a different uniform next year. In fact, the entire team might be moved across country during the off-season, or worse yet, like the hometown factories that used to be part of much of America, might be moved overseas.

In other words, these painted football fans might truly have their fingers on the pulse of the country. Maybe they are showing us that in this time of overpaid players and team owners, all we really have is our friends, our neighbors and ourselves. Maybe they help us see that we—our community—has always been the only real game in town anyway.

GOODBYE, GAYLORD

August 14, 2005

THIS PAST WEEK WE HEARD THAT GAYLORD NELSON died. He was eighty-nine years old. This Wisconsinite, former United States senator and founder of Earth Day, has a Red Cliff connection—one that sets me to thinking.

I have not dug out my old notes and newspaper clippings yet, but somewhere in my boxes and stacks there are those about this man and his struggles to establish the Apostle Island National Lakeshore. I remember the days in the 1960s and early 1970s when folks at Red Cliff were introduced to this Washington politician, and in the months ahead I will be working through those old papers as I attempt to make sense of them. For now, I must be content to simply ponder those times and to raise initial questions about them. The details will come later, after the hard work of reading, thinking and writing.

The 1960s were tumultuous times for many of the world's communities and North America's indigenous peoples were in the thick of it. It was then that numerous human communities stood up, looked around, and announced that they were going to begin to do things differently. They began to talk back to the Man.

As is the case with all Washington politicians, Gaylord Nelson had his cadre of followers who lived in the far reaches of his congressional district and did the hard grassroots work that allows senators and others like them to succeed with their plans. Nelson himself made occasional appearances in Lake Superior Country, but for most reservation residents, his was not a familiar face. He made the symbolic flyovers that high-level power-people are familiar for, and at a very few strategic times, he actually drove into Red Cliff and walked a beach or two. At least one photo of the senator standing on a reservation beach—a leg up on a large piece of driftwood as he looks off into the distance—has become an icon of the political struggles to have the National Lakeshore pushed through Congress. Yes, Gaylord was here back in the 1960s.

But, did the reservation people know him? Did he come to their houses for coffee? Was he seen up at Pit's Store, at the church basement's rummage sales, or out at Raspberry? I suspect he may have broke bread at a local restaurant with the likes of Alec Roye, Teddy Bressette, and a few other community leaders of the times—but the rest of the community? The senator came to Red Cliff but was not known by the people. He did not come among them.

One thing I recall is that initially, he wanted virtually all of the Red Cliff shoreline to be taken for the national park. Yes, plans were to take the shoreline from the far western reach of the reservation near Sand Bay, all around to Buffalo Bay and beyond, nearly to Roye's Point. A road was to be cut through the forest all along the lakeshore so visitors could drive through and enjoy the standard view of the lake from the comfort of their motor vehicles. Interestingly, while the plan was to take this important strip of land where the bulk of Red Cliff's people and their homes were located, all of Madeline Island was to be left alone. If my memory is correct, portions of Bad River's Kakagon Sloughs were to be taken as well. Red Cliff's residents were offered other lands, one suggestion being in or near the Belanger Settlement, miles inland, west of Bayfield.

It remains interesting that Gaylord Nelson's first proposal was to take all the Red Cliff shoreline and move the reservation people away from the proposed park, the lake and the islands. It sure sounds like the old Removal Policy of Andrew Jackson way back in the 1830s, although in the 1960s, hopefully, the people would not have been forced to move by armed U.S. soldiers. No, in our times these sorts of things are done "peacefully" through negotiation—and the courts.

Gaylord Nelson is to be commended for his work to preserve natural areas in this country and he continued with this important work right up to the end. Among his most recent local efforts was his appearance at the Nemakagon River in northwestern Wisconsin where he spoke out against the current attempt to have high-tension power lines erected across this pristine waterway. There is no doubt about it—we are fortunate Gaylord Nelson did much of what he did.

Yet, there is something telling about his early relationship with Red Cliff. Did he fail to recognize the true sentiments of the region's Ojibwe people? How could he, and his assistants, fail to study and understand the history of these people? Did Gaylord Nelson really think Red Cliff would willingly give up its shoreline and move miles inland, away from the big lake? There is something important in all this. What does it say about the way powerful outsiders viewed Red Cliff and its hundreds of residents back in the 1960s? What does it say about the perceived ownership of the Apostle Islands and the Red Cliff shoreline?

And now we are faced with the new name for the park. Recently the U.S. government designated it as a wilderness area. Just this week it was announced that it will officially be named the Gaylord Nelson Wilderness Area. What does the community of Red Cliff think of this new name? Is it comfortable with this historical name right in their midst? Was the Red Cliff community part of this new naming, or was it, as has happened so often in its history, not included in this important decision?

Some Red Cliff members feel that the islands and all the shoreline are still theirs. Names come and go, but these sorts of sentiments, and the land, remain.

HARVEST DINNER

November 6, 2005

NOW THAT THE SUMMER CROWD HAS DEPARTED, it is time for the annual round of Harvest Dinners. Over the past two weeks my wife and I attended two of these feeding frenzies and next week we are scheduled to take in a third. I had better get ready since these fall fundraisers are serious eating events and they can easily throw my diet off. For this and other reasons, harvest dinners set me thinking.

They are warm times, these informal gatherings of good friends, family and neighbors—and we all enjoy warm times, especially in mid-October with the usual nip in the air that tells us summer has long gone, and that soon we must make an appointment with the furnace man.

When my wife and I drove out to the Town of Russell harvest dinner recently we both marveled at the colored leaves all through Red Cliff and out on Highway K. We still call the town hall the Sand Bay School and remark that it is where our Aunt Roseanne Buffalo used to work as a clerk at election time. We easily found a parking space and as we walked to the front door I surveyed the thirty or so vehicles parked there and noted how good they looked. Many appeared to be new and all were reasonably clean and well kept. No junkers here, I thought. Times must be good.

Soon I was in the food line and confronted with the reality of a harvest dinner: mashed potatoes, gravy, green beans, cranberry sauce, coleslaw, and meat—in this instance, an abundance of roasted turkey. A colorful display of cakes and pies rested on a nearby table, and drinks were outside on the rear deck. It all looked and smelled good and I unthinkingly filled my plate.

Later that evening when I sat on our couch trying to get comfortable as another playoff baseball game began, I reflected on what had taken place. A harvest dinner? I had just taken part in an ancient fall ritual and instead of feeling good I was suddenly quite uncomfortable. My stomach was complaining with its mass of undigested food. What had I done? For the last nine months or so I have been on a serious heart-friendly diet and I think my stomach is very appreciative of that fact. After a lifetime of meat and po-tatoes I have changed to lighter fare, then, suddenly here I was again, back into the old meat-n-taters days.

But that Harvest Dinner was about more than meat and potatoes. There were door prizes and a raffle, and ice-cold beer was being sold for a dollar a can. Local merchants donated the door prizes, and after the meal our ticket stubs were pulled out of a box to determine the winners. The raffle was more serious. It was for bigger things, like a weekend at Cable's Lakewood Lodge, and dinners at Bayfield's Rittenhouse Inn. And guns. Three deer hunting ri-fles were the top prizes. Meat and potatoes, beer, and guns.

There was something old fashioned about it all, something that de-manded an explanation. Essentially, I asked myself just what was it that I harvested? And furthermore, what crop had the other eaters in the town hall brought in? What silos, haymows, and granaries had they filled this fall? Were their basements shelved with bright jars of fruits and vegetables canned from their gardens and orchards? Were their winter hams being smoked in the farmyard's smokehouse?

We moderns do not harvest anymore. We don't bring in the sheaves, dig the big crop of summer's potatoes and store them away. Most of us never owned a pressure cooker and would not know how to use one if we did. So what is this harvest dinner business all about?

The lifetimes of heavy lifting our parents and grandparents did are no more. Now the heavy lifting is done with machines—or maybe computers. The tugging, pulling and carrying is done by tractors and big trucks. Do any of us still use a shovel all through an eight-hour shift—like that summer I labored on a section crew for the Milwaukee Road Railroad so long ago?

Is there a connection between our latest national pandemic of obesity and our penchant for harvest dinners? Anthropologists say a culture's tech-nology can change faster than its system of values and beliefs, so although we may no longer be laboring the way we did in the past, we still hold, and put into practice, some of the values, beliefs, and rituals that existed hand-in-hand with our earlier hard-working ways. Cultural lag, they call it. In our world of rapid change, sometimes one part of our culture lags behind others.

Have harvest dinners become old-fashioned? If we no longer sweat and strain in our daily jobs why do we still celebrate all this so-called work? For many of us the coming of fall does not change our work routines at all. We do the same job all year round. Why do we keep flocking to these fall rituals? Are we creatures of habit?—or are we simply reluctant to let go of some of the ceremonies and rituals that we have come to love even though they no longer speak to the way we really live?

IDENTITY THEFT

January 11, 2008

DURING THE WEEK BEFORE CHRISTMAS some ner-do-well out in California used my name and credit card number to steal a large tank of gasoline at a Union 76 station, and then at a Wal-Mart store to steal almost $200.00 worth of merchandise. Christmas presents I suppose. In Orwellian fashion, today we call this identity theft, but no matter what it is called, it is still stealing, and it sets me to thinking.

So far these thefts have cost me nothing other than frustration and an hour or so on the telephone speaking to credit card people in distant places, but I would bet that somehow they, and the thousands of other identity theft cases occurring each year around the world (or is it millions?) are built into interest rates or other credit card fees. I cannot believe these thefts are not costing me a dime.

Identity theft has become so common in America that we seem to have accepted it like the passing imposition of a bad cold. After all, it's no big deal. You just close the old account and open a new one. Those credit card companies can do that in the press of a few keyboard buttons. But, what has happened to us? This latest form of thievery has insinuated itself into our world like mercury in our clear and cold northland lakes. Why aren't we mad enough about both to do something?

This is not the first time someone has used my credit card number to steal. A few years ago a thief in the United Kingdom used it to purchase some automobile parts. In a similar fashion, another scoundrel, in St. Paul this time, stole my checkbook and forged my name to pay for a pizza party. I guess it was kids that time. In that instance I did some detective work and identified the house to which the pizza's were delivered and gave the address to the police, but to no avail. I even offered to take the police to the house but I was strongly advised to leave such things to the men and women in blue.

Then there was the incident in which some outgoing envelopes were stolen from our mailbox—mail that included checks for the payment of utility bills. Those checks held bank account numbers and signatures. I immediately put a hold on them, and quickly changed checking accounts so other than a good dose of stress, no harm was done. I recall at the time how nonchalant the bank tellers were during this transaction, as if it happens all the time.

These thefts occurred downstate, so I cannot blame any of my co-residents here in God's Country, but nevertheless, theft is still theft. It is alive and well in America.

Try as I might to ignore this seamy side of life, its presence forces itself upon me. Like the quiet self-assured arrogance of the well to do, some things will simply not go away. Given the complex nature of our way of life these days, we are connected to all sorts of goin's-on in practically all parts of the globe. Is theft simply part of human nature, and if so, will it always be knocking at my door? Have they found a gene for stealing? Have we met the enemy, and he is us? If it is not illegal steroid use, it is identity theft.

Several years ago a behavioral primatologist working with a colony of South American monkeys determined that theft and deceit were adaptive traits for this species, and, to use Darwin's terms, were selected for. Those individuals without them were at a disadvantage, and those genotypes would eventually drop from the gene pool. This scientist suggested that theft and deceit might still be working for our species today, although we do not want to acknowledge it.

With a little imagination we might think of the psychological highs received when stealing someone's identity. It must be like wearing a really good costume at a serious masquerade ball. It must be like getting something for nothing, and who does not like a free lunch?

I also think about how something like a charge account that used to involve the customer, the local shop at which the account was held, and maybe a town bank has now become a set of relationships spanning a continent, if not the globe. In order to get this theft cleared up, I spoke to a credit card company person in Texas, then with someone in Florida, and later with another in Arizona. Of course, I used their toll-"free" number. My card is from a Minnesota credit union, I use it in Wisconsin, and its number was illegally used in California. Thanks to our culture of cyberspace, this wide distribution of persons and places connected through plastic and theft is hardly unusual. Welcome to the world of 2008.

That recent Visa television ad in which the flow of economic exchange stops cold when someone uses money to make a purchase, is saying it is old-fashioned and downright gauche to use cash. We are to get with it: use plastic, and keep things moving. Be modern. Progress demands plastic.

Recently my new credit card arrived, but I hesitate to activate it. Could I live without it?

THE KEWEENAW

October 15, 2007

AFTER A MINI-VACATION TO MICHIGAN'S Keweenaw Peninsula, I find that I cannot erase images of this beautiful place. It has been a few weeks now, but the Keweenaw comes to mind almost every day. Yes, Upper Michigan sets me to thinking.

Near the end of what had become a very busy summer, I suggested to my bride that after Labor Day we escape for a few days by driving up to Copper Harbor. That, itself, seems incongruous—that anyone would want to escape from beautiful Red Cliff or Bayfield, especially in colorful fall, but my wife readily agreed, so I immediately made the phone calls for accommodations. At my invitation my older brother and his wife, who live near Tomahawk, Wisconsin, agreed to drive up to join us.

What is it about Michigan's Upper Peninsula that appeals to me? Over the past few decades I have visited Sault Ste. Marie, Ironwood, and numerous points in-between, and my wife and I were on the Keweenaw many years ago, but on that trip we spent all our time at L'Ance and drove no further north than the Portage Lake cutoff at Houghton-Hancock. This time we intended to go way up to the tip at Copper Harbor, and so we did.

After a quick breakfast in a small Ironwood café we headed east and soon were in that unbroken land of trees that stretches all across the U.P. Their bright colors foretold what was in store for us further north. An overnight was spent at the casino motel at Baraga where we connected with my brother and his wife.

Before arriving at the motel, my wife and I visited the Catholic shrine for Frederic Baraga and I was struck by the size of that statue of the priest that stands at the lower tip of the large expanse of L'Ance Bay. Whoever designed that statue left no doubt that the intent was to make Father Baraga bigger than life, but for me, his statue pales in importance to the bay. I concluded the Snowshoe Priest was paying homage to that big body of water.

What was just as interesting was the badly faded realty sign at the shrine's entrance. Somehow it had not occurred to me that Bishop Baraga's

37

shrine was a private for-profit business. I found it interesting that religious shrines can be for sale.

After the night at the casino and motel I was eager to be done with gambling and was ready to move on up into the peninsula, but first a stop was made in downtown Hancock to walk Quincy Street before we drove up to Copper Harbor.

Signs of Finnish culture are ubiquitous in Upper Michigan. We visited Finlandia University, the nearby community art gallery—a real treat—before walking to the Kaleva Café to enjoy a hot pasty that, truthfully, had been made that morning, and was about to come out of the oven. We liked what we saw about Hancock.

The city of Calumet was a pleasant surprise. It's historic old downtown district with the large, and often empty, brick and stone buildings told of the copper boom of the late 1800s. We visited some of the shops that were coming to the end of their summer season, but perhaps we were too old to enjoy the usual tourist shop anymore. We wanted something different—something uniquely U.P.

Finally arriving at Copper Harbor we found our lakeside motel and soon were enjoying a very fine dinner at the nearby Harbor Haus, the famed German restaurant. Nice indeed. My brother and his wife still enjoy authentic German cuisine.

We had only three days and on the last one the rains came. But, rather than diminish the pleasure of the trip the rain added a good degree of joy. Few other tourists were evident—something that suited me just fine. A strong northwest wind was coming off the lake and at tiny Eagle Harbor I stood on the observation stand beside the shore to enjoy the large breakers hitting the rocky beach. The light rain, the waves' spray and the loud solitude were just what I wanted.

Our knowledge about the Keweenaw is terribly Euro-based. We know about Frederic Baraga's coming to stay in 1843 after several years at La Pointe far to the west, and of course, we know about the Euro-American mining. The peninsula is dotted with the rusting and rotting remains of these extractive business ventures, and the history books continue to tell, and retell, this story. In contrast, it seems to me that the story of the Ojibwe on the Keweenaw is yet to be written.

Once we got above Haughton-Hancock we saw how few people there were, and how once again a country as beautiful as the Keweenaw has become a place for us to come to for a few days to renew ourselves before returning home. At the time of our visit many seasonal shops had closed, letting a welcome calm pervade the land.

I imagined that except for the abandoned mine shafts, the land really has changed little since the first Euro-American arrived. The deep snows still come and the ubiquitous thimbleberries still make a delicious jam, and even though some minerals are still torn from the earth, the land is still there.

THE LONG PULL OF WINTER

January 14, 2007

It SEEMS LIKE WINTER MIGHT FINALLY HAVE come to the Northland. Last weekend a Bayfield friend casually remarked that he was going to take his boat out of the lake due to the start of the ice buildup. This was on January 11th, a very late time for such things. But, this morning as I sit in my study on our Bayfield hillside and peer out at the ferry heading over to Madeline Island, I see a white world. Lake effect snow has blanketed our yards and rooftops over these last few days. Yes, winter has finally arrived and it sets me to thinking.

One of these Fridays the church basement fish fries will begin and I will have to be there when they do. Nothing fancy, these dinners are old-fashioned fare—just plenty of good food: boiled red potatoes, freshly made coleslaw, home-made cakes and other desserts, coffee, a sugary juice drink, and of course the near endless supply of freshly fried fish. These fish come right from the cold waters of Gitchigami, and are what make the meal. Sometimes we get lake herring, but usually it is whitefish or lake trout. While the food is worth the trip to the church on Bayfield's Catholic Hill, what is just as enjoyable is the chance to see so many friends and neighbors. These fish fries are social get-togethers that seem essential this time of year.

Perhaps some of us do not get out in winter as often as we would like and when Friday rolls around we are eager for company. Solitude has its place but in January it might get old too quick. This calls to mind the words of Henry Schoolcraft, the early nineteenth century Indian agent at Sault Ste. Marie, who seemed to love to write. In his memoirs he told how upon first coming to Michigan's U.P. he struggled to get through the long, cold winters. He remarked that while a famous American New England writer of the time praised the merits of solitude, Schoolcraft wished that this fellow would come to Sault Ste. Marie to see what winter solitude really was like. It sounds like Henry suffered with long bouts of cabin fever.

A long and cold winter can do that to us. Everyone must know about cabin fever, or as a brother of mine calls it, "shack sickness," and how after a long stretch of being indoors you really ache to get out. The long pull of winter is something that all of us are familiar with.

Perhaps we have memories of winters of our youth when we stepped boldly into each day as we began to learn who we really were and how we fit in. Maybe we recall how winter was always an integral part of each year—how the family had to prepare for the cold days and nights. Maybe we remember how the well pump would sometimes get cranky on the really cold days, or how the firewood would run out and we would have to scramble to replenish it. Maybe we remember how in winter it was always a treat to open a jar of fruit or vegetables we helped our mother can last fall. And maybe there was a day or two when we were snowbound until the town plow came by our house.

And this is the time of year for those good, homemade hearty soups. A few winters ago a creative neighbor began a custom of making a large kettle of thick, porridge-like soup and baking a few loaves of crusty bread, then inviting some friends to come and eat. These are good gatherings where everyone digs in and enjoys.

Just as important for me are the impromptu get-togethers at our local main street coffee shop. The random mix of friends who frequent that shop makes for lively conversation. Two days ago I joined in a wide-ranging discussion of the usual political issues, and more. Seated around our few tables were a musical choral director, a school bus driver, a muralist, a railroad section hand, an art instructor, a mental health counselor, an anthropologist, a professional environmental specialist, and a museum quality woodworker. All friends, we clearly were enjoying our chance to get together and converse about whatever came to mind.

This is what winter can bring about. Our summers can get pretty hectic what with all the folks who come to town at that time, but now we have our streets and shops to ourselves and we revel in such luxury. Try as I might, I really fail to see why some of our neighbors go south for winter. All my life I have experienced the wonder of a four-seasoned world and I cannot imagine a year of perpetual summer. It would be like coming to a dinner table and having nothing but dessert.

A year without winter would be like a day without night. The poet, Mary Oliver, has a short poem in which she reminds us that the natural world is always beside us, calling to us, and even though we might feel lonely it is

41

always telling us that we are part of this family of things. That is the way I see winter. Like the calls of our winter ravens as they pass slowly overhead, it announces our place in this quiet, white and wonderful time of year.

Rainy Days

June 24, 2006

THIS MORNING WE ARE ENJOYING AN EARLY SUMMER shower and it is downright wonderful. I am in our hillside home in Bayfield and rain drips from our eves as Madeline Island fades behind a wall of falling drops. One moment the sunshine was here, but now the entire sky is darkened and I need to turn on the study's lamp. It is so cool that our furnace clicks on. A beautiful morning like this sets me to thinking.

In only a few days I will turn seventy. Yikes, but that seems like an ancient age! This morning it feels like yesterday when I was standing on that pitcher's mound, looking in at my catcher as he gave me the sign for the next pitch. That was high school and we were working hard to defeat the boys from a neighboring town. How can those times really have occurred fifty years ago? Sometimes I agree that our lives fly by like that speeding Coors beer train, anxious to get somewhere. Many of my friends are in their eighties and they scoff when I talk like this. They say I am still young, but I know they are kidding. They, and I, are old. We do not have many wonderful summer showers left. We had better relish every single one that comes our way.

This rain is badly needed although the farmers north of town might be both pleased and a bit apprehensive about its coming. Their fields are dry, but this is the last week of June, and it is Saturday. They are hoping for a nice crowd of folks to drive out this weekend to pick this year's bumper strawberry crop, and let's hope for their sake that in an hour or so the sky clears so this can come to pass. I'll settle for that. Those strawberries come on quickly and must be picked when at their peak, lest the crop is lost. We don't want that to happen.

We humans want it all. We want both the sunshine and the rain. And, we get them both. In some ways our lives are like that strawberry-rhubarb pie I baked last week—tart and sweet, all at once.

It is a truism that with the coming of age we start to talk about our aches and pains. So far I have tried to avoid that, but it is getting more and

43

more difficult. These past few months have seen the passing of a few local folks and I miss them. Then, only last week another friend took the $7,000.00 helicopter ride from Ashland to Duluth where heart by-pass surgery was done. And the dreaded C-Word is getting too close for comfort. Cancer comes to town every now and then. Yesterday I heard of another elderly friend who just got the news.

This is the way it goes. Back in those glory years when my curve ball dropped like it was falling off a table and no matter how hard they swung, the opposing batters could not get a piece of it, I did not think of growing old. Heart surgery had not yet come to pass and even though cancer was taking a toll I did not think about it. There were baseball games to play, pretty girls to date, and besides, my two-door shiny sunset-orange-and-white 1954 Mercury Monarch needed a wax job.

What a trip—this life! We know its unbounded joy when young, then in our youth and adulthood we push it to the edge, and now in those fabled twilight years we look back and think about our ride. Some of us must write about it. Some of us draw and paint it. Most of us seem uninterested in pondering its wonder, and we simply live it, then move on. Today I wish a few of my forebears would have recorded their thoughts about what it was like for them. My mother was a musician and when young she wrote a few songs that, in their own way, sang life's praises, but I wish she had written more. Today I yearn to know more about how all those kin who came before me felt about these things.

Nostalgia? Why not? A Saturday shower like this morning's brings it on. Maybe I'll go downtown for the mail, pick up the morning paper, and step into the coffee shop to see if any friends are there. Maybe we'll just sit for a half-hour or so, quietly sipping our coffee while looking out the window at the rain. Then, if it clears up we might go pick a few quarts of strawberries up at Jimmie Erickson's field.

THE RAVEN'S MESSAGE

March 15, 2006

THIS MORNING I AM BEING WATCHED BY RAVENS. They perch in the dead white pine down at the water's edge and crane their necks to peer through the nearby large hemlock to keep an eye on the cabin. A moment ago when I stepped out to the woodpile they were there, talking softly between themselves. What are they up to? These big black birds set me to thinking.

Usually they are more aloof, always lifting off when I come outside, but today they stay put as long as I do not get too close. Is there a deer carcass nearby, left from a night kill? I slept well, hearing no coyotes or wolves, so that seems unlikely. I suspect they are watching for any food I might provide for them, but maybe it is something much more simple, like their possible infatuation with the new day's first smoke rising from the chimney. This morning's smoke lifts ever so slowly and has a gentle twist to it, like the recurring swirl of a soft-haired brush in the hand of an aged Japanese watercolorist. Ravens are intelligent and always inquisitive, and the new smoke from an early morning fire can bring them in just to see what is going on.

Today these birds cause me to wonder what we really know about other forms of life. Zoologists have studied most animals by now and in some ways we seem to have a good understanding of them, but the older I get the more I think about all this. Even though science has most of it figured out, I sometimes feel we still have a long way to go.

The Ojibwe say the winged ones and the four-leggeds, as well as those of the waters and all the others that share this earth with us, live in their own communities and have wants and desires just like we humans do. I find this comforting. Such knowledge suits me and after all my years of walking this earth it helps fill in the missing pieces of the grand puzzle of my life. It fits well with some important conclusions I am finally making. When young I was taught that my people have dominion over the other forms of life—that they were put here to serve our needs. At first I believed these biblical tales, but no more. Such arrogance is not only unnecessary, but can be downright harmful. It makes no sense anymore.

45

For years I called myself a scientist, one who studied people, but for the last many years I have spent time watching, and thinking about, the other forms of life we humans share this planet with. Non-human forms of life have fascinated me for a long time. My switch to a nearly complete vegetarian diet almost a year ago probably heightened this old interest. Maybe the fact that I try to avoid eating any meat causes me to think about animals more than ever before. One thing my years of anthropology have taught me is that we humans are not just ethno-centric—meaning we are so focused on our own culture that we have trouble to recognize and accept others—no, we go far beyond ethnocentrism. Some of us think the entire world was made for us.

Bernd Heinrich, the Maine zoologist, has studied ravens for years and shares his love for them with us. In his very readable books he tells of their social world, a world, I suspect, few of us notice. Among many other things, Dr. Heinrich speaks of altruism in ravens, how they sometimes seem to put their personal needs aside in favor of those of others. Ravens are not just large, crude, black birds that do little more than eat, sleep and procreate. We humans have not yet learned the secrets of their world. Importantly, they have been on this earth for a very long time, and even though they have adapted to our intrusive presence, they still can do quite well without us.

To some Native American communities the raven is a fellow being who teaches humans many things about life. Sometimes they are called Tricksters because their method of teaching is done through tricks played on others, and even on themselves. The birds in the dead white pine before my cabin this morning might be playing tricks on me, and if so, they are successful because I am puzzled. I can only watch and listen as I wait for them to reveal the message in their teaching. It might take years before I learn. They could be Wenabozho, the consummate Ojibwe trickster and teacher. He could be bringing another piece of wisdom so I had better pay attention for there is still so much to learn.

Ravens belong in these woods, and on this beautiful morning their quiet chatter is as welcome as the hot mint tea I sip. Unlike their smaller cousins, the crows, ravens seldom raise a bedlam of loud calls that reminds us that sometimes nature can have a sharp edge. This morning I stand in the cabin's front door, leaning on the hard doorframe, the mug of hot tea warming my hand as I listen to their soft chatter. The rising sun's eager rays glint off their ebony neck feathers like the gleam of diamonds.

ROAD KILL

September 8, 2007

Recently while driving down one of our local roadways I came upon the remains of what was a beautiful young whitetail deer. This youngster's coat had begun to darken and its white spots were fading away, but they were still very visible. It was one of this spring's fawns that almost made it through summer.

There was a time that the uncommonness of the dead body of a white tail deer lying beside our state roadways would turn our heads as we sped by. I recall when as a youngster riding with the family how a soulful click of the tongue might be heard from my mother in the front seat, and a few words uttered about "The poor thing," as if we were at fault. That was a long time ago and now it has been several years that we have been witnessing these—sometimes rotting—roadside carcasses and today they have become commonplace. But, common or not, these dead animals set me to thinking.

What has happened to us now that we have witnessed these dead bodies for several years, and not just now and then, but all year long? Has something changed inside us? What effect might our exposure to these broken and often mangled remains, lying as if they are of no consequence, be having on us?

Here in northern Wisconsin we are a land with dead deer beside our roadways, but I recall how in the first years of our non-removal program it seemed strange to see these animals just lying there as if no one cared. At such times I would eerily hear my mother's clicking tongue and her remorseful words. That was several years ago. By now I suspect most of us have seen quite a few of these roadside remains and that we are accustomed to them. As we hurtle ourselves along in our heavy steel vehicles we might be oblivious to the carnage such speed and weight can cause.

Admittedly, road kill of animals as large as whitetail deer provides food for some scavengers. Especially in winter, crows, ravens, foxes, eagles and more can be seen feeding on these carcasses. Perhaps this is a plus for these other forms of life, since they might be hard pressed to find food in the cold months. But I have heard reports that the same sort of traffic that killed the deer is also a problem to the hungry animals feeding upon them. Speed kills, no matter what the life form.

Today when driving past large road kill I sometimes think of Iraq and how we have been viewing dead bodies from that war for several years now. Baghdad's roadside bombs with their own kind of "road kill" are sadly familiar to us. It may be possible that, as might be the case with Wisconsin's road kill, we are becoming accustomed to this death and destruction. Surely, with all the exposure we have witnessed these last few years, we have had to harden ourselves to the sight of burning vehicles and smoldering bodies. During World War II we had to go to a movie theater to see film footage of battles and the resultant dead, then during the Vietnam War we could witness such scenes on our television sets. In the early Vietnam years some commentator's spoke of what effect the almost instant transmission of this carnage was having on us. Because of our advanced communications technology a war in a distant land was brought right into the sanctity of our living rooms, and on a nightly basis. We at home had suddenly become closer to that war and it was difficult to ignore it.

A few years ago the American writer, Barry Lopez, told how, for a time at least, when traveling across country by motor vehicle he would stop to remove the bodies of road kill from the pavement. Even small birds that were rammed by his automobile's grille would be picked up and carefully placed into the roadside grasses. Lopez does not tell us why he did this, but the piece in which he writes about this behavior is entitled "Apologia."

Perhaps animals have always been an enigma to us humans. Barry Lopez's openness in sharing his puzzlement about them might be indicative about how many of us feel. Some cultures understand animals less as inconsequential forms of life unrelated to us, and more as beings living beside us and involved in important relationships with us. Unless we subscribe to a belief system that dogmatically categorizes animals as having less worth than our species we must face the puzzlement of our relationship with them.

A bloated deer carcass beside the roadway is not one of the nicest scenes for a motorist to come upon. And after witnessing as many of these as we have these past few years we have had to either turn away or begin to ignore them. We have had to push them from our minds, like I tried to do in the case of that young deer with the fading spots. It was just a fawn that did not make it across the road. As did many other passers-by, I went on with my business and tried to think of more pleasant things.

WALKING WITH ROSIE

March 9, 2009

THIS MORNING I TOOK MY USUAL EARLY WALK but instead of a solitary excursion out into our still-winter world, today I was accompanied by Rosie, our daughter's chocolate Labrador. Rosie had a sleep-over and as always when this occured she demanded to be let outdoors right after breakfast. So, after tying on my winter walking boots, slipping into my trusty layered coat, settling my Kormer upon my head and grabbing my pair of leather choppers—and stuffing a plastic bag into my rear pocket—Rosie and I set off. This walk with the dog set me to thinking.

It must be ancient, this scene wherein an aging man and his dog take a morning stroll. Domesticated dogs show up in the fossil record thousands of years ago, so Rosie and I certainly were not doing anything new. And if we consider the Ojibwe origin teaching about how Wenebozho—after complaining of his loneliness—was given Ma'iingan (the wolf) for a companion, then this partnership is about more than mere fossils. It comes from the magical mist of very early, and important, spiritual teachings.

Rosie is a wonderful dog who asks for very little, but she does like to take her morning romp. She comes from the other side of town and when on one of her sleep-overs likes to check out her kinfolk in my neighborhood, so sometimes I play it safe and keep her leashed for a portion of the walk until I can take a reading on which other four-leggeds might be out on their morning constitutionals. These neighborhood mutts often express their proprietary rights when Rosie is visiting and they raise a ruckus that can be a bit noisy. We have at least one neighbor who seems to have a serious dread—or fear, or phobia—about dogs, so I am usually careful to pay homage to his wishes regarding the canine species. I keep Rosie leashed when near his property lines.

Today we headed over to the nearby neighborhood woods where Rittenhouse Avenue comes up the hill and is stopped by a deep ravine. A narrow pathway replaces the street at that spot, and it is a beautiful stretch, just about two blocks long as it meanders upward amidst the trees. No one had used the path after last week's snowstorm because it was filled with two feet or so of new snow.

Rosie knows that hillside well and this morning she plunged on, leaping through the deep snow but always following the buried pathway. I slowly came behind in the new trail she laboriously broke. It was clear we both enjoyed our snowy trek.

Coming from a northern Wisconsin farming background, I am familiar with dogs. There never was a time when we did not have at least one on the place, and usually there were two or even three. Except for a wonderful silver German shepherd all others were the usual mixture of longhaired large farmyard dogs, and all were good with the cattle. In the later years my mother adopted a small spaniel of some sort that was privileged to live in the house, but the others stayed outdoors. With the exception of the spaniel, they were working dogs that slept in the barn and none of them ever saw the inside of a veterinarian's clinic. If these dogs became ill, we doctored them ourselves.

But all that was long ago. These days the dogs Rosie and I meet are of another place and time. Since my farm days a huge pet industry has emerged in America, complete with high-buck pet hospitals, and pet food chain stores. Today I suspect millions (or maybe billions) of dollars are annually made in this industry.

Nextdoor is Sasha, a large Alaskan malamute, said to be a dozen years old, and just down the street lives Bosco, a large French poodle who is usually tethered on the end of a long cable. Then comes Captain Morgan, a longhaired mutt that was rescued from the dog pound by a loving neighbor and ever since shows his joy in being alive. Then it is Roxie, a young black Labrador that has become a neighborhood fixture. This lovable youngster consistently brings a stick or other object to us, and lays it at our feet to block our way, asking us to toss it down the street to allow her the joy of retrieving it only to place it right back before us. This could be repeated ad infinitum. A bit further, on Old Military Road, lives Lucky. This small chunky fellow is a spaniel that, like Captain Morgan, was rescued from Death's Row. His nose seems to be glued to the ground, searching for the scent of a bounding cottontail. It is clear Lucky, too, relishes his comfortable life on this hillside.

Whenever Rosie and I head out on a morning walk it is as if it was our first time. The big Labrador is as enthusiastic about each morning's outing as she was the day before. She puts her nose to the wind, perks up her ears for whatever sounds come her way, and looks around in all directions. She scans her world and never seems disappointed. Her joy of just being out there is inspiring, and I follow behind her like the devoted disciple I am.

School Days

August 17, 2002

IN ONLY TWO WEEKS OR SO THE LOCAL YOUNGSTERS will be heading back to school. These days the familiar music of morning crickets in the yard's deep shadows that linger until nearly noon help to remind me of this. Then, this week my wife and our Bayfield grandchildren made their annual trip to Ashland for their school supplies and new pairs of shoes along with a nice selection of school clothes. This onset of back-to-school days sets me to thinking.

All of us must remember going back to school in fall. And perhaps while we were saddened by the end of another summer we might also have had just a little feeling of joyful expectation with the onset of a new school year. We would miss the long free days of summer but we were ready to meet our old school friends that we had seen little of, or perhaps had not seen at all, since school let out. Then there was the matter of being in a new grade. That business of advancement had its own pleasures and anxieties. No matter how we looked at it, the return of school gave us something to think about.

My childhood summers were spent on Wisconsin dairy farms and since we lived out in the country we did not see much of our schoolmates until the return of September. My brothers and I had no "sleep-overs" like children have today, no pizza parties, or group movies in town on summer evenings. As I recall, to a great extent we stayed put most of the summer—stayed right on our farms. And we had plenty to keep us occupied. As soon as we were big enough we worked beside our parents with the daily round of farm chores and by the end of our high school years we were involved in all farm operations. Our parents, however, did most of the work. When I think of it, I still shake my head in disbelief. How did they do all that labor, seven days a week, month after month, year after year? And there were no complaints, at least none I recall.

There was no kindergarten in my school days. I began in the first grade at what I call a one-room school, although the building had a small gymnasium in the basement. The year was 1942, and except for a young woman who taught us that year, the following seven years were all taught by the same person: Mrs. Klevenow. What a master teacher that woman was!

51

World War II was raging when I began school and I recall how one of our room's bulletin boards was devoted to news items about that conflict, and to our artist renderings of pictures we drew about the war. One day it held an article and picture about one of our school friend's older brothers who was an army pilot. His plane had been shot down and he was killed. That article stayed on the bulletin board all year.

Bayfield's big yellow school busses are being readied for another year of duty at the garage at the south edge of town. Lloyd Turner has been going over those vehicles for weeks now, changing oil, replacing worn parts, and generally preparing them for another year of transporting our scholars. Soon those busses will be making their daily trips up Fourth Street to the school grounds weekday afternoons to load up the youngsters and take them to their homes.

In my grade school days there were no school busses. We walked the mile or two to school, rode our bicycles, or on rare days were given rides in private automobiles. But, now it seems very few students actually walk to school. I wonder about diets, exercise, and the national obesity problem amongst our country's youngsters.

Our teachers never stop to amaze me. I taught for thirty years or so but my students were adults, not young children. Being responsible for a room full of youngsters is something else. How do they do it? Day after day they take charge of those young bodies—and minds—and get the job done. I think our school-teachers still remain in that category of America's workers who are overworked, underpaid, and sometimes, perhaps, underappreciated. Their efforts are crucial to us, but I fear that too often we give them little heed. There is that old view in America that teachers are those who are content to live in the rented apartment above the hardware store down on Main Street and are really not concerned about making money. They love to teach and will do it for practically nothing.

Yes, "Back to School Days" are quickly approaching. Our days are beginning to shorten and these mornings heavy dew is in the yard. Bayfield still has its flow of visitors from downstate—families that walk its downtown sidewalks licking ice cream cones—but in only a short time that will cease. Labor Day is quickly approaching and these families will be back in their homes making those final preparations before the first day of school.

The youngest of the children have finally mastered the task of tying their shoes, zipping their jackets, and doing things right in the bathroom. They have been primed for school. In a few days it is time for classes to begin.

BUYING TIME AGAIN

December 12, 2005

THE PUSH IS ON. THE YEAR-END FRENZY that catches many of us in early December is all around. I have watched it for nearly seventy years and it is as colorful and fretful as it ever has been. One thing for sure—all this hustle and bustle has set me to thinking.

It is interesting how it finally all turns out. My first memories of Christmas-time are of heavy-hipped Germanic grandmothers who had as many hugs as a small youngster could take, and of more distant grandfathers who often had whiskey on their breaths. There always was the real Christmas tree in the front room, as living rooms were called back then. And the wonderful aromas of food! Those farmhouse kitchens surely smelled good! I was born into the time of the automobile so my memories of traveling over the river and through the wood include the warm interiors of Chevrolet or Plymouth sedans filled with my brothers and parents. I did not ride on a horse-drawn sleigh until much later in my life. Jingle bells? For me they always were more myth than reality.

Red Cliff has many stories of such jingling horse-drawn sleighs, or cutters, as the elders like to call them. Horses are said to have been common here until right up to World War II times. Recently Tony Kovachevich told me his parents had six horses on their Red Cliff farm. The Kovachevich place was somewhere back of Bishop Lane. Other stories tell of old John DePerry working a team around the region, hauling just about everything that needed hauling. Horses were part of life here in the early 1900s.

But teams of horses on the dirt roads of Red Cliff are history. Now we see and hear cars and trucks all over. Like in Bayfield, these gas-eaters are part of the scenery. And at this time of year they seem to speed up a bit. Everyone picks the pace up now that we are into the few weeks after Thanksgiving before Christmas. There is shopping to be done and no matter if you are a believer or not, you usually get caught up in it.

This week Christmas decorations are popping up like dandelions in spring. Thanksgiving must be the marker because right after Turkey Day it did not take long before the fake green garlands with little white lights started to adorn porch rails, roof eves and what not. One house in Downtown Bayfield already has its life-sized Santa Claus up, out on the front lawn. At Red Cliff, Lionel Roy's plywood Santa's and Snowmen have been up for a week or so. A few years ago Uncle Lionel won the reservation's house decorating contest and it looks like he will be back in the running this year. That's not bad for an eighty-one-year-old man with a plastic hip. Look out Christmas! Here we come!

A few of those new fangled inflated balloon type things—bigger than life—that we are seeing at several holidays though the year are up too, with their anchor lines fastened to nearby cement blocks or tree stumps. We notice them at Thanksgiving, Halloween, the Fourth of July, Easter, and maybe even lesser holidays like St. Paddy's Day. And with the annual advent of football season in these parts we find those over-inflated caricatures of the Green Bay Packers. I wish I had cornered that market a few years ago when the Chinese came upon the idea. Good lord, they must sell as much of that merchandise as Tyvek does its house insulation. You see it all over.

After so many of the new, fancy decorations, mass-produced in overseas factories, those older plywood cutouts are starting to look a bit genuine, like maybe, the real McCoy. Weird, how things can turn out. I think it might be like those perfectly shaped hothouse tomatoes. We have eaten them for so many years that we sometimes forget how good a real, outdoors vine-ripened tomato is! In fact, some of the younger folk might think that hothouse toma-toes are the cat's pajamas.

Yes, the season is upon us. Neighbors are anticipating long trips here and there, all the time praying for cooperation from the weather gods. Thank good-ness my bride and I no longer have to make those grueling drives to distant places this time of year. Now we stay put on this hillside and wait for the grand-children to arrive. For the most part, our traveling days have come and gone.

But the frenetic behavior continues, even here on the Rez and in small Bayfield. My partner was up at 4:00 a.m. on Black Friday just to be among the first in the stores up at Miller Mall. She came back with huge, colorful plastic bags filled to bursting and with a contented look in her eye. I sighed and gave thanks for another peak experience successfully brought to fruition. Now all I have to deal with is a thick stack of credit card slips.

All this to celebrate the birth of a child. And for those of us who have switched to celebrating the Winter Solstice instead of a middle-eastern god, we stand in wonder at it all. To some, this is a pretty serious season. I watch as much of the action as I can.

THE BIG SNOW STORM

March 21, 2006

At long last we were hit with our big winter storm! It began Sunday night and did not let up until after darkness on Monday. I figure it was almost twenty-four hours of snowfall. Monday morning as I stood in our Bayfield home with an eye toward the lake I was struck by its fierceness. Gusts of wind whipped through the yard, buffeting the large spruce trees and our lone white cedar down the hill at the alley's edge. It kept going all day long. It was a true whiteout, and it set me to thinking.

How beautiful this terrible storm was! How wonderful to stand behind the large windows in the heated rooms and simply watch it! But, it was nothing new, this storm. We northerners expect to witness such fury at least once a year, and usually we do. March rarely disappoints us. My Germanic forebears back in the mid-1800s in the Mechlenburgh region of northeast Germany must have seen many of these snowstorms. I can see them banking the wood fire in the blackened kitchen fireplace in their dark stone walled house dug into the hillside, before snuggling deeply into the soiled featherbeds on wooden pallets in the loft. Germanic peasants, my distant ancestors must have toughed it out through many long, hard winters. And before them, going back into the hundreds and even thousands of years, theirs, and my, even much more distant relatives must have done something similar. We come from a long line of folks who stood amidst swirling snowstorms and did what it took to stay warm.

And I think of those Ojibwe who spent their winters in Chequamegon Country not so long ago. They too, banked their fires before settling into the night under their bedding. But, they had rabbitskin robes, not comforters filled with the down and soft feathers of barnyard geese. And their house walls were made of wooden poles, bark, and reed mats, not stone. These wigwams were cozy, warm places. Like my comfortable glassy house, they kept those who lived in them safe from fierce winter storms.

Just before noon on Monday I was getting restless. I needed to get out into that storm. I did not want to miss it! So I bundled up, strapped on my Yax Trax, pulled my Kromer over the tops of my ears and stepped outdoors.

Visibility was limited as I found Manypenny Avenue and began my careful descent down the long hill to town. About a block away a figure suddenly appeared out of the swirling snow. My neighbor could not resist getting out either. She had walked down to the grocery store and post office more to get outdoors than to get groceries and the mail. As we stood for a moment to greet each other, even though we did not bring it to words, it was plain that we were thrilled to be outside. Like youngsters, we were excited with the storm.

The woman told of the thin layer of ice beneath the foot of snow, suggesting I be careful. After we parted I took a few steps, before suddenly falling to a knee. Further down the hill I slipped again. The wires strapped to my boots did little good under these conditions so I shortened my steps as I carefully made my way.

In a few minutes I crossed Sixth Street and began to descend Cooper Hill. Slipping again, I fell to a knee a third time. Deciding caution was better than a broken bone, I shortened my steps even more. Luckily, I arrived at the bottom of the hill without further mishap. At that point I was protected from the gusting winds and could relax and enjoy the walk even more. Maggie's, the popular eating-place with its loud pink walls and ubiquitous flamingos had its small "Closed" sign propped in the front window. Further along, the lumberyard, with its large storage shed was open, the fragrant aroma of Douglas fir and other fresh-cut woods wafting out onto the sidewalk and I was reminded of the beautiful Cascade Mountains.

Making my way to the post office I found that friendly person who runs the place as warm and outgoing as ever. She too, showed the excitement of the storm as we greeted each other and made small talk before I moved along. Another neighbor offered a ride back up the hill in his big black extended cab pickup truck, and discretion overcame my childlike excitement about the storm. I accepted his kindness. So I stepped up into the high truck cab, strapped the belt abound my body and settled in for the ride back up the hill.

Like the neighbor I met earlier, and the friendly post office manager, my truck-driving friend exuded the quiet pleasure we all felt with being out in the storm. We were children, pretending to be adults. Perhaps we wanted to plop down on our backs and wave our arms and legs to make snow angels. Perhaps we acknowledged our yearning to be out in the world, in all sorts of weather, and experience the joy of being alive.

Back home, as I returned to my study's chair I looked outdoors at the storm and again, seeing its beauty, I acknowledged my gratitude for life.

Sugarbush Time Again

March 30, 2006

IT HAPPENS EVERY SPRING. The earth begins to tilt and the days grow longer. Then the sap starts to move upward, out to the very tips of the trees' highest branches. It is really pretty amazing. Simple, but amazing. And because of these things it is sugarbush time, whether we are ready or not. And once again, it sets me to thinking.

Each spring when I walk into the woods to spend several days in Ojibwe sugar camps I feel like I am walking back to an earlier time. And in some ways this is exactly what I am doing because some Ojibwe sugarbushes are, indeed, very old, and their changes have been slow in coming.

Some of the tall maple trees in these camps might go back two centuries. Because of the ruthlessness of the logging era, there are not many of these mossy backs left in the Red Cliff woods, but a few such trees just might still be here. I do not know that anyone has removed a core of their heartwood to determine their ages, but by the size of their trunks I'd bet they go back that far. If true, that means these trees were seedlings in 1806. That was during the time when the fur trade was getting a bit rough. Competition between the Northwest and the American Fur Company agents was fierce. Then too, the British and Americans were on edge in those years, and finally openly went at each other in the War of 1812.

It was also the time when Tecumseh and his brother were starting their religious and political movement to unite all Indian tribes in a stand against the Americans. That was the time when Red Cliff's Chief Buffalo joined this movement and preached the message of these Shawnee brothers. Contrary to the way some history was written here in Chequamegon Bay, we need to remember that Buffalo was not always a friend of the Long Knives. He was not as pro-American as some would have us believe. Ojibwe sugarbushes can make me think of these things.

When I walk into the Newago Sugarbush at Red Cliff, while I feel that I am walking back into time, I also feel that I am still in the present. It's a paradox. That sugarbush is both old and new. The idea of tapping maple trees in spring, then collecting and boiling the sweet sap into syrup is very old, of course. But perhaps nothing really stands still. Perhaps everything changes.

Today a hand drill is used to make a small hole into a tree and a spigot is tapped into place. It might be a metal, plastic, or wooden spigot. In the past an ax was used to cut an eight or ten inch slash and a wooden trough was inserted at its lower end. The sap flowed down the opening into the trough and fell to a shallow birch-bark container placed onto the snow-covered earth.

These days sap is boiled in large metal drums hung over an open fire. Earlier, I am told, large birchbark containers were used. If placed near the fire rather than right over it, and if kept reasonably filled—and watched carefully—these *makakoon* worked well, but metal kettles and drums were a decided improvement over them so they fell out of use.

In the past the sap was boiled into a thick consistency, and while cooling, worked into granulated sugar, or poured into molds to form hard cakes. Whether in granulated or cake form, it stored well and would be used throughout the winter. Maple syrup as we know it was not important in earlier times since it did not store well and was difficult to transport.

As in the past, today the tapping and collecting of sap and its boiling is all part of the physical work of running a sugarbush. It is spring and such labor, especially if done by family and friends, has a quiet festiveness to it. It is a celebration. Some would say it is sacred.

But, there is more than mere labor to an Ojibwe sugarbush. It is the feeling of the place. It is the "family" of it. When in one of these camps, surrounded with Ojibwe people, I am quieter than usual. I listen to the wind and to the songbirds. I watch for ravens and eagles.

Perhaps the best indication of what these camps are like is to note that infants grow quiet when brought out to them. I do not know what causes it, except that they seem to know they are in a special place. They do more looking and listening, and, I think, they sense a reassuring comfort surrounding them. As with elders who sometimes come to sit beside the fire for a few hours, these little children are at peace. That is what fascinates me. The importance of these camps runs deep.

This is what I mean. Ojibwe sugarcamps bring it all together. They represent a way of life that goes on. They have been in these woods for hundreds of years, during times of thick and thin. The White World has surrounded them so today they are little islands where, in a particular way, nothing has changed. The spirits of the past and of today come together in them.

A Sunday Morning Walk

October 29, 2002

It is Sunday morning and I am about to take a lazy stroll down Manypenny Hill to spend a little time with friends over cups of coffee. My wife left earlier to open the grocery store and get things going down there but I linger here on our hillside before heading out. One must not hurry Sunday morning walks in late October. We have just finished a summer of hurrying, and now it is time to relax. It is time to think about things.

So I slip on my walking shoes and reach for my favorite windbreaker. Finally, I settle my charcoal black Kromer onto my head. Yes, it might be a bit earlier than last year, but today I broke out the Kromer. The mayor has been sighted in his, so I rummaged around in the front hall closet and found the old cap. If it were alive it would have expressed joy in being pressed back into service after another hot summer up on that dark shelf.

Stepping outdoors I was instantly met by the cool morning air. It told me that summer was gone and that fall was thinking about leaving, too. Then, when I turned my attention to the neighborhood I noticed frost on the roof of Vermont and Harriet's house. Yes, it said, get used to it. For a moment or two I reflected on The Johnson's and how many of these crisp late fall mornings they must have enjoyed. I thought of their youthful exuberance for life that stayed with them to the very end.

Once onto Manypenny Avenue and easing my way down that steep hill I let the day take me over. There still are enough leaves on the maples to surround us with oranges, yellows and reds, but they are falling quickly. Soon we will be looking at the blacks, browns and grays of November but this morning it still is October. My eyes reached for every bit of color they could find as if attempting to keep it just a little bit longer. For a moment or two I caught myself trying to hold onto fall and I thought of Blake's famous passage where he admonishes us not to grasp life and hold it tight, wanting never to let go. Instead, he says, we should embrace it warmly as it flies by.

William Blake's image of life as something wonderful, like a glorious bird in flight, that comes to us, receives our embrace, then is gone, visits me

59

often these last few years. Don't hold tight to this world, he says. Don't be caught in the alluring mesh of its tangibles. Like Thoreau said—simplify, simplify. Everything material is transient, and I try to soak up as much of this colorful hillside as possible for as Terry Tempest Williams, the Utah thinker tells us, "Listen. Below us. Above us. Inside us. Come. This is all there is."

It is easier to walk downhill than up and I keep this in mind as I move along Manypenny. I try not to go too quickly, reminding myself to enjoy the downhill journey because on the way home I will be walking uphill and that is another story.

At the corner of Sixth and Manypenny I see that eight or ten vehicles are in the church's parking lot. Unlike during the summer when our town swells with its warm-weather enthusiasts, this morning's pews must have plenty of room.

Reaching Cooper Hill I enjoy the view way down to First Street and the lake beyond. Hardly a car is seen all along that corridor and the blocks click by quickly—past the Kelly's attractive corner home, past Maggie's where the out-of-towners hold court all summer long, past the lumberyard and Tom's neat little bicycle shop. Past the Chamber offices, the Egg Toss and the bookstore. It is almost as if I have the town to myself. What a luxury, I silently exclaim. How delightfully different from my years of life in a large metropolitan area! How I try to embrace and hold tight!

This morning I decide on peppermint tea, and while I savor my iconoclastic drink, I visit with my friend Margie. She and I can agree on things, and we quietly talk about them, perhaps even, in a secretive, subdued manner for the major issues of the day are buzzing through the shop while we practically whisper about different things to each other.

Later, as I depart the downtown area, moving along Rittenhouse and up past Defoe's gas station, I think about how over the 150 or so years of Bayfield's existence, that there have been other walkers who came downtown on a late fall Sunday morning. Was I merely a continuation of those folks? Were my twenty-first-century thoughts similar to theirs? Like me, did they count the number of carriages resting outside the village temples?

This morning as I reached upper Rittenhouse I noted the empty houses of summer folk and I wondered if earlier walkers in other centuries did the same. I wondered if a late October walker might have been amidst the locals who greeted the widow Lincoln when she came a'calling with General Sherman so long ago. Suddenly I seemed to be inconsequential and I wondered if Bayfield has changed at all.

THE SWIM TEAM

November 24, 2007

THERE IS A SWIMMING TEAM IN TOWN but I suspect relatively few of us know about it, and I suspect if I did not have three grandchildren on it I might not know about it either. That is how the business of swimming can be in America–downright quiet and almost invisible. This swim team sets me to thinking.

Let's face it: swimming is good for you. It's proponents tell us it is one of the best exercises there is, and our medical people are quick to encourage we older folks to spend plenty of time down at the pool. They say it has much to do with how when in the water we put many of our otherwise unused muscles to work, and that can do great things. Unlike running–or jogging, as it used to be called–when swimming you are not pounding your feet, knees, and their joints on the roadways. Swimming is gentler on our bones, and the tendons, ligaments, and muscles that control them. And if we push it when in the pool we get one grand workout.

The Bayfield Area Swim Team has been here for a number of years and it has always had its avid members. I am told some of them have gone on to college swimming and beyond. But it all starts with the youngsters. They usually learn quickly, and with the excellent instruction they receive, they soon are in those swimming lanes at regional competitions, going for the ribbons. It is something to see.

Swimming did not come early for me, nor did it come easy. I did not learn to swim until I was seventeen. Unfortunately, in my childhood my brothers and I were not able to get to beaches, swimming holes, lakes or pools very often, and, more importantly, we were not encouraged to do so. For us, it just was not something most people did. Where we lived in southern Wisconsin there were few lakes, and later when we moved to the northeastern part of the state there were even fewer. Our high school was lucky to have a tiny gymnasium let alone a swimming pool. That changed for me when I joined the navy. In boot camp it was learn how to swim or else. And, after a day or two of trying I finally passed the test.

61

Now I watch those kids jump into that lake or pool and take off. They are fearless, and with each passing year they grow stronger and faster. I love to be part of it.

My friend Rainer, who grew up in Europe, reminds me that compared to Europeans, we Americans do not swim. We might learn as youngsters but soon we go on to other things. For most of us it is not a lifetime activity as it is for many overseas. Why it that so? Are we too busy to swim, or is it something else? Do we think there is something better, like playing football, basketball or baseball? Or, does tennis or golf finally pull us away from the water? Up here in the Northland it might even be those ubiquitous ATVs and snowmobiles.

We know that competitive swimming does not pull in the money like the big moneymaking sports. And we know that most of us who take the bait and play one of these other games will give it up after our school years are over. Swimming is not like that. I suspect swimming is like bicycle riding: some of us do it most of our lives. When I see an older person slip into the water at one of our beaches and swim out into the lake I smile a bit. There is something good about an older person swimming.

I recall a day down at the Old Dock in Red Cliff about thirty years ago. A young man had just returned from military duty in Korea and he had not been in the water for many years. There he was, poised and ready to jump into Lake Superior, when he turned to me and asked, "Do you ever forget how to swim?" He jumped in and it all came back to him. I suspect Ojibwe people used to learn how to swim almost as soon as they learned how to walk. Traditionally, the Ojibwe practically lived on the water.

Our local swim team has members from Red Cliff, Bayfield, the township, and Washburn. Once practices begin in late October they run through the winter. Swimming meets are held in Duluth and Superior and teams come from the south shore and general Twin Ports areas. And it does not cost much. There are scholarships to cover the initial fees, and the equipment required is minimal. All it takes is the will and someone to get you to practices. The Bayfield Area team is one of the smallest in this region, but it always has swimmers in the serious competitions. I have been to those meets and can attest to the excitement once those kids hit the water. Bayfield, Red Cliff, the township, and Washburn hold their own against much larger teams.

But, swimming is about more that the competitive meets. It is about our youngsters learning they can do this—they can slip into the water and swim. It's that simple.

TIME

February 12, 2007

SOMEHOW FOR MOST OF MY LIFE I have avoided reading weekly news magazines such as *Time*, *Newsweek* and the like. Then, a few months ago when two wonderful granddaughters brought home some fundraising forms for magazine subscriptions from their grade school and set them before me things changed. How can a grandfather turn down such beautiful kids? The little box for *Time* magazine was checked and in a few weeks that familiar red bordered cover began appearing in our mailbox, right on schedule each Saturday morning. Now, in the twilight of my years, I am reading Time, and it sets me to thinking.

The pulpy bulkiness that I recall has disappeared in favor of a thinner, more suave magazine. It reminds me of Twiggy. It feels a little more slender in my hands. Now it is smoother, actually more slippery as my fingers move over it. But the more important change goes beyond some new fangled plastic spray they use to coat the pages.

Today *Time* magazine tells me that I must be out of the loop. For several weeks I found it difficult to read, then, yesterday it came to me. After I finished studying the classic cover and opened the magazine I struggled in my attempt to determine when the advertisements ended and the news stories began. It seemed like I was turning five or more pages before I came to actual news articles, but I was not sure. Twice I went back to the beginning and turned through the opening pages again, looking for the start of the news pieces. Then it came to me. The format of the magazine had changed. In the past advertisements were clearly identifiable and found only in their traditional places. There were a few at the beginning and although some appeared discreetly placed in the body of the publication, most of the rest came at the end. Now I worked to decide whether I was reading an advertisement or a news article. They looked alike.

Surely this change was planned and carefully orchestrated from some distant suite of offices in a high rise overlooking a magnificent river valley meandering through a cluster of urban canyons. It occurred to me that the pages of *Time* now resemble certain Internet sites where advertisements can pop up almost anywhere and the viewer must study the screen very carefully in order to find what he is looking for. In this new *Time*, advertisements are as ubiquitous as mosquitoes at a backyard evening barbecue. But, their mere numbers is not the issue. The problem is that advertisements are designed to look like news stories, and news stories are designed to look like advertisements. This morphing of ads into news and of news into ads is a sign of the times.

I am reminded of what commercial television has become and why I watch so little of it anymore. The same goes for commercial radio. I cannot recall when I last listened to commercial radio. If I want ads I will go to the *Yellow Pages*.

For the first few weeks that *Time* started coming to our Bayfield home I never really finished reading any one edition. After a few minutes my head began to hurt. It was like I was suddenly thrust deep into that big box on Ashland's East End where you are surrounded with product.

In this day when our names and addresses are sold to all sorts of folks out there in the corporate world we have become the product. A corporate mailing list with thousands of names and addresses must be worth a fortune. Now broadsides, booklets, catalogs and other things come to us almost daily. In America, buying and selling has become our Life Way, and *Time* is in the thick of all this, wheeling and dealing like the rest. Some days when I open our small post office box I must tug and pull to get all these things out. No, I will not pay for a larger box. That would just encourage the scoundrels. That would be like those folks who kept designing bigger and bigger shopping carts. The bigger the cart, the more we put in it.

What I would like to see is for the Postal Service to install a large receptacle clearly marked PAPER FOR RECYCLING in every post office lobby, and then to follow through and actually recycle that stuff, not just toss it in the trash. And what I also would like to see is a *Time* magazine with a minimum of ads and those separated from the news stories.

But, perhaps I need not worry. The print media is said to be suffering with the coming of the computer. Some of the major newspapers are witnessing declining subscriptions as more and more people turn to all sorts of electronic devices to keep informed. Maybe *Time* is on the way out.

The fact that a weekly news magazine has reworked itself to resemble the Internet must mean that most of us have switched our addiction from the tube to the computer monitor. And its all about marketing product.

The insidious presence of the marketplace in our society these days should give us pause. And when it is difficult to tell a news story from an advertisement what is really going on?

Passing Traditions Out

December 3, 2007

L<small>AST WEEK</small> I <small>WENT TO COFFEE WITH THREE FRIENDS</small> at one of our local shops. It was quintessential Northern Wisconsin as we sat in that almost empty restaurant on a white-winter morning. Beside our table were floor-to-ceiling windows that afforded us a view onto the clearing behind the building. Deer, foxes, and more are sighted in that field now and then. Almost idyllic, the setting sets me to thinking.

The scene of a few old folks at coffee on a winter's morn in far northern Wisconsin is one that appeals to me. None of us talked excitedly about news of the day, or of what is going on at our workplaces, or even of our numerous grandchildren. No longer do we get excited about world happenings the way we used to, and since we are all retired we have no workplaces—at least like we did in the past. And although we think the world of our grandchildren we do not go on and on about them. We were relatively quiet, perhaps even calm to the point of not speaking at all. We sipped our coffee, chewed our toast, and passively looked at the woodland scene through the large window.

Only because my bride mentioned it that morning did I ask if any of my companions had put their tree up already, or if they were finished with the yard's decorations. Two responded, saying a grandson now hung their things in the front yard and around their porch. And their Christmas tree was still in its box in the garage, waiting to be brought in and assembled, but that would be done next week.

Then our third companion told how she would decorate the yard and living room year after year with lights, wreaths, boughs and what not. Her tree was always real and its ornaments collected over a lifetime. Some paper and cloth ornaments her children made in grade school would be hung onto the tree, year after year.

But then she told how well into January last year when a daughter came by to help her take the tree and decorations down—when everything was boxed and ready to be put back into storage for another year, she told her daughter to take everything. Yes, to take it to her home. Our friend was finished with it all. Forty-some years of the Christmas decorating routine were enough for her. Now it was the next generation's turn.

We know when we have had enough of some things. And our companion that morning had no second thoughts. It simply was time to pass those things on. I know that feeling, might even say, "Been there. Done that." Lately it has been visiting me more and more. Every time I go into our garage and I see my hammers, drills, and saws hanging where they have been for two or three years now without being touched I am reminded of it. When we reach a certain age there are some things we no longer want to do. For me, that list of such things is growing.

Fortunately, all four of us at that table at coffee that morning are still able to get around and be part of things. We do not feel so old. And we still enjoy most of what we have enjoyed all our lives. We just do not want to do some things anymore. We are as busy as ever, and will tell each other that the days are not long enough to get everything done. But, some things no longer do it for us.

Sociologists used to talk of disengagement. The theory argued that when humans reach a certain age they might start to sever some lifetime relationships, and cease doing things they did most of their lives. Disengagement theory had its detractors who argued it was an excuse for not including the elderly in everyday activities and that it was a way for caregivers to relax. I don't know. More and more, disengagement theory is making some sense to me.

No one around our table that morning at coffee was dismayed at our friend's decision to no longer put up a tree and decorate it. We all knew what was going on. Perhaps we wondered when we would make the same announcement. We still haul out the boxes of ornaments and strings of lights year after year and almost painstakingly place them onto our trees. And we still want at least a few colored lights in the front yard, but our silence around that coffee table held a message.

Traditions can be tenacious although those of us who carry them out come and go. We take part when young and stay with them until, like our coffee friend, one day we are all done. Our friend still celebrates Christmas but she simply does not want to mess with all the decorations any longer.

Maybe she has finally broken through all the hoopla into what this time of year is really about. Maybe she is telling us Christmas and the Winter Solstice never were about bright lights and beautifully wrapped packages. Maybe it takes a near lifetime to figure that out.

We sipped our coffee and brushed crumbs from our chins as we looked out into the winter field.

A White-on-White World

THIS MORNING MY WORLD IS BATHED IN WHITE and looks like one of those oil paintings in which the artist used few other colors to fill the canvas. Except for the brown and deep-emerald tree trunks it is almost a white-on-white world. Earlier when on my walk in orchard country west of town this winter world set me to thinking.

How this morning's simple pallet contrasts with our spring, summer and fall colors! In particular the blazing oranges, yellows, and reds of October stand in stark contrast to today's more subdued hues. As I walked along Betzold Road with Rosie the chocolate Labrador romping on ahead, I challenged myself to see how many shades of white I could find. Whites gave way to uncounted numbers of grays and in turn they to darker browns, greens, and ultimately to deep blacks. While at first glance the countryside might have seemed relatively colorless I concluded that contrariwise, it was full of color.

Those orchards, open fields and bordering forests were a vibrant array of many shades of white. Quiet shadows running across the snow-filled fields suggested tones of blue, and at times they nearly resembled our big lake at this time of year. For a lively change in tone, the tall grasses protruding above the snow at the edges of the open fields here and there held shades of bright yellow running to a deep umber hinting of the dark reds of Cortland apples that only two months ago hung on the orchard trees nearby. The land's winter pallet included just what was needed to compose an eye-catching scene. I saw that winter in Northern Wisconsin is not a colorless time.

Later, in contrast to the nearly solitary walk in orchard country, when entering a downtown coffee shop I found a room filled with people. Not ready to relinquish my contemplative mood I noted how they resembled the snow-filled orchards and woods I had just walked through. Like the trees, they were cloaked in seasonal colors—predominately dark-browns, greens and blacks. And their voices seemed quieted—subdued actually. It was as if the winter landscape had somehow found its way into that shop.

Still filled with the white, gray, and quiet tones of the outside world, I ordered a cup of decaf and accepted an offered chair at a table with a friend and soon was engaged in conversation about worldly things. I heard about my friend's penchant for reading the *New York Times* on Sundays, and his struggle to have the paper delivered on that single day of the week. I took part in the conversation as best I could, but my mind was still filled with the morning sojourn into the natural world. I fear I was not the best of company at our small table in that crowded coffee shop. As much as I need intellectual engagement, my walk into the country just outside of town would not leave me.

White on white. The metaphor of an artist painting this morning's winter landscape stays with me. The subtlety and soft touch required to paint such a canvas and do it successfully is remarkable. For most of the several years I have been dabbling with learning how to paint I felt the daunting challenge before me. This morning I recognize how difficult it can be to paint winter scenes. And writing about winter with its seasonal pallet of whites, grays, browns, and blacks can be likewise. Perhaps the challenge is to make something interesting out of little.

This task of making do with less might be what makes winter in Lake Superior Country so appealing to me. Yes, perhaps this is why I love to spend the cold season here. Obviously, its contrast to our people-filled summers is striking and affords a studious contemplation. Winter is a time to rejuvenate, but its appeal goes beyond that. The simplicity and stark reality of snow, ice and the cold that accompanies them forces us to accept our limitations. A serious snowstorm can literally stop us in our tracks as it reminds us that sometimes we must bow to what is more than us. Sometimes we must simply pause to look, listen and let the natural world have its way.

How can I make room for the *New York Times* when long morning walks wait to be taken? Why give my time to the patter of that busy and distant world when I have quiet, resting orchards to observe and enjoy? Like Robert Frost, I too have woods to watch as they fill with snow.

As long as I can walk through this white winter countryside and become one with it I have no need for the *New York Times*. A presidential race? An assassination in Pakistan? A strong or weak dollar? Certainly these are important, and in time will be given their due, but this morning let me hold the image of our white-on-white world and the pristine freshness it brings. Today I feel my affinity with those snowy fields and sleeping apple trees, with that pair of pileated woodpeckers that sliced through the wonderful silence along Myers-Olson Road as they voicelessly flew from snow-covered tree to snow-covered tree.

Our white-on-white winter helps us see the world.

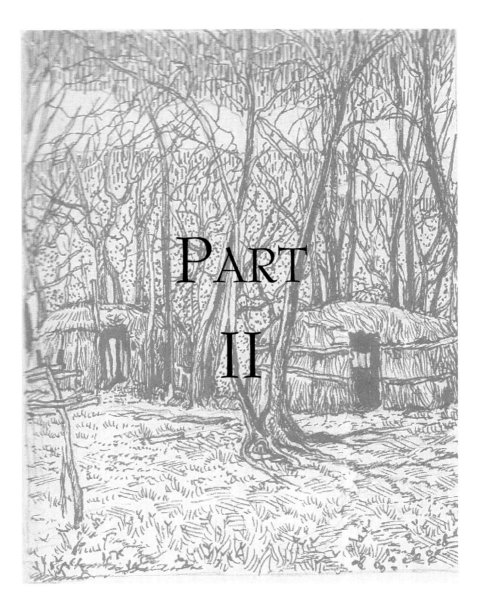

PART

II

PREFACE TO PART II

Our family's Red Cliff cabin has been not only a quiet venue where the muse can come a-calling, it has also inspired essays speaking to the wonder of the woods and those creatures that reside therein. And always, the prominent presence of Lake Superior is just a long shout from the cabin's front door.

Many of these pieces reflect the age-old ambiance provided by such a cabin with its oil lamps, wood-burning stove, welcome cups of hot balsam tea, unleavened bread, and bowls of steaming stovetop bean soup. The creek and lagoon beside the cabin are home to a beaver family, and its activities are observed throughout the year. The cabin has many visitors, like the white-footed and big-eared wood mouse that finds its way indoors each fall, but is quickly encouraged to return outdoors where it must take its chances with the other critters of the woods. Otters, eagles, red tailed hawks, and Canada geese have also made cabin calls, along with an occasional black bear, fox, and coyote. Timber wolves pass through, and of course, white-tailed deer are year-around neighborhood residents. The raspy squawk of the raven is regularly heard as the big black birds come to investigate cabin activities. So far no signs or sightings of cougars have occurred, but in time we expect them to happen too. Each spring warblers and other northern songbirds return to their seasonal summer homes in the creekside trees, adding their voices and the welcome flutter of their comings and goings to life in this woods.

An isolated cabin, however, cannot keep worldly concerns completely at bay, and even here, in these Red Cliff woods, the reality of our distant world is acknowledged. Some of these essays address these perennial matters, but they are tempered and made more palatable by the writer's days spent beside the cabin's creek.

There is much to learn, to observe, and be a part of in Red Cliff, and in different ways this section's essays speak to the deep importance of this community.

ODE TO OATS

March 20, 2003

WINTER IN JANUARY CAN GET DOWNRIGHT COLD, especially in these woods beside this creek. How did those First People do it? How did they stay warm in their bark and reed-mat lodges? Some nights if the fire went out there must have been cold toes, fingers, and noses—and any other body parts that might have stuck out from under those rabbit-skin robes. When they got up, I'll bet they appreciated a good hot breakfast.

This morning as I stood over the barrel stove waiting for the small kettle of water to come to a boil, these questions came to me and they set me to thinking. How did those early Anishinaabeg get through winter without oatmeal?

For some Red Cliff people oatmeal is soul food. It ranks up there with fry bread, wild rice, venison, *lugalade*, and maybe even macaroni soup. In my family it is the stuff legends are made of. Back in the early 1960s when I first came to the creek I was told about oats and how it should be served with grease. Forget the milk and sugar. Not offered in bowls, oatmeal was spooned right onto your plate. A small amount of hot melted salt pork grease was poured over it and maybe some pepper sprinkled on top. You ate it with a fork. Any leftover oatmeal was set aside to solidify into a clump as it dried a bit. Then, at another meal, it was sliced and fried, sometimes served with maple syrup. Eaten this way it was enjoyed just as much as at breakfast.

My love affair with oatmeal became serious forty-some years ago when I first came to Red Cliff. In those earliest years the house I stayed in had no electricity, so refrigeration was available only in wintertime, but it was tricky. Any food left out in the shed overnight might freeze solid by morning. This is why I felt there was so little cow's milk in that kitchen. Cow's milk was quite common in the early 1900s on the reservation—we recall the stories of the Daley, Basina, and Aitken farms—but in the early 1960s all that was in the past. When I arrived here such milk simply was not a common food in the community. Most milk I encountered was condensed and came in small metal cans with those yellowed puncture holes. We drank water, a lot of tea, and a little coffee. All this seemed just fine.

Those First People had no oatmeal, but when I'm honest I have to admit that they did not need it. They had plenty of food without this new grain. The woods, meadows, sloughs, and creeks provided their meats, fruits, and vegetables. The rice fields gave them *manoomin*. The lake gave its fishes, the sky its birds, and the woods its four-leggeds. None of this was processed, reconstituted, extruded or otherwise harmed in any way. Their diet was wholesome. They had maple sugar, much better for you than the cane or beet kind we use today. Their foods were fresh, and sometimes dried and smoked. Fish were commonplace and none of them held any PCBs, mercury or other heavy metals. There was no need for fish advisories in those days.

So with all this food it is easy to see that those people did not need oatmeal. It is presumptuous of us to think that what is dear to us must also have been dear to them, and if they did not have what we treasure it is presumptuous again to consider them deprived.

This is the way the first Europeans coming to Chequamegon saw the Anishinaabeg. The Europeans were certain those early Ojibwe were unlearned, uncivilized and unenlightened. The first Jesuits among them called their religion "abominable." But these outsiders liked much of the food the Ojibwe used. They quickly saw the value of *manoomin*. At times, if the Europeans could not get venison or fish, it was about all that kept them alive through a long winter. But these newcomers sometimes were homesick. They longed for some things they thought all people needed. One such item was wheat and the bread that could be made from it. In 1660 when enduring a difficult winter on Lake Superior's south shore, the Jesuit, Rene Menard, wrote about wheat and how he hoped to get a little patch growing somewhere in spring. Much later the first Protestants on Madeline Island in the 1800s worked to establish a small patch of wheat so they could grind it into flour and make their treasured bread. Manoomin was not good enough for them.

Looked at this way, these newcomers were not good tourists. Today the travel sections of our fat Sunday newspapers sometimes tell us we must be sure to experience the customs of the peoples we go amongst when we travel to other lands. We are encouraged to try their foods for new taste thrills. This is precisely what I try to do when I leave the creek and find myself in Washburn or over in Ashland. I sample their foods to see what it is they are eating now. Lately I've discovered that old trends like pizza and Chinese food are passing. Now it's things like black beans and rice with something called pesto. Very recently I tasted their new wonder green. It's called celantro. Apparently only the very discriminating diner has caught onto this herb. Compared to all this colorful exotica our plain, gray oatmeal must pale in importance.

I don't yet know when oats first made its way to the Red Cliff shoreline. I'll have to ask around. Maybe Fran can find out on the Internet. If not, I'll dig into the old books. One thing seems sure, however. That is that once here, oatmeal quickly caught on.

Today eating oatmeal is said to be a good way to reduce cholesterol levels. Loaded with fiber, it cuts the fat. I don't worry about that hot grease because I get plenty of exercise while working up a batch of firewood or just walking into town. Then there is always that exciting hour or two I spend with Ben Fox as we pick up debris beside the roadway running from his driveway up to the big hill. Of course that is a warm weather activity. In winter I must find other ways to exercise.

As serious as I might sound about oatmeal, in my experience at Red Cliff it has also had its share of chuckles. There were some years that the mention of oatmeal brought smiles and even outright laughter. Back then a nephew or niece who worked in a distant city might joke about how good it was to come home and sit down to a meal that included oatmeal. Everyone understood immediately how the person felt. But this began to change in the 1990s and today while such humor still appears now and then, it is clear that it is on the way out. Some people might disagree, but it seems to me that today it is becoming improper to joke about oatmeal at Red Cliff. Soul food is understood differently now. No longer is it a joking matter. For some the humor might still be there, but I think those persons are becoming the minority.

I fear that this importance of oatmeal at Red Cliff might be best understood by more of the older residents than the younger. In some families that work to keep certain traditions alive this might not be the case, but what about the rest? Might there be Red Cliff young people who have breakfasts of nothing but heavily sugared processed cereals of one sort or another? If so, how is all that excess sugar burned off? I don't see many backyard woodpiles anymore, or youngsters laboring to carry heavy water pails to their grandma's house. And despite the existence of a community-wide garden program I see very few gardens. All these activities provide exercise.

Cold January mornings must have been handled well by those First People. They lived through them for thousands of years. All this brings to mind the words of the first licensed English fur trader to come to Chequamegon Bay. This was Alexander Henry back in 1765. In his memoirs Henry wrote: "The Chippewa of Chagouemig are a handsome, well-made people . . . The women have agreeable features and take great pains in dressing their hair, which consists in neatly dividing it on the forehead and top of the head and in plaiting and turning it up behind." It is clear Henry was impressed with these Ojibwe. The words, a handsome, well-made people, are striking. Well fed, well exercised, and despite how those Jesuits felt about them, these First People must have been beautiful to behold. Oatmeal? They might have felt it unnecessary and even rather lowly. What must it have been like for Alexander Henry to come among these beautiful people? I sit in my cabin beside this creek and wonder. And as I spoon my hot oatmeal into my mouth I also know that they had their own breakfast foods. As my oats suits me, their foods suited them.

Well, these oats are more than mere nutrition. They can help a person understand who they are, where their roots run deep. They can feed their souls.

SUPERIOR WEDDINGS

June 1, 2005

THIS MORNING AS I POURED A MUG of hot peppermint tea I was set to thinking. In only a few days it will be June, the month for weddings, and beside this creek in these Red Cliff woods, it is also a month to pause, look around, and enjoy. Weddings typically are joyful times and the thought of them on such a beautiful late-spring morning makes me feel good. So, I decided to step outside the cabin to sit on the rough pine bench under the big hemlock down by the slough, where I could see Lake Superior at the end of the channel. I would just sit for a while, enjoying the scene.

Over the years I have attended many June weddings here at Red Cliff, but the recent ones are not the usual kind many of us are familiar with—that is, weddings inside Christian churches. No, these newer ceremonies that come to mind today, are held outside, very close to the cold waters of the big lake, and most importantly, they are officiated over by a tribal judge. This is what is so significant about them, and what brings them to mind.

These tribal weddings might not raise many eyebrows, but this morning as I sipped the tangy tea, I sat for what became long moments run together, thinking about them. Such ceremonies demand contemplation because they offer much more than the usual welcome images associated with a June wedding. Their message is personal and political. It's about identity and recognition—about the way a community sees itself and how others see it. Personal identities run deep, are of no little matter, and their recognition by communities outside the reservation is very important.

A lakeside wedding at Red Cliff is something special. If the weather cooperates, the event can be wonderful. The natural setting, the fancy clothes of the wedding party, and all the rest make for a scene that one does not soon forget. The last such wedding I attended had it all. That June morning the sun was with us as we gathered on the pre-appointed spot in the campground at Buffalo Bay. As the time for the start of the ceremony drew near it was evident to all that the unpredictability of the weather was no longer an issue, so we relaxed and began to enjoy the day.

That morning the water was a deep blue, and across the channel Basswood Island was a vibrant dark green. Nodin, the wind, was present, at times causing difficulty for the young man at the portable organ plugged into a nearby campsite outlet. The warm and pesky wind frolicked with his sheet music, but he held it all together and met the challenge. The few women wearing wide-brimmed straw hats also struggled with the wind, but for most of us, it was a welcome member of the party. Nodin is part of life beside this big lake. What would Gitchigami be without its winds?

The Ojibwe people in this particular ceremony were at home, gathered on the lush lawn beside the lake that morning. They readily understood the meaning of the outside ceremony. The others—some from distant places—at first were less at ease, but soon settled in and enjoyed the event.

The tribal judge was efficient. She was introduced, then told the group that the certificate of marriage she would give the couple was recognized by authorities of the State of Wisconsin. It is just as good as a state license, she said. Such recognition was unheard of a few years in the past, but today's world is different. In some ways much good has come about. This point came to me as I lifted my hot mug to my lips and took another sip of peppermint tea. June can be a month filled with good thoughts—and good tastes.

Today the outside world is interested in many things that occur on the reservation. Important news from Red Cliff regularly makes the local newspapers. For instance, these days, news of who is running for tribal council is published in the *Daily Press* and sometimes in the *County Journal*. This was not always the case. A few decades ago the local press did not bother to cover such things. Mostly, the reservation news that appeared in these newspapers was eye-catching in one way or another.

We do not have to go back many years to find times when communities like Red Cliff were barely recognized at all. Events occurred inside their boundaries that hardly caught the attention of outsiders unless these happenings were sensational ones. In interesting ways, reservation communities seemed to be practically invisible to some outsiders. But that was then; this is now. Sometimes I think the changes that have come about at Red Cliff have occurred since the casino was built. This recreation spot has drawn people to the reservation who rarely came before. The chance of winning money can do unusual things.

I hope Red Cliff's future holds many more lakeside weddings. I hope tribal judges are called upon time and time again to conduct these joyful ceremonies.

And I hope that the sound of the drum calls out at these gatherings, letting the surrounding countryside know that another tribal wedding is occurring. In Lake Superior Country, wonderful June is made for them.

A BROWN WINTER

January 3, 2007

TODAY THIS RED CLIFF WOODS IS PRACTICALLY bereft of its winter snow. We still have several inches under the trees here at the family cabin, and the trails to the woodpile and outhouse hold a packed layer of the white stuff, but it is getting soft and if this warm spell continues it will soon be gone. After two weeks or so of really cold days early this winter we were given warmer temperatures right up to a day or two before Christmas when suddenly the snow arrived. This unusual weather set me to thinking.

We almost had a brown Christmas like those snowbirds in Arizona say they enjoy, and I am glad the snow finally came. Let's face it—up here in Lake Superior Country we are supposed to have cold and snow in winter. This is the North, and cold, snowy winters are one of the many reasons we live here.

When at this cabin two weeks ago I woke to the drum of raindrops on the roof. It sounded good, and as such a comfortable sound always does, it took me back to the days when I slept in a second-floor room up under the pitched roof of my grandmother's farm house. Then I enjoyed the music of rain hitting tar shingles only a few feet above my head, but now I feel something other than joy. A night of rain in mid-December is not unknown at Red Cliff, but these days with all the talk about climate change I am caused to ponder what this winter rain really might mean.

Then, this morning on my walk beside the creek I was engulfed in fog. Fog in the Red Cliff woods in early January? The resident beaver family that lives in the slough was not out and I wondered what they thought about all this. I wondered too, if the eagles that work this creek are affected by this warm weather. I have not seen them yet today. Surely, if these temperatures persist lots of changes will take place, for the better or worse.

My firewood pile should last longer with this warm weather, and my snowshoes may stay up on the wall hook. Some of these changes might be enjoyable, but it is the tradeoffs that concern me. I am a creature of habit and I have become used to a white winter. Brown? Brown is good, but not in January.

83

A few weeks ago when on a last minute pre-Christmas shopping trip to Ashland—the Garland City—I noted how folks were quite busy hurrying from one shop to another. Out on the East End the isles of the Big Box were like the streets of Milwaukee in rush hour. Those folks were buying with a passion. I wondered if they were interested in things like global warming, or if for them it was still business as usual.

This is what I notice: We humans must concentrate on the immediate, on what confronts us each day. Our ability to focus on the task at hand is a trait that has served us well for millions of years. We must meet our nutritional needs, protect ourselves from the elements, have children, and raise them. Around the world we all do these things, albeit in different ways. Sometimes I think we should be known as Homo focus. Whenever I am at a casino, which is not often, I am struck by how well we do this as I see those folks bent on focusing on the slot machine screens before them. That is focus of a high order.

But last night's rain might be about more than the immediate. It might be part of something occurring over vast stretches of land around the world. It might be part of changing weather patterns that are only just beginning to make their moves. The rain that hit my cabin roof might be part of what is causing Greenland's ice pack to disappear. It might be part of why the polar bears are beginning to move north, and why the future of the beautiful spruce trees in these Red Cliff woods is said to be suspect.

These are a lot of might-be's but then, this is no little thing. My grandchildren are beautiful to behold, and I want them to live long, wonderful lives. It concerns me that the way I lived my life could have a large negative effect on theirs. That ivory-colored classy 1954 Mercury sedan with the spicy sunset orange roof that I tooled around in almost fifty years ago had a large V-8 engine that spewed carbon into our atmosphere. Every automobile I owned since the Mercury did it. And for a few generations before me my forebears did the same. We lived with little awareness of what we were doing to the earth. We were busy, focusing on the immediate.

A brown winter is all right in Phoenix, Arizona, but not here beside this big lake. We want the cold air to bite our cheeks when doing that last minute Christmas shopping, and likewise when we spend those sunny January Saturdays out at Mt. Ashwabay. As usual, we humans have a long list of "wants." And we want snow. I think of what we might have to do to ensure that our winters remain white.

Cleaning the Cabin

September 2, 2007

Y ESTERDAY MY DAUGHTER AND I HIKED the mile or so into the Red Cliff woods and did some much-needed work at cleaning the cabin. It had been a long time and even though we labored for two good hours there is still much to be done. The woods, the cabin, my daughter, our working together—all that sets me to thinking.

What would we humans be like if we did not have family? And, what is it like not to have a daughter? And just as importantly, not to have one who loves the Red Cliff woods and is willing to spend a few hours hard at work cleaning a very messy cabin? At times, when I think about it, I have been fortunate.

The cabin really was a mess. A family of mice had wintered over in our little barrel stove, almost filling it with bits of a cotton blanket and other material. The white-bellied, big-eared woods mouse is nice to see in its own element, but not inside our cabin. Maybe an occasional one passing through is all right, but a family settling in for the winter? When mice are in the cabin I think of the Hantavirus, that deadly virus that if picked up by we humans can do us great harm. No, I do not like mice in the cabin.

For years we had a little brown bat that spent its summer days hanging up in the roof rafters. It preferred a spot directly in the center of our largest room, depositing its droppings in a neat pile on the floor. Upon coming to the cabin after a week or so absence we would sweep up the droppings and that would be that. The bat did us no harm and we were pleased to share the cabin with it.

Yesterday we cleaned out the stove and then moved it to a better spot on the floor. In the process the stovepipe was disassembled and put back together, and finally a fire was lighted to see how the draft would work. All went fine and now the stove is ready for its fall fires.

Another job was to clean and do a few repairs on our dozen or so kerosene lamps. Previous visitors to the cabin clearly were not familiar with the workings of these lamps for they had let the flames blacken several chimneys, and in

85

some cases they lost the wick down inside the oil. I held my tongue, but wondered about today's young folk who know nothing about how to operate an oil lamp. Growing up in a home lighted with electric lights can cause us to forget how to do without them. As I carefully washed the glass chimneys and tinkered with the thin brass lamp fittings to make them operable again I wondered about other things we moderns have forgotten. I wondered if some of our cabin visitors knew how to use the outdoor toilet.

My daughter is in her forties so she has witnessed plenty of cabin dirt before. She did not complain as she set some water on to boil and began to clean up here and there. It was good to work together and see the cabin begin to take shape again. We talked about trying to make it mouse-proof and whether or not it was possible. Is there such a thing as a mouse-proof cabin? We wondered about that, but decided to give it a try. We intend to spend a few weekends this fall working to do just that.

A family that works together stays together. That is not exactly the way the old familiar saying goes, but I like it. My daughter loves to dig in and get her hands dirty, and over the years she has had ample opportunity to do just that. She must have gotten that from her mother because that woman is a working machine.

Yesterday as the cabin's varnished floorboards began to take on their bright shine again and the round and heavy wooden table was cleaned I stood aside and smiled. "Nice." I muttered, "This place is looking nice again." A sparkling clean, but still rustic, cabin is a special thing.

We'll go back in a few days and do more cleaning. And we will get up in that gable corner where we think the mice are entering and decide on what needs to be done to seal it up. Then, there is the matter of a supply of firewood for the winter. That work is best done in fall when the air can have a nip to it. Working up a large batch of firewood in October or even November is an activity that I have been part of over the years and so far I have not tired of it. Soon I hope to get my grandchildren involved in such work. They are big enough to carry and stack sticks of firewood, and maybe, if I am lucky, they will actually like it.

Well, cleaning a messy cabin might not be the most exciting thing for some folks, but yesterday when I worked with my daughter I felt something downright enjoyable. Even though there were just the two of us it was still a family activity and it went well. Even in this modern world, families and cabins are still special.

CABIN HEAT

July 30, 2007

THIS MORNING IS DOWNRIGHT WARM here beside the creek. The cabin is sheltered by towering hemlock and white pines but it still is cooking. No air moves, making things quite uncomfortable. All this summer heat sets me to thinking.

The weather folks say we are in an eight-year drought and today I believe them. It is as dry as British humor and this morning I have had enough. We need rain, and badly. Last Thursday evening's shower was wonderful but as usual this year, we need more.

The creek is the lowest I have ever seen it, but out in the main channel it still is flowing. This is a spring-fed waterway, and thank-goodness for that. Without those springs quietly bubbling up along the creek's banks there would be no water at all. Yesterday I checked for this year's wild rice crop but there were no rice grains to hang low as they finished ripening time, and there was no wind to make them sway here and there. It was deathly still— and overly warm. I came back to the cabin and drank a long draught of cool water as I silently gave thanks for this precious liquid. Icy spring water in the heat of July is one of life's sweet pleasures.

The wood's critters are lying low in this summer heat. They must take on a near nocturnal lifestyle these days, nodding off in a shady place during daytime and moving around for food at night. Even the ravens and their airborne cousins are not to be seen. And those pesky *ajidamoog* (small red squirrels) are quiet, hiding out somewhere, waiting for cool times. When outdoors on more comfortable days those little red fellows watch my every move as they send up a chatter that can last for hours.

This heat makes me think of earlier days when I took pride in my ability to labor out in the hot sunlight at haying time. Throughout my farm years— the 1940s and 1950s—I was part of the family crew that put up the hay crop. This was used for fodder for the dairy herd through the cold winter months and was always important. Once I recall how the season's crop was not as good as needed and we had to scramble to find cash to purchase a semi-load of baled hay to carry us through. My father was not pleased that we had to buy hay.

July was haying time and it was approached with apprehension but if the crop was particularly good and the weather cooperated it was also looked to with joy. A good hay crop usually meant it would be a good winter. I recall that throughout my farm years we put hay up a number of different ways: loose, in heavy wire-tied bales, and then in smaller, string-tied bales. In later years we chopped it when dry and blew it up into our haymows with a belt-driven blower. In the last years we chopped it while still quite damp, and blew it into our silos to be fed as fermented grass silage, something the cows ate with relish. Whichever method we used, it always called for much physical labor and my teenaged brothers and I took pride in getting out there, stripping off our shirts and digging in. Like our deeply tanned skin, the sweat running down our chests and backs told of our youthful, and prideful, labor.

Those haymaking days are long gone and their memory tells me how time has sped by. Today in hot July here at the cabin I have all I can do just to find shade and sit tight. I don't move much in this heat as I take my cues from the absent and silent critters hidden somewhere in these woods. Let the young fellows strut their stuff out there in the sunlight. I'll sip my ice water on the sidelines.

The earlier Ojibwe seemed not to complain about this kind of heat. The elders tell how it was just something they lived through. As is true today their summer villages were always beside a body of water. Summer was the time to travel to visit friends and distant family, and for most people travel was done by water. This meant that if one became overly heated a cool dip was not far away. Water, or *nibi*, as it is called, is one of the spiritual treasures of the Ojibwe people. It has its own presence, must always be treated with respect, and at appropriate times is to be honored with proper ceremonies. Today this cabin heat calls this to mind and making spiritual offerings to water sounds like the right thing to do.

On these hot days I try not to cook my food, but yesterday I brought in some fresh sweet corn and had to boil it up for supper. For such tasks I use a small propane stove. The heat from the barrel stove would drive me outdoors. I will save that for the cool mornings soon to come. For now, propane does the trick.

Here at the cabin my carbon footprint is small. Oil lamps light my evenings and plumbing is non-existent. A deep hole by the spring is my refrigerator. For me, these things work just fine.

THOSE MELTING GLACIERS

January 6, 2007

Ever since driving over to Northland College several weeks ago to view Al Gore's film on climate change I cannot get those photos of Greenland's melting ice out of my mind. As long as I can recall Greenland has been nearly completely covered with ice, but according to those time-lapse photographs there is very little of it left. Greenland soon will be green. I suppose neighboring Iceland will also change. Such things set me to thinking.

It is not just Al Gore's film. Almost a year ago I attended a University of Wisconsin workshop on climate change where a few science types presented data on how the climate of our state has been changing for a long time. Long-term studies of ice thickness on our lakes attest to this. It is clear that we are not just experiencing a minor cyclical phenomenon. This is something different.

So what about this melting ice? If I trade in my gasoline-powered automobile for a hybrid will it help? I recycle, in fact all the "trash" I generate at this Red Cliff cabin is carried out and placed in my recycling bins at my Bayfield home. And, perhaps most importantly, when at this cabin I am off the grid so I am not contributing to the pollution from those coal-fired power plants.

But, why now? Why be bothered by voices that tell me about melting ice? I sometimes think I have enough on my mind with our two current middle eastern wars. The faces of those dead soldiers I see every few nights on that public television news show won't go away either. Wars and melting ice are a double whammy, and at my age I do not need such things. I am supposed to be in my retirement rocker, looking out at the green meadow in front of my house, with a restful smile on my face.

This morning when I stepped out of the cabin to go to the woodpile for an armful of dry birch, I saw a few chickadees flitting from branch to branch. Such wonderful birds are always a treat to witness, no matter what time of year, but last week in Bayfield, my wife said a neighbor reported seeing a robin. Could these birds still be here? This is January and they should be far to the south.

Bob King, the kind fellow who shovels the snow from our driveway has had very little work so far this winter. If this warm spell continues he might be hard pressed for income until the grass comes up. Mr. King also trims lawns around town in summer so for him it might be a tradeoff—less snow shoveling and more grass cutting.

For others it might not be so easy. Jerry Carlson out at the ski hill has been busy with his snow-making guns this year so things seem to be going well out there. But what about the Book Across the Bay—and those dog sledders who like to come to Bayfield and run their pups? With more thought we might come up with all sorts of people who could be adversely affected if this warm trend goes on and on. And it is not just people. We should be thinking about the non-human companions who share this planet with us. Already we are being told that this year will be an unusually warm one.

I might have to go visit Greenland soon to see for myself. So far I have noticed no reports out of that part of the world as to how things might be changing with the loss of all that ice. If that newly uncovered ground is cultivable maybe those Greenlanders might go into farming.

But, it is not just Greenland's ice. Canada's polar bears are supposed to be facing severe problems since their ice is melting, too. Surely we will rally to save the polar bears even if we have to put them all into zoos in order to save them.

I hope these Red Cliff woods do not change too much due to our warming trend. Predictions of such things tell of some plant and animal species that will die out or migrate northward with the long-term upswing in temperatures. Some evergreen species, for instance, will be in trouble. And the white birch trees as well. All sorts of things might change.

If all of this is really happening, and if it is because of our behavior, then we have cause for thought. Do we want a Greenland without ice and a Canada without polar bears? Scientists tell us such bears are white because of the cold and ice so if they somehow survive will their color eventually change? Could we take brown polar bears—and a truly green Greenland?

Well, maybe I should listen to my mother-in-law. Many years ago she once said, "Those people! They think too much!" She was commenting on some white-folk (my mother-in-law is Ojibwe) who lived in a fast-paced distant city and were struggling with tough problems of their times. Maybe I think too much. Maybe, when out at this great cabin I should turn it off and just enjoy the simplicity of these Red Cliff woods. But, a Greenland without ice? How could that be?

THOSE JESUITS, TOO!

November 10, 2002

THE OTHER DAY I WALKED OUT TO THE BEACH and just sat for awhile looking at the islands. It was one of those typically November days, overcast and grey all over, and quiet except for the squawk of an overhead raven now and then. Life is good by the creek, even though some friends say the trees can crowd around too much. Out on the beach things sure can open up, even on a cloudy day. That morning while contemplating the channel between Oak Island and me, I was set to thinking.

This was the same channel that the Jesuit, Claude Allouez, paddled through back in 1667 when he went on that canoe trip up north to visit some folks at Nipigon. Surely his gaze must have passed over this beach, over the very spot where I was sitting. My mind's eye saw him out on the lake in his black coat. He wore an old, dusty wide-brimmed black felt hat, and his birch canoe was powered by a native bowman and steersman. There was a second canoe with two more people who had a large gray canvas bundle of provisions between them. It was a colorful image, and I even heard the rhythmic dip of the four paddles that dark day. Claude Allouez was the second Jesuit priest to come to Red Cliff Country back in the mid-1600s. He was not the last.

Of course back then there was no Red Cliff as we know it today. People were living along this shoreline and amidst these islands, and they likely had villages and encampments at the proper places, but most seemed more focused on the big island—Madeline—and that needle-like point to its south, and the lower reaches of this big bay. The books tell us that in the 1600s it was the Odawa and Huron who were living here, not the Ojibwe. The Ojibwe were to come after 1680, but I don't believe it. I feel, like William Warren did, that the Ojibwe were living along this shoreline, in these bays and amongst these beautiful islands, long before the coming of the Jesuits. I think they never left. And sometimes when I sit on that log back on the high water line at the beach I imagine I can still feel their presence. Their bones are in this ground all along this shoreline.

Those Jesuits were something else. They were not native to this land. They were cut from another cloth. After years of hearing of them, and reading what others have said about them, I finally sought out the words of the priests themselves. Last year I found copies of the *Jesuit Relations*—all seventy-three volumes—and started to read. The *Jesuit Relations* are a mixture of reports, some written by church leaders at the various North American mission stations, some written at Quebec and Montreal. And some come directly from the field. Some come from places like Sault Ste. Marie, Keewenaw, and Chequamegon Bay. They all are quite interesting. No, I have not yet read all seventy-three volumes. So far I have completed only the very earliest ones, and all those pertaining to Lake Superior.

Something happens to my head when I read such writing. I'm not sure exactly what it is, but one thing is becoming clear. Those *Jesuit Relations* are troubling. Sometimes they are downright hard to read. It's not that the words are too big or the syntax too archaic. The copies I read are the English translations by the early Wisconsin historian, Reuben Thwaites. His English is from the late 1800s, written over one hundred years ago, but it's not difficult to understand. In fact it's very easy. If you read French you can do that too, because Thwaites provided the original French right beside his English, but I don't read French, so I'm stuck with the English.

The trouble I have when reading the words of Claude Allouez and his colleagues has to do with their certainty. These Frenchmen were sure they had it right. They were certain they were superior to the native people they had come amongst. It is this arrogance that I struggle with. This is one reason I leave the creek now and then to come out to the beach. Maybe the open sky, the big water—the obvious space—will help clear it all up.

Historians tell us that the first Jesuits to come to Lake Superior were Charles Raymbault and Isaac Jogues. They were at a Feast of the Dead ceremony on Lake Huron where some Ojibwe from the far eastern end of Lake Superior asked the priests to come to their village. The priests did, coming to what is now Sault Ste. Marie. That was in 1641. It is likely Raymbault and Jogues did whatever Catholic priests did in such places back then, but they did not stay at the Sault very long. After some weeks they returned to Lake Huron.

We do not know for certain why those Ojibwe wanted those priests to come north to the Sault. I suspect it had more to do with trade goods from Montreal and Quebec than with any religion. The Ojibwe people knew about economics and politics and the like. According to William Warren they had been making regular long paddles to these eastern trading centers for years and years.

Raymbault and Jogues, it seems, vainly felt they were invited to the Sault because of their religion, but I think it really was about economics and politics. These Ojibwe had their own religion and it suited them just fine. It doesn't make sense to think that they were willing to cast their powerful Midewiwin aside for the religion of these two Frenchmen.

Raymbault and Jogues never came to Chequamegon Bay. They had their hands full with the Odawa, Huron, and Iroquois. It was twenty-some years after 1641 that the first Jesuit came to western Lake Superior. This was the Frenchman, Rene Menard.

Rene Menard's trip along the lake's south shore was not an easy one. The priest was getting up in his years and it seems he was not a pillar of physical strength. He wintered in Keewenaw in 1660-1661. Some writers think he never made it to Chequamegon Bay, that from Keewenaw he went into the woods of northern Wisconsin to aid some Huron people and died on the trip. Others feel Menard made it to Chequamegon in the spring of 1661 and after some months went to the Huron village. I agree with them.

After Rene Menard it was Allouez. He came in 1665, left in 1667 to go back to Quebec to get someone to help in his work at Chequamegon, and came back with another priest, Louis Nicholas. We do not hear much about Louis Nicholas at Chequamegon Bay, but he was here—he worked with Allouez briefly—then apparently tired of it all and went back east to a more comfortable life. After he left it was not long before Claude Allouez did the same. Chequamegon's people were not listening to his sermons so he went south to Green Bay to be with the Potawatomi. He had come to Chequamegon Bay in 1665, left to go back to Quebec to get Nicholas in 1667, returned to Chequamegon that very year, then when Nicholas left in 1668 Allouez followed a few months later. Claude Allouez had been in Chequamegon off and on for only a little over two years.

In 1669 the fourth Jesuit arrived: Jacques Marquette. He brought Louis Le Bohesme (or Boehme) along, a Jesuit lay brother who was a blacksmith skilled in making and using armory. Marquette and Boehme left less than two years later, in 1671. Most historians say they left because of trouble with the Dakota. This is the story we have been told for years and years. Reuben Thwaites, in 1890, wrote that Marquette and Boehme "were driven like leaves before an autumn blast"—meaning the blast of a Dakota war party. I do not believe it. I think Marquette left because he liked big rivers and the Illinois people. The Illinois had been coming to Chequamegon Bay and Marquette listened to their requests that he come south to live with them. He liked them. They treated him well and were persistent. Besides, Marquette had heard about the big river in their country. He was still young, an accomplished mapmaker and must have had ideas.

So, with the departure of Marquette and Boehme the time of the Jesuits at Chequamegon ended. This was a span of only ten years and out of these they were actually at the bay for at most only a little more than five. Some writers say the Jesuits failed at Chequamegon Bay, that the people there rebuffed their attempts at religious conversion. We have many pages of the Jesuits' accounts of these times but little of what the tribal people said or felt. Europeans did all the writings of those times, so we must be very careful as we try to make sense out of them.

Maybe this is what I think I sometimes hear out at the beach. Maybe it is those muted voices of all the early people who lived here in the 1600s and watched those four Blackcoats come and leave. Maybe their voices are in those channel winds, or in the calls of the gulls, ravens, eagles and others who fly in this channel sky. And maybe their voices are in the waves that come to the beach, sometimes loud and forceful, but most often much more quietly as they meet the pure sand, over and over. The music of these smaller, recurrent waves is gentle but strong. It is so persistent, and it keeps coming even on the most windless days. Day after day that gentle sound can be heard. It never ends.

These quiet voices stand opposed to the loud pronunciations of the Blackcoats. Way back in the 1600s those loud voices came, stirred things up for a while, then suddenly left. They are gone. But each time I go out to that beach the other more gentle voices are still there. Even on the calmest days like that overcast November day last week, I still hear them. I am not sure I understand their message yet, but I am beginning to like what I hear. It pleases me. When I hear it I feel good.

I have much more thinking to do about those Jesuits. They are not easily put aside. Their words, especially those of Claude Allouez are so loud and so certain. And Allouez, like the others, was an educated man. Must arrogance and education go together? I must think about this. I will have to ask a few people on the Rez. Maybe Acorn Gordon, Clara Cameron, or Billy Joe would know. Maybe I will have to write about it again.

WHITHER THESE KAYAKS?

September 12, 2004

SOME TIME AGO I NOTICED A STORY about this person who paddled a kayak all around the shores of Gichigami. (I forget, and my newspaper is recycled by now—but, he was a Native American. Was he Ojibwe?) It was an interesting article, well written and it even offered a photo of the chap—a nice looking fellow. He set me to thinking.

This was not the first time someone kayaked around the big lake. A woman did it a few years ago, and published a book about it. Such a trip is no little feat. It takes courage, determination, and all sorts of other good things. The old books tell us that the Jesuit, Claude Allouez, circumnavigated Lake Superior in 1667—in a canoe, not a kayak—but I don't think he put a paddle in the water on that trip. Those Jesuits traveled with an entourage of native paddlers.

I think I understand why this latest fellow made his long trip. If I was younger, stronger, and if my legs were shorter, I might want to do it myself. A person's life can open up on such challenges. Your mind could be cleansed of years of rubble. And if you were a believer, on a trip like that you might even meet your maker. That could be downright scary.

But this sort of question—why today someone would paddle a kayak all around Lake Superior—is not the most interesting that comes to mind. That fine article about this recent fellow caused me to think about kayaking itself. Here at Red Cliff kayaks have become like locusts on the prairie. These summers if kayaks had wings their annual coming would darken the sky.

How long will this last? Surely, this too shall pass. With kayaks come the entrepreneurs. There is money to be made on these trends, and over the last few hundred years Red Cliff has witnessed many such comings. Maybe Pierre Esprit Radisson and his brother-in-law, Medart Chouart, Sieur des Groseilliers, back in 1659, were the first. They were adventurers—seventeenth century thrill-seekers—but they didn't come just to paddle, to view the scenery, and to clear their minds on the big lake. They were business people. They came for furs, but really for the cash furs would bring them.

With these earliest Frenchmen were the Jesuits—the priest Rene Menard came on the second Radisson-Groseilliers trip. It has been said that the Jesuits were very involved in the fur trade, even controlling as much as ninety percent in the 1600s. Perhaps in those early years all Europeans who came to Lake Superior were in business. Maybe they all were after money. Almost immediately after the coming of Radisson and Groseillers the floodgates were opened. We all know the story of fur traders, loggers, fishermen, land speculators, railroaders, anthropologists, social workers, construction companies, novel writers, dram shop keepers, developers, life insurance salespersons, bankers, outdoor recreationists, so forth and so on, that followed.

Big things seem to draw humans to them. Gi-chi-gami. Big lake. Really big lake. The migration that the Ojibwe teachings tell about was probably all about this. Those people kept coming down the St. Lawrence River way, through the eastern Great Lakes. They were like salmon, swimming upstream, looking for the source. Finally, many stopped here: Madeline Island and this Red Cliff shoreline. Some went on to the very end of the lake, to Fond du Lac, and some even continued on to the prairie. But this place, Red Cliff and its big lake, might have been the destination all the time.

These earliest folks did not come in kayaks. They used birch canoes. Kayaks were part of life for those humans far to the north. These vessels were often made of wooden frames covered with sealskin. The Inuit people used them to get food. They took fish, seals, and at times even caribou from their kayaks. Those vessels were tools the people needed to survive in their land. At times their lives may have depended on their kayaks. This is what interests me.

The kayakers we see at Red Cliff do not use these thin, sleek, narrow vessels to get food. Their lives, those of their families and communities, do not depend on kayaks. These kayaks are for something else. Even though it appears to take a good deal of physical effort to get around in a kayak, our kayakers are really playing in those boats. Red Cliff's current "coming" is all about having fun, about getting away from the work-a-day world. This is called recreation, not food-getting.

And this is at the nub of my interest. Something has occurred in the lives of these people that causes them to feel a strong need to get away from their chosen jobs—or careers—for a few days, or weeks, or maybe longer. They leave their workstations and come to the big lake to play. Could it be that their jobs are not fulfilling? Something must be missing in their lives.

Among other things, this is what is so interesting about that fellow who paddled around the big lake. He was Native American. Up to the present time I know of no Ojibwe people from Red Cliff who feel the need to take a kayak out on the water and challenge the big lake like that.

The kayaking thrill-seekers must come to this lake for the same reason many others do. The promotional brochures I have read speak of being low on the water, feeling it, even tasting it. It's like immersing yourself in the lake —physically and mentally. Maybe it's like a Christian baptism. Water has been called the universal mediator, meaning all over the world humans use it as a symbolic connector between themselves and the spirit world.

That's pretty heavy stuff. Once this summer when I was on my way to 'Da Lanes for one of those great noon specials—I think it was that excellent homemade chicken noodle soup Bilzo Gordon makes—I saw several kayakers in Buffalo Bay. They were in a big circle with one kayak in the middle. For a moment I thought it was a ceremony, a communion of some sort. I don't know. There must have been some teaching going on there. (Is there a Church of the Kayak?)

Our kayakers are fair-weather paddlers. Maybe sometimes they get caught in a storm and must deal with rough water, but most often I see them out there when things are calm. Sometimes on a bright summer's day when they are on the water along with a lot of sailboats it almost looks festive. Especially if there are big doings on the Rez or in Bayfield, it nearly has a carnival character to it. On such a day if I dare venture into town and walk the streets, as I pass the shops and see the tourists buying fudge, ice cream, and t-shirts, with a little imagination I might think I am at Wisconsin Dells, or at least that single block on Hayward's main street with all the tourist shops. On the sidewalk on such a day I see that, like me, people are doing a lot of looking.

And on Lake Superior kayaking must involve a lot of looking, too. The brochures and videos like to show kayakers at the caves. Those "sea caves" seem to be a fascination. They must be looked at a lot. Imagine all the snapshots taken of the caves! And the reservation's beaches have been known to pull the kayaks in too. Kayakers have been found out at Point Detour Campground where sometimes they try to get to the water without paying a fee. But, I suspect most kayakers are friendly, law-abiding folk. Like the rest of us they must love this land and the lake, and they respect the rules of its use.

Kayaks have become playthings. They are on the water for recreation. Kayaks on Lake Superior are not working fishing boats. For some of us the big lake itself might have become a plaything. Look at all those sailboats going 'round and 'round. And besides, what is so different about the kayakers and those of us who build our houses facing the lake? Folks in those new, big, glassy houses are looking at the lake, too. It's the thing these days.

So. I'll just leave kayakers alone for now. So far none of them have come up the creek. I suppose if that ever happens I'll have to be nice—maybe even ask them in for coffee.

NEW YEAR'S EVE

September 21, 2004

W E ARE IN THE MIDST OF "THE HOLIDAYS" and once again the revelry is underway. By now Thanksgiving is ancient history, the Winter Solstice, Christmas, Hanukkah, and the onset of Kwanzaa, have come and gone, and we are facing New Year's Eve. For the past month or so we have been knee-deep in holidays. It's enough to set an old man to thinking.

In winter here at the cabin it all looks the same no matter what the holiday. The woods is at rest and our winter birds are lying low. Ravens have been quiet for a few weeks. I suspect they are miles away, searching for road-kill, but in time they will be back, flying quietly overhead, keeping an eye on things. I love to have them around. Their chatter is an important part of this woods. Their guttural croaks are friendly, familiar statements, but it is their deep, throaty, gurgling calls that intrigue me. Very intelligent forms of life, ravens make many different noises, all interesting. They have a lot to talk about, no matter what the season.

This winter I find coyote tracks now and then, and deer sign is in its usual places. In past years I found what had to have been tracks of timber wolves, but I look in vain for cougar sign. *Makwa*, the bear, is sleeping so I will not see its sign for months. The other four-leggeds come and go—fishers, minks, otters, martens, porcupines, and bobcats—leaving their trails in the snow. And, of course the squirrels are constant companions all year long. It is way too soon to look for snow fleas.

Over the years I have spent a number of holidays at this cabin beside this creek. I like it that way, but must still keep things quiet on the home front so at this time of year I am obligated to leave this sacred sanctuary to make token appearances in various family houses. It always takes me a period of adjustment to step out of these woods and re-enter life out there where the others live.

In the days before the missionaries came the old Ojibwe people embraced this time of year in a deep, religious way. Winter was a quiet time when teachings went on. Elders stepped up and taught the young what they needed to know.

Most *manitos* were sleeping so stories could be told about them. With the breakup of the peoples' fall villages they moved to the winter hunting regions where a nuclear family or two might live alone far from others. If hunting was not good, it could be a hard time, meaning the food caches that had been filled in summer and fall might be depleted before spring. But, like the other seasons, winter was a good time. Much knowledge could be passed on in the winter lodge. And, it is important to recall that we need not speak in the past tense when discussing winter activity for the Ojibwe people. This old-time winter teaching goes on as it has every year since its beginning. Much too often, American Indians are discussed in the past tense by people who should know better.

This year my New Years reveling will be low key, as it has been for years and years. No longer do I imbibe to the extreme. It was many, many years ago that I grew disenchanted whenever I had to be in the company of family and friends who were consuming too much alcohol. Now I use it for cooking, and maybe enjoy a glass of wine now and then, but the rest is history. Those beer commercials on TV during the football games are overdone, and perhaps, even obnoxious. Maybe such things are only for the young. I still have not explored all the beauty of this world and my time is winding down, so I want to be as clear-eyed as possible every minute of every day. Let me see, hear and acknowledge all this wonder.

So a new year is upon us. I try not to think of the wars we are involved in, of the violent deaths occurring as I write this. I try not to think of those wealthy politicos and gesticulating generals whose epaulets are tossing here and there as arms are raised to make important points. Republicans? Democrats? Conservatives? Liberals? Sacred writings? Give me these ravens and the occasional eagle overhead. They know nothing about politics and economics, or religion and war—and I like that. Give me these Red Cliff woods with their winter silence. Give me nature and its welcome regularity. Out here beside this quiet creek there are no leaders arguing about this or that. There are no concerned citizens worried about tax rates and failing schools. The Winter Solstice has done its thing and the days are growing longer with each sunrise. For some time the nights will still be cold but my woodpile is adequate, and my larder is filled. It is winter, and even after all these years I am still able to walk out to this cabin and spend time here. For that I am glad. Any reveling that I do will be done quietly, beside this creek. I need not go into town. There is enough power right here.

Cold Winds and Warm Fire

November 1, 2005

T HIS MORNING WHEN STEPPING from the cabin to go to the woodpile for another armful of dried birch, I caught myself uttering a brief but serious shudder from the icy wind that met me. It was not much of a wind and it was not really as cold as it would be later in the winter, but it was still downright chilly. That little wind set me to thinking.

How I love to mess around with firewood and my wood-burning stove! Surely, that dusty and sometimes smoky stove is one of my little treasures. How different it is from the modern natural gas fireplace my wife and I have in our Bayfield house! My stove is the classic barrel type, made from a thirty-five gallon steel barrel. When I do it right, and when the wood cooperates, it can heat the cabin to the point of extremes. There have been times when I had to throw open the cabin door and let the heat escape—that's how hot it can get. Usually, however, I am more careful and do not let the fire drive me outside. After all, it is my cabin, not the barrel stove's.

When my wife and I sold our house in a distant city a few years ago and came home to northern Wisconsin we left our wood-burning stove behind. It was one of those newer ones with cutting-edge engineering that meant little firewood was wasted. The wood burned so efficiently that hardly any smoke seemed to go up the stovepipe. And it had a large glass window that allowed for a constant view of the ever-changing fire. I think I loved that stove and when we walked out the house that last time I recall taking a moment of silence before it, like I was saying goodbye to an old friend. I miss that stove. I miss its altar-like presence in that house. I hope the new owners appreciate it and are taking care of it.

Perhaps such a high-tech stove would be out of place in this rough cabin. Most often, I suspect, such expensive stoves are used in modern houses with all the usual amenities like dishwashers, in-floor heating, fancy plumbing and what not. Maybe that stove would not have been happy in my dusty cabin. Maybe such things come from another place, a place with different values and assumptions. Maybe that stove would not have adjusted to these Red Cliff woods. But, I am guilty of anthropomorphizing. Stoves are not alive, and they surely are not humans. They are machines and even though some of we woodsy types might treat them as if they were human beings, they are still inert masses of matter, completely in our control. They are mindless and without a culture. They are man-made tools that exist only because we allow them to.

Yet, I think about other wood-burning stoves I have had the pleasure of knowing here in Red Cliff. My wife grew up with a classic pot-bellied stove with Eissenglas windows. That stove stood in the middle of the living room floor and did yeoman service in heating her parents' little old, three-room house. Eventually it was replaced with another classic, the famed Ashley wood burner. Over the years the Ashley Company sold many stoves in Red Cliff. Some people still recall how they had to go way out to Ehler's store in Cornucopia to purchase them. Mike and Babe Newago had another favorite of mine. It was a scaled-down model of the potbellied stove. That little marvel sat in the Newago kitchen and sometimes would drive folks outside. Then, there are the wood-burning stoves that worked so well in the Newago Sugarbush's cabin all those years. How different all these stoves are from our fireplace!

Even though our fireplace throws off some heat–especially if I activate its little blower system–it is still an embarrassing fake. I click it on and off with a remote control. There are no ashes and there is no smoke, at least any I can detect. And, sadly, its flames are almost always the same. They are like a painting of flames instead of the real thing. Sometimes I think our fireplace is like a plastic flower–colorful but unchanging and without a perfume. But when in town on these ever-cooler evenings I sit beside it as if it were the real thing. I pretend.

Some folks I know love their natural gas fireplaces. They remark about their cleanliness and how easy they are to operate. "No more woodpiles and no more dirty curtains. And no more problems about what to do with all those ashes," they like to tell me. I don't know. Sometimes I think of that natural gas and where it comes from. I think of all the pipelines crossing our land. There is nothing about the natural gas industry that appeals to me. The same goes for those oil refineries.

At the cabin this morning it is just cold enough to make me really appreciate my barrel stove's heat. But, it is more than the mere heat. I like to hear the wood popping and cracking as it sometimes does. And when I step outside, like this morning, I glance up at the stovepipe chimney and watch the smoke lazily curl up and out as it rises far above where the ravens and eagles fly.

THOSE WARLIKE SAVAGES!

August 25, 2005

Even though our summer has been downright comfortable I still occasionally kindle a morning or evening fire in the cabin's barrel stove to take away any chill that the big lake might bring our way. I sometimes have a supply of newspaper on hand to make this enjoyable chore a bit easier, and now and then I re-read one of those papers before it is used to ignite my firewood. This morning I read that back in June some Pennsylvania students were working to stop their high school from giving their personal information to military recruiters. This bit of old news set me to thinking.

That article claimed that under the Bush administration's No Child Left Behind Act, public high schools must give personal information about their students to these recruiters. Under this act if a school does not release the students' telephone numbers and addresses it runs the risk of losing significant federal funding.

A big part of my spending so much time at this isolated cabin is to get away from such news, so I struggle with my penchant to read these outdated newspapers. Maybe I must bring other kinds of paper to kindle fires, or better yet, keep a supply of birchbark on hand. Even though I try to escape the daily patter of what is called network news, it occasionally finds me, even at the cabin. This is part of why Red Cliff has had such a strong appeal to me for the past forty-or-so years. It seemed to be far away from things like wars, army recruiters, and pompous presidents. I know I was not being realistic when I viewed Red Cliff this way, since a serious study of its history shows an almost regular engagement with military things. I have to go deep into denial to view Red Cliff—or any Indian reservation—as an isolated place, safely out of reach of wars and presidents. Reservation cemeteries make it very clear that indigenous people have done their share of fighting our country's battles.

Yet, I still am puzzled. What logical connection is there between the No Child Left Behind Act and military recruiting? Why does this act require a school to give the telephone numbers and addresses of its students to the Army, Navy, Air Force, Marines, and Coast Guard? Could the thinking behind this act be that those students having problems getting educated via the usual public schools, might benefit from spending time in the military? Is it felt that they might even get an education while serving their country? Or, does the No Child Left Behind Act show that the present administration wants to be sure that no child will be left behind regarding the opportunity to be part of our military forces? Put even more crudely, is the "Left Behind" Act meant to help ensure that military recruiters meet their quotas?

I think of that bank robber, who, when being asked why he robbed banks, said, "Because that's where the money is." That must be why military recruiters are like seagulls hanging around the fishing boats. Recruiters come to high schools because that's where the young men and women are. And even though two of our present wars involve many National Guard and Reserve personnel, most of our troops in Afghanistan and Iraq are younger persons. Recruiters like to meet young men and women who are still in their teens. It seems that teenagers are easier to get excited about going to war than older folk.

To add to my consternation about all this are the numerous military vehicles and personnel in Red Cliff this summer. For the first time in my memory, the military has a very obvious physical presence in the community. Camouflaged humvees can be seen in Red Cliff as well as on the streets of Bayfield. When I see them I think of their ultimate purpose. These vehicles have to do with war.

Our present enemies in the Middle East are said to be warlike people. A few years ago when we were fighting in Somalia we were told our troops were going against guerilla fighters led by tribal warlords. Today, tribal warlords are supposed to be active in Afghanistan and possibly in Iraq. Democracy is supposed to replace these traditional leaders. This causes me to ask what warlike means? And, just what is a warlord? Surely the people we are fighting in the Middle East look upon us as being warlike, and maybe even consider our leaders to be warlords.

In the early written history of the United States, we see where writers said European colonists came among warlike savages to "settle" this land. Do our leaders view the Middle East as a place where we are destined to go and "settle" things? We do not hold public beheading events but have our bombs and missiles beheaded anyone? And playing with these words and images a bit further—what could be more public than a screaming American bomb or missile flying into an Iraqi city?

Maybe I have been spending too much time at this cabin, but I ask again, what logical relationship is there between the No Child Left Behind Act and military recruiting? Have I missed something? And what about our ease in using words like warlike and warlords? Just who is calling the kettle black?

THE JOY OF THE SUGARBUSH

April 12, 2005

W E HAVE HAD SOME SNOW AND COLD WEATHER this winter but for the last week of so things have begun to change. The longer days and the occasional drip of the roof's icicles have ridden in on the coattails of warm air. I like it, yes I like it all, and it sets me to thinking.

It's sugarbush time. Each year when February starts to pack its bags I begin to think of what Mike Newago used to call "The Bush." "Who's goin' to shovel out the Bush?" he'd ask. "Who's goin' out to cut the wood?" You could tell he was itching to get out there. I think that man loved his sugarbush.

His brother Sam was the same. These fellows came alive in their sugarbush. I think when they were out in the woods they were at their best. They seemed to belong in that woods. They were happy there.

And I was happy out there too. For years I was able to spend a few days of my Spring Break with them, cutting, hauling and splitting firewood, and hauling and boiling sap. It was hard work, but our working together made it easier. We all dug in and got it done. There usually was something to do, whether working with firewood or the sap. Mike was a stickler for removing most of the snow from the boiling area. That camp resembled his yard at home. Each winter that yard's snow was painstakingly cleared, by hand—and it was a big yard.

Sam was usually the one to tap the trees. Like his older brother Mike, he was very strong and could turn that hand-drill with little effort. The number of taps varied each year, ranging from a hundred or so to more than twice that many, but I don't think we ever knew exactly how many taps were put out. The number depended on who was tapping the trees, and what the weather was like. The hole was drilled, the metal or wood spigot tapped in, a small nail pounded in beneath it and a large food tin hung on the nail. When the weather was right the tins would be emptied at least once a day, but each season was different. You could not predict how much sap you would get.

What I liked was the isolation. After months in the city I was suddenly out in the woods. The rough cedar cabin with its wood-burning stove, its sleeping bunks and cots, and the soft glow of the oil lamps at night, all added to my joy. The trail in was almost a mile long and most of us walked it. Once in a while a snowmobile was used, but not often. Walking in was a rite of passage. I felt like I was entering a different world. The rush of urban life would fall away with every step. It was an act of decompression. Walking out was the same, but in reverse. Coming out of the bush was a mental preparation for being back amidst people. It was a twenty minute hike, during which I got ready for returning to traffic and the rush of the city. I liked the walk in better than the walk out.

Most Red Cliff folks do not have sugarbushes anymore. They might talk about them and say they are important, but that is about the extent of it. They welcome the dark and smoky syrup when given some but apparently not enough to set up their own bush. Maple syrup from the Rez is like wild rice. It's Ojibwe soul food. As such it has heart-felt meaning and continues to be very important to those who feel deeply about Ojibwe things. These days an Ojibwe sugarbush is about much more than making an old fashioned sweetner. It's about staying in touch with the ancestors, about being out in the wonderful world of trees and other important things. And it's certainly about family.

Today I see young people on the rez who might really enjoy working a season in the bush. Exercise, home-cooked camp food and being outdoors seems like a good idea to me. And imagine how a few weeks away from the television and computer would free-up your mind! But these days young people like their electronics, and there is that thing called school. It is interesting how school sometimes takes youngsters away from some real important things. Adults have similar problems. Working a job from eight to five makes it difficult to set up and run a sugarbush.

Maybe most folks don't have sugarbushes anymore because there are few maple trees left. The Red Cliff woods has been logged and logged again. There are plenty of aspens but few hard maples. Wouldn't it be neat if the community established a few sugarbushes for those who would want to work them? Are there enough large maple trees left, or would they have to be planted? And is there the patience needed to wait for a maple seedling to grow into a large tree? Would it be practical to use ceded lands? Are there any granting agencies that would jump at funding a project to reestablish several sugarbushes at Red Cliff?

Questions, questions, questions. Asking them is easier than coming up with answers. Good answers to tough questions are the hard part. But—is there a maple grove on that old Aitken Farm? And what about that nearby forty acres that is now known as the Bayfield School Forest? That forest is within tribal boundaries and might be just the place for a new sugarbush. Who knows? Such things could happen. All it takes is for a few determined folks to make it so.

Well, after a year or more Ben Thinken is back. It feels good to be writing this column again. It's been a long time since I have written one—a long time without much thinkin'. With a little luck—and good health—maybe I can keep it going every month.

ANOTHER OJIBWE SUMMER

July 3, 2005

IT IS EARLY JUNE AND HERE BY THE CABIN I feel the cool air from the big lake. Some mornings it is almost too cool, but this is what I have liked about this Lake Superior country for the forty-some years I have been spending time here. I'll take the cool—even cold—days over the stifling hot days any-time, besides, these cool mornings set me to thinking.

Last year we had a cool spring too, and shopkeepers in Bayfield com-plained that it kept visitors away. It was not until well into June that things began to warm up and the days' cash receipts began to grow. In spring (and summer) cool days can be poor for business. It seems warm days bring the folks with the fat wallets.

This is what I loved about Red Cliff from the first time I saw it. It was so far from the major population centers of Wisconsin that few people came here. There was peace and quiet in these lakeside woods. There was no casino, no "Lanes," no gas station, gift shop, fire hall, health center, administration building, or anything else like that. There were no housing projects. There was no wastewater treatment plant. There was the Catholic church, the old community hall and that tiny little building in a small grove of trees nearby that served as the dentist's office whenever one came to the Rez. And of course, there was "Pit's," the small grocery store just off the Rez, at its south-ern extremity. Essentially, Red Cliff was a community of houses scattered along the highway and out along Government Road, and except for the land, trees and shoreline—that was all it was. To me, that was always enough.

I recall lying on the lawn in a yard on Highway 13 in "Downtown Red Cliff" in the early 1960s with an elder on a lazy Saturday afternoon when hardly any traffic passed by. We talked about a myriad of things as we kept an eye on what came down the road. Most of what passed was pedestrian traffic on its way up to Pit LaPointe's store. Pit and Lucille LaPointe's gro-cery store was also where a thirsty person could buy a drink and a bottle of Rhinelander Shorty beer, and I recall that many folks availed themselves of this refreshment in those days, especially on the weekends. In later years it was turned into "The Outpost." This was strictly a tavern, the grocery line discontinued by new owners. Later, when this establishment folded, the building was moved across that boundary line and became today's Peterson's Foods.

Back in the 1960s that elder and I would remark about the occasional boat and trailer that came along, as we stretched out on the grass and enjoyed a bottle or two of amber glow ourselves, but boats and trailers were few and far between. In those times Highway 13 was a pretty quiet stretch of road. I liked it that way. In summer there usually was some activity at a nearby home called "The Ponderosa" (named after the popular TV western of those years) just a short distance from where we reclined in the yard with the apple tree. Sometimes a runner would be sent out from the Ponderosa for replenishments from Pit's Store. Once this person carried a scribbled note, written on a small swatch of birch bark. We laughed about the historical significance of that.

There were no pow wows in Red Cliff in those years. All of that had gone long before the 1960s and would have to wait several more years before it returned. Now, especially when I attend one of Red Cliff's traditional pow wows on the weekend of the fourth of July, I think about what has changed. Today's pow wow has become a welcome institution, not just to some of the local people, but to many from other parts of Indian Country who travel long miles to get here each July. How important these wonderful gatherings have become!

For many years summer has been the time for Ojibwe people to come together and enjoy each other's company. With the advent of the European fur trade in the 1600s, people came to Chequamegon Bay in spring to meet with the new traders and to regroup with native relatives and friends. This was a ceremonial gathering after sugarbush time, and of course, after the sometimes long and hard winter when small family groups would be off in the woods, separated from others. Summer was a time for traveling to renew friendships and to establish new ones. The ice had left and now the water highways were open and ready for the canoes. In old Ojibwe culture it was a busy time and religious ceremonies took several of its warm days.

In some ways, not much has changed. Ojibwe people still gather together in summer, just as they have been doing for hundreds of years. They travel, and they hold spiritual ceremonies where the drum and pipe play important roles. And here at Red Cliff even though some summer days can be almost unbearably warm, there are not many of them. Besides, as these chilly mornings in June at the cabin remind me, cool air is never far away, even on the hottest summer day. Lake Superior stands by, ready to bring it to us once the wind shifts. And of course, nights beside this lake bring a welcome drop in temperatures.

Yes, summers in Red Cliff are still good times.

THOSE SOPHISTICATED FOLKS!

October 14, 2005

ONE THING THAT KEEPS ME COMING BACK to this rough Red Cliff cabin is its simplicity. In the sailing season I can spy fancy sailboats passing out on the lake as I sit beside this creek, relaxing in my favorite rocker. I suspect that in some ways, those boats and their occupants come from a world far different from mine.

Then, last week I was reminded, again, that although we humans are very similar, we can still be very different. After many years of studying this paradox, it continues to fascinate me. It came to mind recently at breakfast, when I was listening to WOJB and its broadcast of National Public Radio. Cokie Roberts, a news commentator from inside the Washington, D.C., belt-line, was remarking about Cindy Sheehan, the woman who is camped outside President Bush's ranch in Texas. Cokie Roberts called Cindy Sheehan "an unsophisticated woman." She did not bother to tell us which way she was using sophistication in this remark, but from the context of its use, it was clear to me that she used it in a derogatory way.

I consider Cokie Roberts to be a self-assured upper-middle class person, formally educated, and coming from a background where national and in-ternational political awareness is highly valued. No doubt, she sees herself as being educated and well informed, even worldly. A few months ago I heard another of her news reports in which she said she was pleased to see two for-mer presidents—Bush and Clinton—travel together to Indonesia to the areas of the tsunami tragedy. She said the friendship of these two former adver-saries testifies to the value of the American political system and how it is so much better than that of other countries where "tribalism" still exists.

I do not know what Cokie Roberts meant by tribalism, or what she knows about the lives of today's tribal people. Her remark suggests to this writer that she sees tribal political systems as archaic, and inherently inferior to hers. I suspect she feels that today's tribal people are horribly out of date, and that surely, they are unsophisticated.

Several years ago, during the final years of my teaching career, I would hear the word—sophisticated—coming again and again, from the mouths of people who saw themselves as educated. They may not have been from the upper-middle class, like I suspect Cokie Roberts is, but they no doubt held some of the same "truths" she does. I was told by these voices that I was to work toward "the sophistication of my students." I was to make them informed.

What does sophistication mean? My several dictionaries offer numerous definitions, but finally, all focus on one underlying referent. To be sophisticated is to layer oneself with sensitivities, characteristics, and knowledge that cover our natural simplicity. Put more plainly, all definitions finally state that to be sophisticated is to be artificial.

The term, sophisticate, originates from early Latin and Greek. It is related to sophism, and sophism refers to a method of argumentation that, some say, is intended to deceive. Yes, deceive. The early Sophists were teachers, skilled in their use of words and reasoning. (They remind me of many American politicians who came to Ojibwe Country in the early years.) The Sophists were said to be wise, but with a twist. They used false, or artificial, reasoning. Their arguments were fallacious, and often specious. Deceptive, fallacious, specious, artificial—these four words are deeply embedded in the noun, sophistication.

I suspect that the word, sophistication, has become part of the vocabularies of many Americans who see themselves as knowledgeable, informed, well-traveled and certainly aware of what is occurring in the world. I suspect they see themselves as sophisticated.

However, there is another word that needs to be mentioned here. It is arrogance. Perhaps all of us have shown features of this characteristic at one time or another. It refers to a sense of superiority that stems from notions of possessing something felt to be valuable, like knowledge. And it also is related to power. The word, power, has been defined as the ability to make decisions that affect other people.

Well, perhaps it is time to set the dictionary with all its definitions aside. The English language is enjoyable, but too much of it can be overbearing. There are many languages in this world and we need to remember that our American-English is just one of them. It holds only one set of truths among this world's many.

What interests me is how some of us who have experienced years of formal education use words like sophistication. We become loaded with assumptions. Here is another fascinating paradox! That is, after years of formal education we can be some of the most unknowing people in the world. And if we couple our success in academe with success in wealth acquisition, we too often, it seems to me, become arrogant. Our successes can cloud our reason to the point that we start assuming that what we hold to be true should be the truth held by all people. To use another interesting word, we become ethnocentric. Although we will deny it, we assume that our way of life is really the best in the world. And, like Cokie Roberts, we might see others as unsophisticated.

Well, if I ever leave this creek to take a stand somewhere, I think I will head to a certain ditch in Texas rather than that crowded place inside the Washington, D. C., beltway.

FOLKS IN SCRUBS
OR: THE VIEW FROM A HOSPITAL GURNEY
June 7, 2005

THERE IS STILL A LOT OF SNOW IN THE WOODS, but finally the melt is underway. The hard crust that held my snowshoes up for most of the month of March is turning soft, making it difficult to get around. It's been another good winter and once again I am grateful for the opportunity to have been part of it, but it also was a season of some trepidation. This was the winter of my first bout with serious health problems and it set me to thinking.

I guess I had better expect these things, given that I have been walking this earth for nearly seventy years. But unexpected health problems can be an eye opener. Mine began with a severely sore throat and soon gave way to an angioplasty. A stent was inserted into a heart artery to clear a blockage. It went well, but I don't relish the notion of a wire being run up into my heart.

We have a good health care system here in the Northland. Those folks at the Red Cliff Clinic were, as always, top notch. I feel at home there. It was there, during the process of checking the throat, that an irregular heartbeat was detected. An EKG was immediately taken, but before this matter could be checked further, the throat suddenly took a turn for the worse and two days later I found myself at Ashland's Memorial Health Center's Emergency Room. Those Ashland folks were wonderful. Treatment was administered to the throat before I was turned over to "Robbie and Pam" of St. Mary's Lifeflight Helicopter crew that whisked me to Duluth. It was amazing. I think I will not forget that flight crew. Then, even though heavily medicated, upon arriving at St. Mary's, I was impressed again, this time with more people in hospital scrubs who hovered around me. Two days later, after the throat problem was stabilized, it was time to address the irregular heartbeat. A series of tests was given, the stent inserted, and in days I was back home.

Soon I was sweating on the machines in the Cardiac Rehabilitation Center at the Ashland Hospital. For several weeks Mary Defoe and the rest of the crew did an excellent job of putting me through my paces. Under such

116

good care it all went well. What a difference it makes when health care people look you in the eye and seem to be genuinely concerned! How nice to make new friends at this rehab center!

But my story is not unusual. There are those who have more serious health issues than I, and the medical professionals who helped me have gone on to meet the needs of many others since I passed through their lives. They give this great care every day, on every shift. And this is what struck me as being noteworthy. These good people do this all the time, day in and day out. It simply is what they do.

It has been two months since this happened, and for me, life goes on. Yet, I cannot forget those people. I rarely saw the physicians who made the high-level decisions in my case, their time being at a premium. My memories of the others who wore hospital scrubs are clearer. Their salaries were more modest, their wages not as high. These are the folks who brought my meals, checked me at night, cleaned my room, bathed me and walked me down the halls. Others, who were expert with needles, hooked me to the plastic tubes leading to suspended bags of medications. Then there were those highly skilled folks who ran the very complicated machines that magically showed what was happening in my heart. And I still see that helicopter crew that gave me such comfort in my time of stress. All of these medical workers were wonderful to behold. These were just people at work who took the time to care for a stranger who unexpectedly crossed their lives. Like me, they were ordinary folks.

Perhaps I overdo this, but I think not. When hospitalized I watched the new television show about Auschwitz. This was the computer-enhanced series that candidly showed the details of the engineering and construction of those dreadful death-camp buildings, and most importantly, the cold indifference in the minds behind it all. It showed the people who were brought to the site, to be slaughtered like cattle. Over the years I have seen several such films—although none with this new technical side—and was once again taken aback. Those fellow humans were brought to Auschwitz and coldly put to death.

Once again I was struck by the insanity of the Holocaust. I compared what happened there with what was happening to me. Why was it that I was being treated so extremely well and those people were put to death? How am I any different from them?

I make a connection between all this. My joy with spending time at this cabin in these unbelievable Red Cliff woods is somehow related to my feelings for all the persons in the medical profession who cared for me. And I think of those millions of other humans who were not so fortunate. Those workers who helped me were good people. I offer a sincere "Thanks," to them all.

THAT OLD STUFF

October 14, 2004

T HIS WINTER HAS BEEN MILD and so far we have had little snow. The cabin is comfortable, so I don't turn in as early as usual to burrow into my cot to stay warm. Usually I find myself sitting up late by the barrel stove and oil lamps, reading. My books are old ones, some with rounded corners. They're about early times in Chequamegon Bay—and they set me to thinking.

Reading this old stuff is almost like listening to an elder telling those great Ojibwe lodge stories. That is done in wintertime too, when so many of the *manitos* are asleep under the snow. It's proper to tell such stories in winter. It's a quieter time and it feels good to cozy up beside a hot fire.

For years and years I ignored such old books. I didn't like them. When growing up my high school history texts told about European kings and queens and American presidents. In college it was the same. Those profs liked to talk about the power brokers of the Euro-American world. I wondered where the rest of the people were—folks like mine. I couldn't relate to kings, queens, presidents, and industry's tycoons. So I ignored history, focusing instead on the real people of my time, those common folk Red Cliff's Frank Montano sings about. (That Frank sure can sing!)

Some folks might have called me a-historical in those years, but I had my own history, my common folk history, and I thought about that a lot. But times change and lately I've picked the old books up again. They show me how those early writers saw things. Here in Chequamegon Country they show me how those writers viewed the Ojibwe People. It's downright interesting.

Take Guy Burnham for example. He had the *Ashland Press* over a hundred years ago and he sometimes wrote about the folks at Bad River and Red Cliff, but he didn't really say much about them, as if they weren't important in the doings of his time. How could he write a history of Chequamegon Country and mention the Ojibwe only at the very beginning?

Closer to home are the Bayfield newspapers from way back in the 1800s. They tell us a lot about how Bayfield folk saw their Ojibwe neighbors in those days. And Benjamin Armstrong's book is good too. It's about his life here in the bay. For some time he lived out on Oak Island and claims to have been an adopted son of Chief Buffalo. Then there is the Hamilton Ross book about Madeline Island. He felt that Indians were interesting but at the same time were destined to pass. They were people of "long ago." Ross gave each chapter a biblical title. (Now, that's a story right there.) Another favorite of mine is the book on Chequamegon Bay by the Ashlander, Walt Harris. I don't know about Harris. He too seemed certain "the Indian" had to give way. He wrote a lot about "progress" and had a boosterism style that puts me off.

Many years ago I discovered old books on Ojibwe culture. I gobbled them up like a starved pup eats his late lunch. Talk about old stuff! Those writers served it up on big platters. It was like the Bingo Hall feasts we enjoy here on the Rez today. The amount of food is overwhelming.

Yes, that old stuff is good stuff, and in time we can learn to appreciate its value. When we read it we might begin to understand where we come from. How can we be sure of who we really are if we don't know who our forebears were, how they lived and loved, how they raised their families, how they made it from year to year, century to century?

Years ago I asked a Red Cliff elder a question about Wenebozo. This man, who was born right after World War I, looked at me, uttered one of his famous profanities and said, "We didn't hear Wenebozo stories when we were young. We learned about Jesus." I don't know if I can believe him or not but if he was right I have trouble with that trade-off. I'd opt for the Wenebozo stories. They have more to do with this big lake, these woods, and creek. They fit better here.

Some time ago I was told that a Red Cliff person had recently been asked what he thought about the old Ojibwe ways. He raised an arm, as if to brush something behind him as he replied, "I don't want anything to do with that old stuff." Well, to each his own. Surely we can "do" with whatever we want to, but if we turn our back on old traditions and beliefs because we feel they offer us nothing then we are attempting to live without the traditions of our ancestors. It would be like someone trying to move forward without an adequate understanding of where they have been.

My newer books sometimes talk about the word tradition. They tell me that it doesn't mean something from long ago that never changes. They say a tradition is a process, meaning that it flows, moving with the times. It's as if a tradition is alive. Some historians used to write in ways that put traditions in boxes that sat on museum shelves. A writer writes for a purpose. What could the purpose have been to view traditions this old way?

I think I understand what these new books mean. They're saying there can be old ideas, customs, and ways that are useful in these new times. I could be wrong, but aren't these new historians saying what the old Ojibwe teachings have always been saying? One of my newer books puts it in an interesting way. In it an Ojibwe woman up in Canada says, "We change to remain the same." Think about that. That lady knows what's what. Traditions are never just old or new. It's a mindbender, but they are always both old and new.

Maybe it's like those fancy new ribbon shirts we see these days, worn by some of the Rez men. Sometimes it might be hard to spot them, what with all the Packer sweatshirts around, but I've noticed them being worn at especially important doings. When a man has one on he walks a little straighter—seems to feel good about himself. Those new ribbon shirts are old stuff, but they sure look good in these new times. I like to see them being worn. I like to see the set of the jaws of those who wear them.

Maybe if we don't learn about our old stuff we are like these balsam trees growing by this creek. They get pretty tall but when a strong wind comes along they can be uprooted. How could they even begin to weather a storm? They reached for the sun, but shallow rooted, they had nothing to hold on to.

OUR CURRENT OCTOBER

October 1, 2007

Recently I spent a full day in the Red Cliff woods with several members of my family. We went to our cabin to do some fall chores as well as simply to spend what was a beautiful day in a place we enjoy. Rosie, our daughter's chocolate lab was with us and she had a good time, too. As the memories of this great day begin to slip into the past, they set me to thinking.

Much has been written about the wonder of October and that is what this piece is about, but there is more. What is it about this October that causes me to pause and do some thinking? How is this October different, and perhaps more important than many of those in my past?

This fall the usual changes seem to have come much more quickly than ever before. The shorter days that bring the colored leaves, the onset of decidedly cooler temperatures, the silence of our summer songbirds—these and other seasonal changes came in like a sudden windstorm without much advance notice. And although it probably happens each year, with the coming of Labor Day a few weeks ago it was like someone had turned down the flow from the spigot so that now in October our almost steady stream of tourists that we have witnessed daily from Memorial Day is reduced to a trickle. Seasonal changes that took their time to develop now seem to come much more quickly.

This year October is galloping in like our grandchildren to the dinner table. Some days I wonder if I should not just stand aside and make room while the rush passes me by. Is this sort of thing common when a person reaches their seventies? Paradoxically, do some things slow to a lazy drip and others speed up to a torrent? What's going on?

When at the cabin we all, even the youngsters, were captivated by the beauty of the fall woods. Some of the youngest gathered fistfuls of brightly colored leaves that were placed on the dining table. Others explored the creek, and excitedly chattered about how the many frogs usually found there supposedly had started burrowing down into the mud for their winter rests, while some of the older youngsters seriously helped batten the cabin down for November's cold winds.

We were busy that day and at times I stepped aside to watch and enjoy the scene. Yet, I was struck by other thoughts. I have been watching the new films of World War II being run on public television these past two weeks or so, and try as I might to exclude them, those terrible images of men at war kept intruding. I wanted to concentrate on the great mix of colored leaves with the pleasant laughter of grandchildren, but I kept seeing that fighting. The contrast was compelling.

Then, while World War II was fought over sixty years ago, and those old films showing Germans, Americans, British, Japanese and a few other nationalities killing each other are really quite old, I realized that our newer wars have replaced those old battles. War never ends, it just leads to newer kinds. Now it is Middle Easterners, Americans, and the British shooting at, and bombing each other. In the beautiful Red Cliff woods on that recent great October day, I had to accept the fact that we were still at war.

And, as if that is not enough, I also thought about the extremely low level of the creek. My grandchildren probed the very depths of that waterway in ways they never had been able to do before. It too, had been slowed to a trickle. Global warming, or as our Current Occupant calls it, climate change, had apparently reached into the very heart of my sylvan sanctuary and began to deprive me of the pleasures of a full-bodied, fresh-water creek.

Sadly, as I continued to dwell upon the negative, I thought of images of frogs with a third leg growing out of their chests, or with untold other deformities, and hoped our youngsters would not come upon any such monstrosities. Then, suddenly I was struck by what was happening to me. The singularity of our Current October became as striking as the singularity of our Current Occupant, and the juxtaposition of the beauty and wonder of our fall day at the cabin with the awfulness of what is going on in the Middle East threatened to overwhelm me. I struggled to put the reality of our warlike national character and the foreboding reality of global warming out of my mind.

We do not use compact fluorescent light bulbs in the cabin because we have no electricity. And we heat with wood, a renewable energy source but, I suppose the sweet woodsmoke I enjoy so much is polluting our air and that the remaining water in our creek has PCBs and whatnot in it, but, hey, it is

October. I cannot correct the problems of the world even though I doubtlessly am implicated in their existence. When the time is right I will try to share my thoughts about all this with my grandchildren, but that is still a ways off. Now I say let them enjoy this wonderful month of many colors. Let them revel in the magic of life.

WOODSMOKE AND CABIN THOUGHTS

October 28, 2006

Each fall when I start keeping the cabin's fire going almost all day its sweet smell of smoke is especially welcome. Whether I am returning from the outhouse, the woodpile, or just from a short stroll along the creek to check out what the resident beavers have been up to, this old-time smell sets me to thinking.

At this time of year, cabin woodsmoke tells of the end of another summer and the start of winter's long heating season. It is a pleasure that is receding into our country's past as more and more we turn to natural gas. I do not know the specifics, but it seems natural gas burns cleaner than wood so with gas less air pollution is occurring. I guess less sweet woodsmoke means cleaner air and that means less global warming—something we should all strive for. But I still love that old woodsmoke smell and its passing is another sad sign of the times.

When at the cabin in fall I often take long walks to check out the woods and big lake. These are times of physical exercise and I usually feel a bit of fatigue when coming back. As I climb the hill up from the creek, if the wind is right, the sweet smoke greets me. It is like the hail of a good friend and if I have a kettle of homemade vegetable soup simmering on the stove it is especially welcome. Homemade vegetable soup and cabin woodsmoke make a good combination.

This is the smell early writer's sometimes mentioned when they told of entering an Ojibwe wigwam in winter. Johan Georg Kohl, the German mapmaker who was here in 1854 spoke of his joy in being invited to join an Ojibwe family for a meal of hot venison and vegetable stew inside their toasty wigwam. When reading Kohl I sometimes imagine what he met upon entering these homes. I can hear his mixture of French and Ojibwe coated with a thick German accent as he tries to express his pleasure with his hosts' hospitality. Kohl spoke fondly of the Ojibwe people and their way of life. Unlike the Americans who had surrounded them by the middle of the nineteenth

125

century, he did not preach to them about changing their world. The smell of their fires must have been very welcome to him. Unlike American writers of his time, Johan Georg Kohl appreciated the Ojibwe people and was grateful they let him warm himself by their fires.

In the past, sometimes I was chastised for smelling too much like woodsmoke. When returning home after a winter's weekend stay at the cabin I might be told to immediately change clothes because "they smell like smoke." This often happened after a week of work in an Ojibwe sugarbush, where I had tended the large outside boiling kettles. For some, woodsmoke might be best if left in the woods. Today I am more careful, being quick to remove my cabin clothes upon entering the house. Like pets we have had over the years, you might say I am house-trained.

But there is more to keeping a cabin then its woodsmoke. An isolated forest cabin beside Lake Superior in late fall can be a place to retreat to after an almost hectic summer. After such a season—a season filled with fellow humans—the solitude of a cabin can be comforting. Adding the smell of woodsmoke on a crisp early November morning makes this scene even more inviting.

But some readers might not find these things interesting, especially if they are young and still hurrying about in their quest for that place their life is leading them to. My grandchildren, for example, can appreciate my feelings for the joy of woodsmoke, but if I wax on and on about its pleasures their eyes will soon roll and they will run off to other things.

Some mornings when I am at our home in town and step out to begin my morning walk I head down the street to Old Military Road where a neighbor who burns wood lives. On occasion I am treated to a whiff of woodsmoke from Eric's basement fire. Its singularity is striking since no one else in our neighborhood burns wood anymore. There was a time here in Bayfield when, I suspect, everyone burned wood and doubtless on some days there was a gray cloud hanging over town from these many household fires. That time has passed and although we are now pleased with our clean air, I still think about what we have lost. Today few folks have woodpiles in their back yards with a chopping block and its pleasant scattering of wood chips. And the nearly musical ring of a heavy splitting mall as it hits a steel wedge again and again is slipping away.

So far our start of gray November has been a chilly one and today, as I rest on the crude wooden bench under the tall hemlock on the hillside before the cabin I enjoy the warmth from the mid-day sun. Coupled with this is the occasional whiff of sweet woodsmoke that comes down the hill. I lean back and relax, watching the wind ripple the surface of the creek's blue water and conclude that I am in a good place.

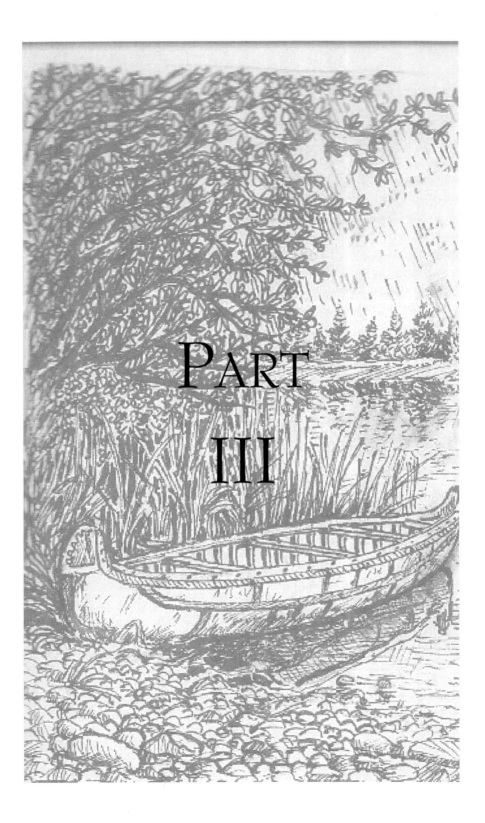

PART
III

PREFACE TO PART III

THE FOLLOWING PIECES FOCUS on the Anishinaabeg of Chequamegon Bay. Moreover, they address events from Ojibwe history, and in general, on life at Red Cliff today. Several important issues are introduced and discussed, but always from the view of the writer. This is an outside view, although tempered and influenced by decades of sometimes-intimate contact, by the reading of Red Cliff's long history, and by listening to nearly fifty years of an oral retelling of these early times. It has been said that a people's past is visible in their daily lives as they interact with their world, and that an interested onlooker needs only to watch and listen to gain at least a rudimentary understanding of its prominent characteristics. The written record suggests that Red Cliff's origin reaches back at least to the early seventeenth century, when the first people who later became known as the Ojibwe may have come to western Lake Superior, but there are voices that insist these early inhabitants have been here much longer than a mere few hundred years. Some Ojibwe say they were created here, and some insist these tribesmen were always here.

Important aspects of the rich Ojibwe foraging culture of the distant past still exist at Red Cliff, and threads of their influence can be encountered daily. Within the last few decades a serious interest in the old Ojibwe language and the culture's religious, political, and other social institutions has been rekindled. Today Red Cliff is acutely aware of its past, and seriously focusing on its future, and these short essays speak to one writer's view of this dynamic. It is a time of major change for the community, while simultaneously a time of on-going persistence of an ancient and rich way of life.

COMFORTABLE WITH CROWS

September 14, 2002

LAST WEEK'S *COUNTY JOURNAL* HELD A PIECE by a Bayfield writer who complained about this season's crows that woke her (or was it him?) too early on recent sunny summer mornings. The writer noted how there were complaints from others, and we readers were asked for "a solution on how to get rid of the noisy crows." This was not a short comment, made in passing. It sounded sincere, telling how the birds were making "life miserable for a lot of people." It went on for some length, and it set me to thinking.

Then, a few days later, my wife unexpectedly remarked about that writer's dismay with the black *aandegwag* and I started thinking again. During my forty-year marriage to this woman I have learned that she feels close to crows, those "*andegs*" as she calls them. Occasionally she speaks lovingly of a long-gone Red Cliff aunt of hers, an "Auntie Aandeg," who was an important part of her youth on the reservation. And I recalled how Louise Erdrich, today's famous Ojibwe writer, fondly includes crows in the novelized account of her ancestor's origin and exodus from Madeline Island so long ago.

To Ojibwe people crows can be very important. They might, at times, bring some noise, but they are never said to, as the Bayfield writer did, "make life miserable for a lot of people" no matter how early they start calling on a fine summer morning.

Like that writer I too have known times when I felt a certain disaffection towards these large black birds. Several of my youthful years were spent on northeastern Wisconsin diary farms, years that included crows. My brothers and I tried to kill these birds—shooting our rifles at them. We were never successful in hitting a single bird for they quickly learned to stay out of range of our long-barreled guns. We were certain crows came to our newly planted fields each spring to dig up the kernels of corn and oats we deposited just a few inches below the warm soil's surface. Those black birds were stealing our treasured grain.

But that was nearly fifty years ago. Over those five decades I, and maybe the crows as well, have changed. I'm certain I am not the same person I was fifty years ago, and I think the crows have changed as well. For the past many years when traveling on our northern roadways and coming upon a few crows interested in a deer carcass beside the highway I notice how the birds barely move with the approach of my vehicle. Years ago they would have lifted off and flown away with the first sound or sight of me, but now they no longer seem frightened by human presence.

The big change in me is that I no longer consider crows as adversaries. To me, they have become like most other forms of life, companions—fellow travelers on this roadway of life. But suddenly, in the words of that Bayfield writer, there it was again: that old disdain for crows. Although I have changed, maybe some of my fellow humans have not.

What is it about these bold black birds that offends some people? Is it really their loud calls that wake us too early on a fine summer day? Or might it be just their deep, obvious blackness? Or, is it that they sometimes do not act as birds usually do? Some spring mornings I am wakened by the loud music of songbirds, especially at the family cabin. Yes, the music is loud, so wonderful that it pulls me from sleep. Now, isn't that a great way to be wakened on a fine morning? That music can be like a symphony—but crows, on the other hand, do not sing. They caw. And perhaps cawing is too harsh for some human ears.

There is more to crows' behavior that might be contrary to our notions of how birds behave. When on the earth's surface crows rarely hop like other birds often do. No, like us, these black birds walk on two feet—first one leg is thrown forward, then the other—as bold as a biped. Who do they think they are?

And they are smart. In fact, yesterday's St. Paul paper carried a story of new laboratory research with crows that shows they are much smarter than we thought. They make and use tools. This is no little discovery. The researchers clearly documented that crows are toolmakers. While several other animals use what can be called tools, the fact that crows make tools is another matter. For years the art of tool making has been reserved for humans and their closet cousins, the chimps. What's going on with these black birds? Might it be that they are not simply too noisy but that they are too smart?

The University of Maine zoologist, Bernd Heinrich, in two wonderful books, tells us about his research with ravens. Now—ravens are not crows.

These are two different species in the genus Corvus. When reading Professor Heinrich's books I feel his love for ravens come through. Sometimes he seems awed by their behavior. Clearly, he has broken through to a higher understanding of another way of life.

But, crows are not ravens. We have both of these birds in Chequamegon Country, and over my many years in this land I have become somewhat familiar with them. For the past fifteen or so years each March I have been fortunate to spend a week or more out at Eagle Bay in the Newago Sugarbush. Both ravens and crows come a'calling in that sugarcamp. They are always welcome—even that handful of crows that sometimes wakes me at sunrise. Good alarm clocks, those birds tell me it is time to roll out—sometimes as early as 4:30 or 5:00 a.m. It is spring—the March breakup is underway, and the sap is running. There is work to do.

Very recently I spent two weeks in Bayfield, staying at a house on the hill by the old courthouse, and for a few consecutive mornings loud crows wakened me. They were up, going about their business of their day, so I rose to start mine. I came downstairs, put the coffee on and soon was out on the front porch watching the sun come up. Sunrise is still a thrill. If it ever ceases to be this way then I'll have a serious problem.

In some Native American worlds, especially those in northwestern North America, the crow is the Trickster. Like Wenabozho here at Red Cliff, he is a supernatural figure that teaches humans how to make life meaningful. In the Manidoo World of the Ojibwe the *aandegwag* are not typically considered to be tricksters, but they are persons—and as such are a natural, and important part of the world. A world without the Crow People would be a world incomplete.

Perhaps crows are like Bayfield's summer visitors, only they stay with us all year. They become loud with the warm weather and quiet down with the arrival of the cold. And although crows do not take our favorite seats at the Pier—or Maggie's—and they do not jam the parking spaces outside Andy's like our summer people, when they move throughout town they seem to be everywhere. They come into our neighborhoods, even peer into our houses, and sometimes they become noisy—yes, sometimes they become a nuisance.

This morning's St. Paul paper tells of another Wisconsin town with a perceived problem with birds. Manitowoc feels it has too many seagulls so its leaders have decided to start shooting them. Seagull droppings have become unsightly on the lakeside walkways and litter the citizens' pricey upscale pleasure boats moored dockside. So the federal authorities have given the approval for the killings. I believe in the case of crows that the state of Minnesota has an open season on shooting them, and maybe Wisconsin is the same. All this reminds me of the coot shoots that took place in this country just over a hundred years ago. They were festive affairs during which citizens gathered together to blast the ivory-billed small black birds from their waters. We were certain these mudhens were useless and that they bothered the ducks that we hunted and liked to serve as food on our tables. At these weekend "hunts" coots were killed in great numbers, sometimes left where they lay.

Crows can be pesky, cantankerous, wonderful, teachers, clowns, good company at the cabin on a crisp fall morning, jokers, and noisy. In all these ways they are necessary. They bring a needed thoughtful joy into our lives. If in some future early spring that familiar call fails to wake us we would notice that something was amiss. Our spring would be incomplete. We should be glad the crows share their world with us.

DAGWAAGIN: ANOTHER AUTUMN IN OJIBWE COUNTRY

October 21, 2003

Fall came early to Red Cliff this year. It was in mid-August when it started hanging around the cabin. The first hint of its presence was seen in the movement of the sun when it started its annual trek southward. Then a swatch of orange maple leaves beside the trail made it clear. The air definitely had taken a turn to the cool side, and finally, as I kneeled before the barrel stove one morning to kindle a fire I was set to thinking: summer really was over and fall has arrived.

Perhaps for all of us fall is a time for contemplation. Even though it brings a list of chores we must hurry to complete before the arrival of cold weather, it is still a time to pause and watch the changes occurring all around us. Maybe most humans ponder their mortality in fall. Despite its wonderful colors, fragrances, and tastes, it is still the season of endings. By this time here on the Bayfield Peninsula our prized roadside lupines have gone to seed, most songbirds have departed along with the heavy flow of summer folk, our old friend—goldenrod—is in bloom, and the obvious activity of open schools has returned. Then, on this morning's walk I noticed that the wine-red high bush cranberries are ripening.

We revel in the joy of another harvest of crisp and juicy apples as we breathe in the pungent earthy smells these fruits and other things bring. For some time we have been enjoying the palate of bright new colors brought by the grasses, bushes and trees. And lately the *aandegwag* began acting differently. Their calls have changed. These large black birds seem quieter—as if they know cold weather is ahead. The cooler air brushing our cheeks is part of this change. With its arrival we put the summer clothes away.

At Red Cliff the age-old rhythm of the change from summer to fall continues. Ricing is over, and deer hunting season imminent. Raspberries, thimbleberries, and blueberries have come and gone and weeks ago the last of the blackberries were picked. Perhaps it is a little early to check any trapping or snaring equipment, or to repair a broken snowshoe, but maybe someone is tuning up a snowmobile, anticipating what is ahead. The commercial fishermen are trying not to think of the rougher water they will soon face. And the subsistence fishermen are preparing their nets that will be set in shallower water, near shore.

Some distant voices might say that fall on the reservation is the same as anywhere else in Lake Superior country. They might argue that the old Ojibwe seasonal round of food-getting practices is long gone from places like Red Cliff. These onlookers seem to be certain that so much change has come to the reservation that they question "the Indian-ness" of its residents. Over the years folks living in nearby towns have told me that the area's "real Indians" are gone and that Red Cliff's people don't look like Indians anymore. When I hear such remarks these days I no longer get angry, I just pause, and try to understand. Usually, after the silence I say something like, "Well, things certainly have changed, but what's new? As members of the human species, Red Cliff people have always been changing. Everyone has." The record of human life is well over a million years long and if anything, it is all about biological and cultural change.

And I wonder about my own background. I am a third generation German-American and for at least the last few hundred years my forebears were all 100 percent German. Photos of my earliest immigrant relatives hint at resemblances but I really do not look like those people. They were considerably darker, shorter and simply very different in appearance from me, yet I call myself German. Even though I do not resemble them, they are my ancestors.

The above remarks from nearby townspeople tell me that America is still fascinated with Indians. Sometimes it seems that this country wants today's Indians to look like those that found Columbus. What's going on here? Could it be that some onlookers need to feel that "real" Indians never change? If true, why would anyone have a need to feel this way? Even the Masai, those fascinating cattle herders in east Africa who have been working hard to resist Westernization for years, and who we love to watch in those National Geographic television shows, have always been changing. Change is the Human Way.

I say that in some important ways the old Ojibwe seasonal round is still going on at Red Cliff and that it shows itself each fall. Parts of its physical form have obviously changed, but other aspects of this cycle of food-getting activities are still here. For instance, entire families no longer pack up and move their abodes to the autumn ricing camps, the spearing lakes and sugarbushes in spring, or the hunting areas in winter, but this does not mean the seasonal round no longer exists. The ricing fields, spearing lakes, sugarbushes, and hunting areas are still out there and in proper times the people go to them. Furthermore, it is not insignificant that in the past several years we have seen a resurgence of interest in these things. A rice seeding program is going forward at Red Cliff, walleye spearers go to the landings each spring, new sugarbushes are being established throughout northern Wisconsin, and Ojibwe gardening is still practiced. In a complicated and very interesting way important aspects of the Ojibwe seasonal round we read about in the old books are still alive. Each fall I watch as their customs unfold once again.

And I wonder about those community members who choose not to knock rice in fall, spear walleyes and make sugar in spring, or set nets and hunt. They see others doing these things and perhaps they hear stories from elders about how they used to do them. They certainly see the wild rice dishes and pans of roasted venison at community feasts. They see the walleye filets each spring, the deep fried whitefish and lake trout and all that fried bread. Maybe they even taste the hard maple sugar cakes, the light-brown granulated sugar, and the sweet syrup someone might give them at Christmas time. They know about these things. Perhaps they feel "modern" but I think about their reaction to all this soul food that shows up at funerals, weddings, graduations and other important times. This treasured food feeds self-conceptions, and these deepest inner identities are very personal things. The arrogant assumptions of onlookers about these identities are not only grossly uninformed, they are also absurd.

For years at Red Cliff, fall ushered in herring fishing. Folks made good money picking these fish from gill nets in commercial fishing sheds that dotted Bayfield's waterfront. "Picking fish" has become part of Red Cliff's past. It was a change that came and went. Importantly, it was not really something completely new that the Ojibwe people took up years ago. The advent of picking fish did not altar their lifestyle. I see Red Cliff's years of picking fish as a custom coming out of the age-old Ojibwe practice of fall net fishing. Such fishing was always a major part of preparing for winter. Picking fish was a form of wage labor and the custom of working for wages was a change that Ojibwe communities made long ago. Taking part in a cash economy has not altered their deepest identities.

In some Red Cliff homes fall still brings thoughts of firewood. These are the homes whose yards offer the sweet-smelling smoke of woodburning stoves in the cold of winter. And there are the fall ceremonies. These religious events are ancient. Some might take place in distant communities, so arrangements for traveling and time away from one's workplace must be made. And in fall there still are those who go to the woods for harvesting medicines.

The line between sacred and secular in all these activities is clouded and often non-existent. The reservation's fit of old tribal religious beliefs and practices with Christianity is fascinating. Always complex and forever deeply meaningful, this relationship is an ongoing adaptation at places like Red Cliff.

Lately out on the water sailboats and kayaks are no longer as evident as in summer so a subtle sense of normalcy has returned. Now the lake is not so busy and the woods is settling down. In fall at Red Cliff the land becomes quiet again.

This thought-provoking season gives me assurance. Here in Gichigami Country it comes every year and as I approach the end of my seventh decade I like this regularity. The cycle goes on. My time is winding down and these days my body has its share of aches and pains, but fall still comes and it is as good as it has ever been. Like Ojibwe culture with its myriad of rich and colorful customs, it persists. In some future year I will not be here to spend time at the cabin, marveling at the cool air, as I breathe in its rich fall perfumes, but this wonder-filled season will arrive as usual. Each year at summer's end fall will come strolling down this trail.

FOOD AND FAMILY

January 1, 2006

Now THAT THE WHITE HEAT OF THE HOLIDAYS has subsided it is time to take stock and contemplate what happened. For most of us, I suspect, it was a good time, filled with the pleasures of friends and family as we came together and celebrated many things, all warm and wonderful. In the midst of this celebrating was food. No doubt our kitchens were busy places as folks worked to prepare the many meals served over these past several weeks. How important the connection between family and food is! Today, in the deep of early winter this connection sets me to thinking.

Recently I heard a conversation between Eric Shubring and Joy Schelble over radio station WOJB from Reserve, Wisconsin. Eric is familiar to me since I hear him nearly every day but Joy Schelble's voice was new to these old ears. She works for the University of Wisconsin Extension at Ashland and deals with matters of food, nutrition, gardening and what not. Joy and Eric talked about how the foods we eat are part of the way we live. Among many, one of the points Joy made is that "a disconnect" between food and family has occurred in America. While aware of this problem for some time, I had never put it into words as well as Joy Schelble did. She has much to say about food and family and it would do us well to listen to her.

In Ojibwe culture food and family were as intimately connected as water and Gitchigami. You could not conceptualize one without the other, and to some extent this is still the case today. But, here at Red Cliff, for some folks —as is true across America—this is no longer so. Something has happened with our foods just as something has happened with our families. Too often the two no longer exist in the wonderful partnership they enjoyed in the past.

I am not speaking just to the special act of eating food when we gather around the table and break bread. No, I am speaking about how we procure the food that enters our homes—where we get it, how we get it, and lastly, what we do to it before it appears on our tables, ready for consumption. To a great extent in the past, at least for some of us, these steps involved most family members, often working as a team. How much of this team effort exists today? How many of us still work side-by-side in the family garden, and again, in the kitchen preparing food for consumption?

Herein is the disconnect. Today too many of our foods come from cardboard boxes and plastic bags. Too many fruits and vegetables have little paper stickies, telling us they came from Mexico. Today we might ponder the tons of jet fuel burned to bring us grapes from Chile and apples from New Zealand. Is this the best use of our world's resources? Why bring apples from the far Pacific when excellent varieties are grown right here on the Bayfield peninsula? Do we really think those crunchy Fujis are better than our local Cortlands? And also, must we have a bowl of those sweet, juicy Florida oranges and yellow Central American bananas on our kitchen counter all year long?

My childhood involved family outings to harvest hickory nuts from roadside ditches in southeastern Wisconsin. We sought out wild plums, cherries, elderberries, and gooseberries, bringing them home to be cleaned, cooked, canned or frozen for our winter meals. Then there were those Saturday morning forays into the family's woodlot for wild mushrooms that my mother and grandmother put up in one way or another.

These were some of the wild foods that were part of our year-around menus, but most other foods came from our gardens, henhouses, and cattle barns. We raised much of the food that we prepared and ate. Our recipes were passed from generation to generation. We shared many food traditions, and not just of the wonderful times of gathering around the table for a holiday meal. Our traditions involved the selection and saving of garden seeds from year to year, the knowledge about proper times to search for and gather wild foods, the right way to raise a flock of chickens and geese, how to feed and care for beef cattle that ended up in our freezer, how to grow, harvest, shred and season a large crock of sauerkraut—and on and on.

As we sat around a table for the evening meal we thought about, and conversed about, what we were eating. In that radio discussion Joy Schelble mentioned the "mindless eating" that inflicts us today. We no longer seem to think about where our foods come from, and how they were grown and prepared. Today, could our teenaged youngsters plant a garden, raise a flock of chickens, or net, clean and prepare a catch of whitefish for winter's use?

We have witnessed a tradeoff between homegrown foods and those from distant places. For too many of us the wonderful and healthy connection between our foods and our families is no more. We have become mindless eaters.

The opportunity to change this is within our grasp. Some of us are making these important changes. For them it is like a welcome homecoming.

THOSE OLD INDIAN TREATIES

May 21, 2004

F OR THE PAST SEVERAL WEEKS I have been reading about the Ojibwe treaties of 1837 and 1842. These were the two major land cession treaties for northern Wisconsin and anyone who is interested in the history of the region should be familiar with them. There is a lot to read, and I do not pretend to understand all that went on beside this big lake back then, but one thing is certain: these treaties set me to thinking.

By 1837 treaties were not new to the Ojibwe people. It is said that La-Pointe's Buffalo may have been among the signers of a treaty back in 1795 with General Anthony Wayne at a place called Greenville, Ohio. The written record claims that a contingent of Odawa people from Mackinac was delegated by some Wyandot leaders to come to LaPointe and ask its chiefs to travel to Ohio and be part of the treaty gatherings. It is said the Odawa made the trip to LaPointe and met with its leaders, one who would have been a relatively young Buffalo. (At that time he could have been thirty-seven years old.) There is no written record of this LaPointe meeting but a name among the Lake Superior Ojibwe chiefs who signed the Greenville treaty was recently translated as "Young Ox," and since there were no other Lake Superior chiefs with that name at the time, it may have been Buffalo's.

This Ohio treaty conference was no little matter since at the time the new United States was eager to diffuse the anti-American sentiment of western tribes that were pro-British during the American Revolution. We know that the western Lake Superior tribes were British allies in those years, and that there is a long history of Ojibwe people from western Lake Superior traveling down the Great Lakes to eastern destinations to meet with Europeans.

Thirty years later, in 1825, Buffalo was one of the signers of the Treaty of Prairie du Chien in far southwestern Wisconsin Territory. A year after that he was signing another treaty at Fond du Lac in what is now Minnesota. Then, I believe, he was at the 1827 signing at Butte des Mortes in southeastern

Wisconsin Territory. None of these were land cession treaties, but they were still very important. They all established boundaries for tribal land holdings and they were setting the stage for the next big push from Washington in which the land would be taken.

The 1837 treaty was signed at St. Peters, a place now called St. Paul, Minnesota. The papers say that LaPointe's Buffalo did not do much speaking at St. Peters, at least not much that was written down. But he signed that treaty, and many acres of land in Wisconsin and Minnesota territories were sold to the United States. Five years later at LaPointe he was asked to sign again, and he did, this time selling all the Ojibwes' land along Lake Superior's south shore. Obviously, these huge land sales affected the Ojibwe people in a big way.

We might wonder why Buffalo and the many other leaders agreed to these sales. Today, folks at Bad River and Red Cliff are working hard to get some of that land back. We wish them well and hope they use all due speed in these endeavors. These days, the recovery of their lands is a major movement in Indian communities across America.

Perhaps few of us ponder these things since the treaties were signed nearly two hundred years ago. For some folks history has limited appeal, and history nearly 200 years old might have none at all. Maybe they have neither the time nor ability to find interest in such things, but for others, reading and thinking about all these treaties can become a passion.

In the early 1820s some LaPointe Ojibwe began taking part in commercial fishing that was started in the western lakes by the American Fur Trading Company, so at these early times some tribesmen were being pulled into the emerging American national economy. But, by the 1840s many Ojibwe were still relying on hunting, fishing, gathering and gardening to feed themselves and their families. To a great extent their original culture was intact.

Yet, change was in the wind. By the 1830s the fur trade remained an option for tribal people but it was obvious that it was a dying industry. Surely, leaders like Buffalo were well aware of the pending death of this long-time trade. By that time the people were experiencing much pressure from missionaries and government agents to change their entire lives. There was a lot for an Ojibwe person to think about.

Historians have shown that Ojibwe leaders were deceived at both the 1837 and 1842 treaty gatherings where, some claim, "heavy-handed tactics" were used by American officials. The Ojibwe thought they could stay living on their lands but soon were confronted with demands to move far to the west. Today, when I look at this creek and these Red Cliff woods, 1837 and 1842 do not seem so long ago. There is a great peace here today, but I must remind myself that in those treaty-signing days this was not the case. In those times the Ojibwe were under great adversity and I struggle to understand the legacy of that hardship for today's people.

La Pointe's Indian
Agent in 1843

March 16, 2007

Several days ago I finished reading the memoirs of Alfred Brunson, an Indian sub-agent at La Pointe back in 1843-1844. After years and years of neglecting these early historical writings I am finally reading them—and they intrigue me. Among other things, Mr. Brunson was a U.S. soldier in the War of 1812, a Methodist circuit rider in Pennsylvania and Ohio, a legislator for Wisconsin Territory, a judge at Prairie du Chien, and a missionary to the Dakota Indians. His life of well over seventy years was full of interesting events but it is his connection to Chequamegon Bay that sets me to thinking.

Alfred Brunson was the third La Pointe Indian agent and served for only a year or so, right after the Ojibwe and Americans signed the major land session treaty of 1842. The agency was located on Madeline Island in those times, but Brunson, who was living in Prairie du Chien, never moved his family north. In fact, it appears he came to Madeline only twice during the year of his appointment, before he resigned.

Whenever I read historical accounts like Brunson's memoir I learn a little more about what life was like here in Chequamegon Country over one hundred and fifty years ago, and I am becoming aware that what occurred back then is not unconnected to what is happening today. This winter when at my cabin with its outdoor plumbing, oil lamps and wood-burning stove, I reflected a bit on how in some small way I am experiencing what those folks back then went through, but I know my life is still far removed from theirs.

The wide chasm between our material culture and that found here in 1843 is significant, but what about the other aspects of our lives? How do our beliefs, values and assumptions about how human beings should live compare to those the Americans brought here back then? Is it possible to understand the deep effect people like Alfred Brunson had on the Ojibwe?

In December of 1843 Alfred Brunson set out on the long trip from Prairie du Chien to the big lake as he departed on foot with a small party of lumberjacks. In a few days they arrived at Chippewa Falls and found Lyman

Warren and his family at their farm on the river. Warren agreed to take Brunson to Lake Superior and in time the party set out with a horse pulling a narrow wooden plank sled loaded with oats and bundles of hay for the animal, and amidst the hay sat the new Indian agent. A team of dogs pulled a smaller sled with provisions for the party. At least two feet of snow covered the ground.

It took fifteen days to reach Lake Superior. This was fifteen days of finding their way through woods and along frozen streams and rivers in winter. There were no roads and Brunson tells of his appreciation for his buffalo robe when sleeping on the snow-covered ground. He also notes his gratitude for the efforts of an Ojibwe woman who traveled with the small party. She and her trapper husband were returning to their northern home after a trip south, and it was this woman who prepared the food when the party stopped for the night. Brunson praised her ability to cook a delicious dinner of venison, vegetables and freshly made bread.

They arrived at the big lake in darkness and decided to cross the channel to Madeline Island, but they found the ice unstable—with large cracks—and after struggling with the horse, the party retreated to shore to spend yet another night. The next morning they made it across.

At Madeline Brunson had a long talk with Chief Buffalo and other band leaders, but unfortunately he did not share its details with us. Instead, the new agent said simply, that he "urged upon them the necessity of their adopting civilized habits." In the 1840s Alfred Brunson's voice was added to the many that were admonishing the Ojibwe to "become civilized."

Brunson claims in those times Buffalo's oldest son and his wife, along with a few followers, started using log homes instead of wigwams and began dressing like, and in other ways, living like whites. This led to their being recognized as "The Pantaloon Band" at La Pointe. Chief Buffalo, himself, took a contract to cut firewood for the fur company in order to make some money, but according to Brunson, also to show his people that they should make similar accommodations to the whites. Yet, Chief Buffalo is known to have held out for many of the old Ojibwe ways.

They were interesting times, those 1840s at La Pointe. The fur trade was coming to an end and the lumber era was on its way. The Ojibwe people were under the gun to make major changes in their lives. What must it have been like? When I sit in my Bayfield study I can view Madeline across the channel and see the village of La Pointe—the place where Buffalo and Brunson met. I try to imagine the meeting of these two men and how different their worlds were. Alfred Brunson and Chief Buffalo are long gone, but, even though much has changed, the big lake, the island, and the Ojibwe people are still here.

SAME OLD APPLES?

October 1, 2003

L AST WEEKEND I SAW THAT SHODDY WEBER is selling apples already. Her paper sacks of tart Paula Reds, early McIntoshes and sweet Whitney Crabs set me to thinking. In only a few short weeks the Bayfield Apple Festival will be here.

The folks who gather at Glady DePerry's most Saturday mornings were talking about it last week when I dropped in for coffee. Fran had taken his apple-red shirt out of storage and was going to iron it soon. Glady had her little apple earrings out on the counter and her apple sweat shirt—the one with the green apples—was hanging in the hall. I could see that people were getting ready.

That morning the talk soon turned to the festival. Someone mentioned how years ago it was so much fun to set up a stand and sell things downtown. One year a group of family members had such a stand. They sold homemade vegetable soup, fried bread, Spanish rice, hot dogs, coffee, and pop. Then one time it was apple pies—Glady and Auntie Roseann baked for two full days getting them all ready. Back then a fresh homemade pie went for two or three dollars.

Those were good times, fun times. It was always much work, but when most folks chipped in it became play. Those times were like the threshing bees of my youth down the line in Wisconsin. Back then the neighbors worked together at harvest-time, moving from one farm to another and everybody worked, but it was enjoyable.

But for the past several years, for most of us at least, all that is history. Now and then someone from Red Cliff might put up a stand in downtown Bayfield, but there aren't many that do anymore. It costs too much. And if you're thinking about serving food there are those health inspectors. Things have to be "certified" these days, checked out—stainless steel kitchens and the like. The casual seller can't take part. If you're not a Chamber of Commerce member you pay what to me at least, are big bucks.

When the apple festival began (was it way back in the 1960s) it soon over-shadowed the older Bayfield Strawberry Festival and seemed to grow and grow each year. I think it was started by the apple growers living on the hills just northwest of town. Those apple growers were the apple festival in those years. I get a bit nostalgic calling those times to mind. At those festivals the people sell-ing food, paintings, handicrafts, and so forth were largely local people. The whole thing was about the region. Most food stands were from kids up at the school, or else from town organizations of one sort or another. Now such fund-raising attempts must compete with Famous Dave's and other professionals. And many of those talented folks who paint those great pictures of "The Islands" are highly schooled and from posh suburbs downstate.

These days an event like the festival used to be might be called provin-cial, or even parochial—you know, "too local"—for many folks who come to visit the area. But I wonder about that. Do we really like all this up-scaling? Bayfield still has its apple growers, although some of the names have changed, and its arts people are still here. An obvious surge of art and craft work is being done these days at Red Cliff and in town. How about reserving a sec-tion on main street just for them? Maybe they should be allowed to set their stands up, free of charge, just to bring a little local color back. Sure, local peo-ple have always been represented among the festival's many vendors, but more and more it is hard to find them. There has been an inrush of newcomers.

I like to buy my apples from Bummy Rabiddeaux. When I do go into town Apple Fest Weekend I go looking for Bummy's truck. He always is pleased to sell me a bag or two of crisp Cortlands—and I get some good old-fashioned wisdom from him in the process. That's free.

But last year when I decided to leave the creek for a few hours and go into town it took me longer than usual to find the Rabiddeaux stand. The crowd was thicker than at the Minnesota State Fair. I got lost, pushed down a side street, and had to work through all kinds of Christmas tree ornament stands, water music stands, blackened whitefish stands, western-organic-spices stands, and more. For block after block I looked for apples but found none.

Yet, I was not completely in a foreign land. I saw some things I knew, even recognized a few familiar faces. There was that nice Hispanic couple I know that I often meet at other festivals. They were selling those colorful bulky Ecuador wool sweaters. Once again they humored me as I tried out my poor Spanish on them. And that middle-aged bald man—the really friendly guy—that set up at all the summer art and craft shows in Wisconsin, Michigan and Minnesota, was there, selling his fancy wind chimes. (Where's he from?—Little Chute?) And that group of fine Mayan musicians from southern Mexico that you often find at Twin City street doin's was there. They stood on the corner by the Egg Toss, blowing their bamboo pan-pipes —and had quite a crowd around them. Their music was exotic, not from Lake Superior Country. Out-of-towners.

Famous Dave's Barbecue wagon was on the street last year, too. I guess he doesn't miss many such gatherings. I don't remember Famous Dave's red wagon at earlier Apple Festival's, but then, I haven't been at many lately. Years ago there were no fancy rib stands. The meat of choice was bratwurst. Brats were new back then and quickly caught on. I bought mine from Barney Cadotte at the Legion stand. Like Bummy Rabiddeaux, Barney Cadotte seemed to belong behind a stand on Bayfield's main street on Apple Festival Weekend.

That Saturday last year after working through the crowds I found an open spot on one of those benches in front of the old Bayfield Press building on main street right across from Vic and Irene Gruenke's old place. I was in the shade and for a few minutes was able to relax and look around. In places the trees up on Catholic Hill were visible. They told me it was October. The maples were as colorful as ever, the white pines, balsam and spruce as green as other years. Then, when I turned to Madeline I saw that the big lake was still there too. And a few white gulls—those old-time Lake Superior gulls— glided aloft down at the docks. The birds are still here, I thought.

Most of the faces on the streets, however, were new. Those behind the stands, like out in the street, however, were strangers. For a moment or two I wondered if maybe I was spending too much time out at the creek. Maybe I was out of the loop. But then, I saw them, those welcome, familiar, smiling Red Cliff faces. Now and then one or two, or more, beamed out of the crowd. A young couple with a new baby here, an older fellow there. An elder with her grown daughter. The daughter with her man. Some things haven't changed after all.

I thought of the Minnesota writer, Jon Hassler. Hassler has put Ojibwe characters in several of his many novels about life in the upper Midwest. Once when I asked him just what he was saying about the Ojibwe people by including them in his writing he thought for a moment, then replied, "Well, they're always there. They're always around, out there nearby."

Some folks tell me the Bayfield Apple Festival has become too big. I don't know. In America we used to think bigger was better. In last week's *County Journal* Barb Meredith wrote about how the shop and inn-keepers in Bayfield had to work like beavers in the short summer months and how they counted on Apple Festival Weekend to help pay winter's bills. I guess that's it. The Apple Festival is a money-maker. The queen candidate who sells the most tickets wins.

Some Red Cliff people tell me they have had enough. They prefer to stay out of town from Friday to Monday. They wait for the crowd to leave. If they need groceries there is Peterson's—and Basina's. Sometimes they might even take "J" around town and drive to Washburn. But, sometimes the Bayfield Apple Festival is still exciting, still a lot of fun, still wonderful. It's fall—the colorful leaves, crisp air and freshness of it all are as invigorating as ever. And it's a pleasure to meet friends in that crowd. We greet each other with smiles. And I hear that there isn't as much open drinking going on like there used to be. That terrible habit seems to be passing.

But, I don't know if I'll go downtown this year. Those beavers from the slough have started working in that aspen grove on the hillside where the creek makes that sharp bend. They do most of their work at night, but if the woods is quiet enough they'll come out in the afternoon. Maybe I'll pack a lunch, take my books, camera, and a folding chair, and sneak over there and watch them instead.

RABBETT

July 1, 2006

Recently I attended the reception for the opening of a new art exhibit at Mary Rice's gallery in Downtown Bayfield. It is located in what used to be Bates' Bar on Broad Street just up from the post office, and the artist is Rabbett Strickland, a long-time Californian who is a Red Cliff Ojibwe. It was an unforgettable evening, and one that surely set me to thinking.

Rabbett Strickland is a tall, well-apportioned man of about forty or so years. Several weeks ago he was a guest on a weekly radio show on the Red Cliff station (WRZC-92.3FM) I have been a part of for the last two years, so he was no stranger to me. At the reception, when I was able to get his attention, he gladly answered my questions about a few of his pieces, and he was quite kind in the process. I am a newcomer to the deeper workings of the world of art and these are big canvas oil paintings—really big. I readily admit that for a few moments they were overwhelming, but their importance is about more than their mere size, even though some of them seemed to be eight or ten feet square. Only someone with a very large wall could hang one in their home, so they are more appropriate for a large public hall of some sort. As they are big in physical size, they are even bigger in their emotional power and impact. In all aspects, these are no little paintings. Only the determinedly non-observant person, or someone deep into denial, could witness them and not be moved. Never before have I seen Native American paintings that speak the way these do.

The gallery's viewing areas were not crowded, in fact there was plenty of room. Several comfortable chairs were placed in appropriate spots and at times a few of us used them. It was interesting to stand back and watch the folks who took a chair and poured their attention onto the large canvas confronting them. And confront us they did. These paintings shouted their messages.

And just what were these messages? Brief written explanations were posted at eye level beside each canvas so there was to be no doubt about the artist's intent. These beautiful paintings are about the tragedy of colonialism and its ugly arrogance in North America.

This was the show's opening night and after my initial viewing of each piece I grabbed a chunk of creamy brie cheese, a cracker and a glass of wine. These were not heart-friendly foods, but I felt I needed strong fortification at this show. No Styrofoam cups here—happily, the wineglass was actually made of glass. And these standard hor d'oeuvres were complimented with a large bowl of newly picked Bayfield strawberries. Nice, indeed. It was pleasant to mosey amidst the small crowd and large paintings, greeting friends and meeting new ones with this very fine fare in hand. The Bates' Bar I recall of over forty years ago is no more. That old tavern is now filled with art. For a second I pondered if upscaling might not be as bad as I usually feel it is.

When I first saw one of Rabbett Strickland's paintings I thought of Medieval artists, but Steve, who helps run the gallery—and has a degree in art history—suggested it was the European Renaissance. These paintings of Strickland's are, indeed about a re-birth—a spiritual, intellectual, and certainly political re-birth. But, they are not about a European re-birth, not by a long shot. These are about the Ojibwe.

Strickland's Ojibwe figures are large, muscular and downright beautiful. These people are not in the least bit inhibited—or as they were often described in the Euro-American literature in the Chequamegon Bay of the early nineteenth century—subdued. No, Rabbett Strickland's Ojibwe figures are not defeated people. They are under attack, but are not defeated. They are big, bold and pristinely beautiful. They filled me with an instant sensation of positivism. This is what is so poignant about them. The powerful, healthful, and simply good awareness they immediately project is sharply contrasted with another aspect of the paintings' content. They show this beautiful Ojibwe community and way of life being attacked by the Europeans who had no doubt they were doing the right thing. This deep and obvious contrast in all the paintings can take a viewer's breath away. To me they are about Manifest Destiny and the beautiful way of life this self-serving notion was bent upon destroying.

I studied the gallery visitors as much as the paintings and looked in vain for the present movers and shakers in the Chequamegon Bay area. Hopefully, these important personages will find their way to Bates' Art Barn during the month of July while the show is still up. What a loss if these politicos stay away.

There is no fee to view these important paintings. We should thank Mr. Strickland for bringing his art to us. And just as importantly, we should thank Mary Rice for hanging them for this free public viewing. I only hope the regional communities avail themselves of this very important opportunity.

WHO WAS GREAT BUFFALO?

October 18, 2005

RECENTLY I WAS CAUSED TO THINK of Great Buffalo, the prominent Ojibwe leader in Chequamegon Bay in the1800s. While flipping through a new travel guide to northwestern Wisconsin to see what it said about Indian communities in our area I was surprised to read that with the signing of the 1854 treaty between the Ojibwe and the United States "the Protestants went to Red Cliff and the Catholics to Bad River." This was news to me, and it set me to thinking.

Long ago I learned that it was just the opposite—the Protestants going to Bad River and the Catholics to Red Cliff. This travel guide's error suggested that Great Buffalo, as the leader of LaPointe's Ojibwe who eventually went to Red Cliff must have been a Protestant, not a Catholic, as popular history has long claimed.

This brought to mind the incident last summer when I looked over a Washburn shopkeeper's display of regional books. They were all about lighthouses and shipwrecks so I asked if she had any on the local Ojibwe communities. "No," was her simple reply, but perhaps to show all was not lost, she offered a little history on the area's Indians. Among other things, she said "Chief Buffalo of Bad River signed the last treaty in 1854." When I replied that I thought Buffalo was better associated with Red Cliff than Bad River she corrected me by saying, "No, he was the chief at Bad River, not Red Cliff." Somewhat surprised, I thanked her and left the shop, taking her poor history with me.

I suspect many of us have learned poor history about Buffalo. That new travel guide and the shopkeeper's remarks led me to ask myself what I was sure I knew about this major historical figure. Over the years I have thought of him often, struggling with the fact that he signed that treaty. How could he give up so much for so little?

What do we know about Great Buffalo? One thing is for sure. That is that in the 1800s there were several leaders named Buffalo in the western Great Lakes and it was not unusual for any one to have multiple names. No wonder we are confused by them.

We know some of the military and diplomatic events LaPointe's Buffalo was part of, but little about his personal life or what kind of husband, father, and friend he was. We do not know for certain when or where he was born, who his parents were, or if he had any siblings. Written history has locked Great Buffalo into an image of a wise and prudent leader who was a good friend of the White Man. Two busts in the Washington, D.C., capitol are said to be of LaPointe's Buffalo, but there is controversy about their authenticity.

Great Buffalo has become a mythic figure. We read that he was "temperate . . . very industrious . . . of immense frame . . . with an iron constitution . . ." and that he was a "renowned man of conscience, empathy, fairness, and social mind." We cannot be sure of all this, but that has not stopped us from constructing a popular history of the man.

One of the more interesting things we know is that in the early 1800s he fervently embraced the new religion of Tecumseh. In these years this Shawnee leader worked with his brother (the Prophet) to unite all Native American communities against the land-hungry Americans. Emissaries of Tecumseh and the Prophet came to Chequamegon Bay to gain converts to their religion which like all religions, had a political component. Tecumseh and the Prophet were allies of the British and their new religion was seriously anti-American. It had a large following in Chequamegon Bay and William Warren said Buffalo was a "firm believer of the prophet," and that he "undertook to preach his doctrines." The fact that Great Buffalo preached the doctrines of the new Shawnee religion shows us the severity of the challenges his people faced in the early 1800s.

Warren claims that in these times 150 canoes of Tecumseh's followers left Chequamegon for an eastern site to meet the Prophet and have him bring a dead boy back to life. A recent writer feels Buffalo was in this group. Out on the water they met Michel Cadotte who convinced them to return to La Pointe. I think they were more than a group of religious converts going to witness a miracle. It is probable they were intending to join other easterly tribesmen in military action against the Americans. Both Michel and his brother Jean Baptiste Cadotte were pro-British and fought the Americans in the War of 1812. It remains puzzling why Michel would have turned those canoes back given his alignment with the Red Coats. William Warren downplayed this anti-American stance of the Cadottes, perhaps wanting us to see the Ojibwe as peaceful and from the start, aligned with the United States. I wonder about William Warren and his motives.

And today I wonder about Great Buffalo and his religions. I feel his only lasting religion was the one he learned from his forebears. He accepted baptism into Christianity but like the busts in D.C., this is clouded with uncertainty. One writer claims Buffalo refused baptism until only a few days before his death in 1855, but others say he was baptized in 1835. This controversy, like that of the sculptured busts shows more poor history. In time both issues will be resolved, but until then we are left with uncertainty.

These thoughts about Great Buffalo might be uninteresting to some people today. Perhaps we are so caught up with the present that we fail to find much meaning in Indian affairs of over150 years ago, but to some of us Buffalo remains very important. I think we should learn all we can about him and his times. I certainly intend to. Furthermore, thoughts about Buffalo can lead to many important questions. One is, if back in 1854, the Protestants went to Bad River and the Catholics to Red Cliff, where did the Traditionalists go? Surely in the mid-1800s not all Ojibwe in Chequamegon Bay were Christians. Could it be that the writers of this early history have assumed that in those days there was only one religion, and its followers were either Protestants or Catholics? Could it be that those writers never really knew the Ojibwe people they were writing about?

REMEMBERING SANDY LAKE

July 28, 2006

Each summer Sandy Lake, Minnesota, continues to attract some of us who live in these north woods. Last Wednesday I was able to drive the three hours to get there from my Bayfield home and once again it was well worth the effort. I went to be part of the annual commemorative ceremonies held at the Ojibwe monument at the northwest corner of the lake, a trip I also made last year and hope to do so again in 2007. Each year these ceremonies celebrate our Northland in a very important way.

Too many folks do not know about Sandy Lake. I suspect to some of us it is known only as a great fishing lake, one with a modern campground, and a good place to spend a weekend with the family in summer. Perhaps we do not know that an Ojibwe community is found there, one alive and well and serving as host for the ceremonies.

This year the heat made the gathering a bit uncomfortable, but we toughed it out, and even two of my young grandchildren stayed for the completion of the event. Sometimes I suspect those youngsters thrive in summer's heat. As I stood on the mound where the monument rests and where the ceremonies take place, I thought the day's hot temperature was an apt counterpoint to the biting cold the Ojibwe found at Sandy Lake in the winter of 1850-1851. That was the time over four hundred of them perished in that cold, and although at this year's ceremonies we were uncomfortable in the heat, our discomfort was nothing compared to theirs.

A second counterpoint to the events of 1850-1851 was the food. This year we enjoyed another bounteous feast of traditional and other dishes, served in great amounts, but, those folks over a hundred and fifty years ago waited weeks for their promised provisions and when they finally were provided they were spoiled. This was the way the United States treated the Ojibwe in 1850.

For some of us the Sandy Lake story will never grow old. It speaks to something very important and we hope never to forget it. This is what is so striking. Sandy Lake marks an important event in America's past, yet there are so few Americans who seem to take note. This year's gathering saw about seventy-five people in attendance, a larger number than last year.

Yet, there was something special about the small number of participants. It was like we were sharing a secret that only a select few were privy to. Most who came were Ojibwe and they all held strong feelings about being there. They are quiet folk, but their strong sentiments run deep. They are wonderful and they come year after year.

This year I was able to visit with one eldery couple in particular—our good friends, Kenneth and Rose Tainter of Lac Courte Oreilles. After the ceremonies we sat in the shade near the monument and brought each other up to date on what was going on with our families. Kenneth is originally from LCO and Rose from Red Lake, Minnesota, and they both know the importance of Sandy Lake.

But, what was the Sandy Lake tragedy, and why did it occur? Why did over 400 people die that winter? To answer these questions we must familiarize ourselves with what life in the western Great Lakes was like for the Ojibwe people back then. By 1850 the French and British had withdrawn and the Americans were closing in. Ojibwe communities had been ravaged by smallpox, and liquor was taking its toll—both maladies brought by the Whites. The fur trade was almost over, but the mining and logging industries were cranking up, pulling more and more Americans to Ojibwe Country, and land speculators were everywhere.

Many Americans wanted the Indians moved west of the Mississippi River so they would be out of the way of "progress" but this really was not the reason some leaders worked for the removal of Wisconsin's and Upper Michigan's Ojibwe people. The names of two of these leaders stand out among the many involved: Alexander Ramsey, the governor of Minnesota Territory, and Henry Rice, an aggressive investor and a founder of Bayfield. Both expected to gain financially if the Ojibwe could be moved west. Both worked hard to have President Zachary Taylor issue the Ojibwe Removal Order.

To entice the people to move it was decided to distribute the annuity payments for 1850 at Sandy Lake instead of the usual location—Madeline Island at La Pointe. That is why so many Ojibwe people trekked to Sandy Lake. The annuities were payment for the sale of their lands in the Treaties of 1837 and 1842.

This year once again we formed a circle around the monument and listened to the words of the leaders who spoke in the Ojibwe language about those fellow humans who perished so long ago. That rich and beautiful language is coming back to Lake Superior Country. And the drum spoke too, with its deep, heart-felt beat. And of course, tobacco was offered.

The Sandy Lake Tragedy must not be forgotten. Thankfully, those folks at the Great Lakes Indian Fish and Wildlife Commission at Bad River work to help us keep its memory alive. *Miigwech* to them!

Gashkadino-giizis: Giving Thanks Time

November 4, 2002

It has been a month since the Bayfield Apple Festival came and went. Red Cliff gets caught up in the excitement of this annual gathering, but by now things are slowing down. November is at our doorstep—and it sets me to thinking.

This is Gashkadino-giizis—Giving Thanks Time. With practice these Ojibwe words roll from the tongue. They can begin to sound downright good. They belong here in Lake Superior Country, and today they are telling us that November has arrived.

When I was young I had no problems with November. It was a wonderful month, filled with serious preparations for the cold weather we would soon face. And near its end was Thanksgiving—a holiday my family enjoyed. My youth was spent on northern Wisconsin dairy farms and even though November had its share of work it still held the hard-earned pause when we gave thanks for another successful season of labor. The hay mows, granaries and silos were filled with our livestock's winter fodder. Our basement shelves were lined with jars of colorful food; its bins held green and gold squashes and mounds of earthy-brown potatoes. For weeks a few hams and slabs of bacon hung above a slow apple wood fire in our smokehouse. Then, at the end of the month we did what we thought all other Americans were doing. We celebrated Thanksgiving as we ate our big dinner and gave thanks to our Middle-Eastern god.

Those farm years were times of long ago and I still treasure them, even though things have changed. For the past forty years the majority of people I spend my personal life with have been Native Americans, not German-Americans. While most of them do not hesitate to celebrate Thanksgiving with a turkey dinner and a Christian church service there are some who choose not to acknowledge the event this way. They honor this time of giving thanks, but they do it in a more traditional Ojibwe manner, with minimal Christian intrusion. How different this is from my earlier years! And how

161

fortunate I am to have had things turn out this way! These changes in my life have caused me to look at myself—at where I came from and just who I am. The tension between my earlier years of mainstream living and my last forty decades or so of being influenced by an Ojibwe community is quite manageable, but at Thanksgiving, it makes me pause and think.

As we near Thanksgiving a scene comes to mind from my grade school years in the early 1940s in southern Wisconsin. In November our school's bulletin boards invariably were decorated with paper cut outs of Pilgrims and Indians. Those Pilgrims always wore black-and-white clothes and the men held long barreled guns. Some carried a dead turkey over a shoulder as they returned to the village. A smiling, bare-chested Squanto was present, often with outstretched arms as he offered several ears of corn to the newcomers. I do not recall any Indian women or children in those fanciful scenes. It was only this single male wearing a buckskin breechcloth and a puzzlingly, stoic smile. In those years we were in World War II and perhaps we were too busy to raise political questions about Pilgrims and Indians.

Those grade school bulletin boards offered their image of cultural diversity without calling it that. Such buzzwords were far in our country's future. Today we are inundated with messages about diversity's value but I suspect for most of us all this remains pretty shallow. We nod our heads in agreement when someone tells us of the richness of other cultures and we readily accept the truism that travel to different lands is wonderful. Friends of mine have great pride in taking trips "overseas" as they put it. They revel in "international" experiences, assuming that those of us who prefer to stay at home are missing out on something important. Too often, I fear, when these friends think of cultural diversity they think of exotic foods, ceremonial clothing, music, and art. They seem not to be able to open up the word culture to rightfully include all of its components—economic and political systems, family and kin systems, religious beliefs, and much more.

Sometimes I play with these friends' beliefs. I send them a postcard from an Indian casino saying that I am enjoying a truly international experience on an Indian reservation and I did not have to travel overseas! When I next see them I ask if they received my card and after they say yes, they quickly go on to another subject. They seem uncomfortable with my underlying message. Why is it difficult for us to view Indian communities as nations? We have no problem conceptualizing China, Japan, Canada, and England this way. Why do we hesitate with the Ojibwe, Odawa, and Potawatomi? What does the word nation mean to us? Just how do we define this important concept?

Surely if we studied the history of the Ojibwe nation we would have something to think about. In such a study we would learn about the assumptions underlying the beliefs of the early Europeans who came to this continent and how these self-serving "truths" were motivating forces behind the newcomers' relationships with tribal nations right from the beginning. Recent scholars like Robert Williams (see his *The American Indian in Western Legal Thought: Discourses of Conquest*) lay bare the arrogance—if not hidden agendas —in these intellectual maneuverings.

The careful work of historians like Robert Williams causes me to think about what the word belief refers to. I say beliefs are assumptions held to be true. Such assumptions cannot be proven true or false, and as such they fall outside the realm of objective thought. We humans need our beliefs. As is the case with our rituals and ceremonies, if we had no beliefs we would have to make some up very quickly. That, I suggest, is how important they are to our species. Beliefs are culturally specific and they give life meaning and purpose.

Perhaps all human cultures believe their way of life is the best. This is not the problem. The problem is that throughout history some have had the power to press their beliefs onto others. Power is the ability to have others do what you want them to. And beliefs can drive the use of power, as we are witnessing in the case of our recent invasion of Iraq. All nations have interesting religious beliefs, but if they have little economic and political power their beliefs may remain just that—interesting. We observe them, perhaps are even titillated by them, then quickly move on. They may not cause us to consider ourselves except perhaps, to have us conclude that our beliefs are the only true ones.

No doubt there are voices that have grown weary of all this talk about the politics of Thanksgiving. "Come join us in this great way of life we enjoy in America," they might say. "We cannot change the past so put all this 'Pilgrims and Indians' talk aside. We are tired of it, and it is time to move on. There are more important issues today—like the Middle East, the Philippines, Kosovo, Colombia, the environment, the poor, health care, Social Security."

These voices miss the point, or more likely refuse to think deeply about the politics of holidays like Thanksgiving because this would cause them to confront the assumptions underlying their beliefs. The way Thanksgiving is perceived has a direct relationship to the way other incidences of the use of political and economic power in America's history are understood. We cannot separate the beliefs behind Thanksgiving from the rest of our way of life. In this way we see that a kind of colonization is still going on in North America. It is a very subtle and perhaps, silent, colonization. It asks us to stop thinking about holidays like Thanksgiving in a political way. It admonishes us to deny the deep way beliefs can be embedded into a society's institutional framework, and yes, into our self-conceptions. So finally, the way we celebrate Thanksgiving is a statement about the way we understand ourselves.

Yesterday when walking down the wooded trail to the cabin I thought about all the beauty I was strolling through. Even though the days were growing shorter and the skies were often overcast, I still felt a goodness all around. November does that to me. I was pulled into the world of those trees. Most had lost their leaves so they stood naked in the forest. I saw how white, yellow, grey, brown and black trunks and branches contrasted with the few green conifers scattered amongst them. Many different kinds of trees mingled, accepting each other's differences.

The apple festival was over for another year, Halloween was fun while it lasted, and in a few weeks we would have Thanksgiving. I felt, however, that I was already giving thanks. Gashkadino giizis was only days away. My personal larder was filled with the produce from living in this land through another great season of growth. And interestingly, the imminent arrival of Giving Thanks Time helped me feel that I was somehow freed from earlier youthful convictions about life and about how we should relate to people who are different from us. As I slowly moved along the trail I gave thanks for being here.

What's Behind Our
Street Names?

July 16, 2006

RECENTLY AT LUNCH I SAT WITH A FRIEND who has lived just outside of Bayfield for the last twenty years. As we both were enjoying our bowls of hot homemade soup in our favorite local cafe the question of writing came up and before long I mentioned that I was working on something about how Bayfield's streets got their names. This friend's remarks set me to thinking.

With tongue in cheek, he said he always assumed that Rice Avenue was named after Mary Rice, the contemporary Bayfield benefactor. While Mary probably should have a street named after her in recognition for the good things she has done, and still does, for the community, I had to tell my friend that Rice Avenue was named after someone else. That someone is Henry Mower Rice, an early mover and shaker in these parts back in the mid-1800s.

My friend professed to never having heard of Henry Mower Rice and I suspect many other local folks also do not know the origin of the street name. I wonder too, if they know where other street names—like Manypenny, Rittenhouse, and Old Military Road came from. It interests me that we might walk or drive on a local street almost every day and not know from whom—or for what—it was named. I wonder to, if many folks know why Bayfield is called Bayfield.

Many years ago when I discovered that Bayfield had a street named Rice I suspected right from the get-go that it was for Henry. I knew about this man from studies I did regarding the history of Minnesota and I was aware that he had an early connection with Bayfield, but I did not want the street to be named after him. I remember how I fantasized about how nice it would be if that street had been named after rice, the grain. White, brown, or wild, a street named after rice would have to have something good about it.

I recall how a few years ago on a colorful fall day I sat on a porch and studied the street before me. The name on the signpost at the corner just a few yards from where I rested said Rice Avenue, and in that warm morning's shaded sunshine I thought about what it would be like if the street was named after *manoomin* (wild rice). Given the history of the importance of wild rice for the Ojibwe people who first lived on the site where Bayfield now stands—and whose descendents still live here—the name would not be out of place.

The houses along the section of Rice Avenue I studied that morning are pleasant to look at. Not large, glassy, pillared, and pretentious, they are smaller and much quieter. That fall morning they sat peacefully as yellow and red leaves slowly detached from overhead branches, and like falling feathers, gracefully zigzagged to the earth. It was an inviting scene. All seemed right in the world.

Henry Mower Rice is known as a founder of Bayfield. He was one of the land speculators who operated in northern Wisconsin in the days when the government was signing land treaties with the resident Ojibwe. His behind-the-scene financial machinations are disclosed in documents surviving from that time. Rice is said to have been a good friend of the Indians, but there is something disquieting about that, and also about claiming that he is a founder of Bayfield when people had been using the site for their homes for a century or two before he arrived. The first grid pattern for Bayfield's streets was overlaid on footpaths used by others who "founded" the town site long before Henry Rice appeared.

Henry Mower Rice was one of the persons responsible for Zachery Taylor's 1850 Ojibwe Removal Order. This was the presidential order that would have seen the local Ojibwe moved out of Wisconsin to what was then Minnesota Territory. The Ojibwe did not want to leave and were successful in having the order rescinded, but it took much hard work. Their efforts overcame those of Mr. Rice, but not before over four hundred Ojibwe died in the Sandy Lake Tragedy of 1850-1851. These deaths are directly connected to the activities of Henry Mower Rice.

Working with Alexander Ramsey, the governor of Minnesota Territory, Rice schemed about how to move the Ojibwe out of Wisconsin so their annuity monies would come to Minnesota. This would have been good for his and Ramsey's financial investments. In one of his letters Rice remarked of "the annoyance" the Ojibwe were to him. Then, about four decades later, in 1894, Vincent Roy, a well-known nineteenth-century figure in Northern Wisconsin, reportedly remarked that Henry Mower Rice "was practically a god among the Chippewas."

With today's hindsight we see that Mr. Rice's record of involvement with Indian people is, to say the least, interesting. It is also interesting to consider how relationships between those with power and those without power have played themselves out in America's past. Perhaps some things really do not change. Today, Bayfield's Rice Avenue is a nice quiet street in this small mid-western town, but at times it speaks loudly to those who care to listen.

HOUGHTON POINT

September 16, 2004

THERE IS NO DOUBT THAT THOSE OF US LIVING in Ojibwe Country here beside Lake Superior appreciate the beauty of our surroundings. These wonders are regularly depicted in the works of our local artists—whether painters, photographers, writers, or whatever. Recently the fact of all this beauty in our backyard struck me once again when I made a visit to Houghton Point on the shoreline just north of Washburn. This trip set me to thinking.

Houghton Point, or Houghton Falls, as it is also called, is a landmark in Lake Superior's Chequamegon Bay. It is well known by local residents as a place to go to for picnics, swimming, or just an outing. The water in the cove is usually only a few feet high, and given its sandy bottom, and the high rock walls that protect it from most winds, it is a great place for wading or simply splashing around on a warm summer day. The numerous aging initials carved into the table-like sandstone rocks found in the cove attest to the area's early attraction. Those carvings remind us that we humans are like dogs and cats that leave their marks for others to witness. Houghton Point is not a huge place, but its beauty is striking. There is no doubt that it is one of the premier natural sites in Chequamegon Bay.

According to Hamilton Ross, the early Madeline Island writer, the Ojibwe named it Neiashibikang, which Ross translates as 'A Rocky Point of Land Extending into the Lake.' Its second name is that of Douglass Houghton, the early nineteenth-century physician who joined Henry Schoolcraft on his 1832 expedition to the headwaters of the Mississippi River. Today Douglas Houghton is perhaps most often remembered for the city in Michigan's Upper Peninsula that bears his name, but here in northern Wisconsin we might remember him for this relatively small scenic site on the west side of Chequamegon Bay.

On the 1832 expedition Houghton was assigned the task of giving smallpox vaccinations to the native people encountered on the trip—a job he accomplished with few difficulties—but, he was also familiar with geology, and in his short life went on to spearhead the Euro-American initiative to bring mining to what is now Upper Michigan. Ironically, in 1845 at the young age of thirty-six, after all his traveling on Lake Superior, he drowned in the big lake because he mis-judged the seriousness of its heavy seas.

Douglass Houghton kept a detailed journal of his 1832 trip with Schoolcraft, but unfortunately the volume describing the portion of the trip from Sault Ste. Marie to Fond du Lac is lost, or destroyed, so we do not have his words about Chequemegon Bay and its point of land now bearing his name.

What we do know is that way back in 1659 or 1660, the Odawa people built some sort of fortress on or near the point, and that in those times the site was an important marker for Radisson and Groseilliers when in the area. There is no doubt that the spot was significant to several Indian nations that resided here in those early times. We know that its cultural and historical importance goes back at least that far, so there must have been many folks who regularly enjoyed it long before the nearby city of Washburn was established.

The reason for my recent visit is that today something is occurring to this important place that is happening all over our Northland: one half of Houghton Point is for sale. Placed on the market about a month ago, the approximately eight-acre parcel of land on the north side of the cove is offered at nearly one and a half million dollars. Apparently, there is the danger that this important site may soon become another prime real estate location filled with large houses, all "with a view."

How can this be? How can such a beautiful and important historic site be used in this way?

Unless we have a boat that allows us to come to Houghton Point by water, I suspect many of us have never visited the site. Today, to approach it by land, the visitor must use a private road, so perhaps this keeps many of us away. This might mean that most of the point's visitors come by water, in either a kayak or sailboat. I suspect that the times of casual visits by local folk who drive, bike, or walk out to the site might be over.

These days, large, glassy, shoreline houses, carefully positioned to afford a maximum view of a body of water, have become almost commonplace in America. Perhaps we have learned to expect them whenever coming upon a spectacular stretch of lakeside land. In the boom times of the nineteenth century these houses were built near the center of our towns so the mansions' imposing presence could easily be witnessed by passers by. Not much has changed since then.

What strikes me is how easily we Americans understand an unbelievably beautiful natural place like Houghton Point as a commodity with great marketable value. This is what the early tribesmen were so perplexed at, and what some still are. How can we Americans assign a dollar sign to our land, water, and air?

THE OJIBWE PEOPLE AND THOMAS MCKENNY IN 1826

February 10, 2005

THIS PAST WEEK I FINISHED A SECOND READING of Thomas L. McKenny's book about his 1826 trip to Lake Superior Country where he and Lewis Cass officiated at treaty negotiations between the Ojibwe people and the United States. Maybe it was the deep quietude of January that caused me to comb McKenny's words and take pages of notes, or else maybe I was just struck by what the local Ojibwe people were up against in the early 1800s. Whatever it was, McKenny's book set me to thinking.

In the nineteenth century such travel books were popular and served to earn good money for their publishers. There was interest in the western frontier and there was a fascination with Indians. But, who reads these old books anymore? I personally know no one who has ever read McKenny. Maybe that is part of the fascination I have for these sorts of things—the feeling that they are ancient treasures, filled with long neglected riches. While many of my contemporaries entertain themselves by watching the latest high-tech investigative crime television shows, I prefer to study these old forgotten manuscripts. The TV shows are fabrications, but my old books are genuine.

The book's title is *Sketches of a Tour to the Lakes, of the Character and Customs of the Chippeway Indians, and of Incidents Connected with the Treaty of Fond du Lac.* Such long titles were in style in the nineteenth century. McKenny retells his experiences after leaving Washington, D.C., on May 31, 1826, until his return, four months later. He traveled approximately 4,000 miles, much of it in birch bark canoes.

His traveling companions included some heavy hitters of the day, like Lewis Cass and Henry Schoolcraft. They traveled with a small unit of soldiers from the U.S. Army, and a group of native people. McKenny took horse-drawn coaches and canal boats until reaching Detroit where he stepped into a birch canoe. After Detroit his party encountered native people regularly all the way to Fond du Lac. On July 24th they reached Madeline Island—in their day it was known as Michael's Island—where they stayed for a few days. Michel Cadotte and his family were their hosts.

They embarked from Madeline on July 26th, a beautiful summer morning. After passing through the channel between Madeline, Basswood and Oak Islands, the party made the turn at the tip of the peninsula and stopped at Point Detour for a fried fish lunch on the large flat rock before moving on to Fond du Lac. When nearing the treaty site Lewis Cass ordered that some of the soldiers bring out musical instruments, and as Old Glory fluttered overhead, they played "Hail Columbia." Upon arriving at the landing they switched to "Yankee Doodle." America had come to Fond du Lac! It is quite unfortunate that we have no accounts of the Ojibwe interpretation of this sight.

Thomas McKenny was a fine writer. He used colorful prose and had an eye for detail. He noted numerous Ojibwe customs and claims to have witnessed the ancient wabeno and jiisakaan ceremonies. In fact, to the interested reader his book offers much about the Ojibwe way of life of the times. But after these praises, we must also say that Thomas McKenny missed it. He did not get the picture. He could not move beyond his own assumptions about what constitutes a proper way of life. To some readers his book will cause anger.

"Poor," "naked," and "wretched" were three of his favorite words. Like other writers of his day, he could not get beyond these negative adjectives when describing Indians. McKenny said this about the Ojibwe, "Nothing can exceed the poverty and wretchedness of these people!—and their love for tobacco and whiskey." These words came from the pen of the Commissioner of the Office of Indian Affairs. Blinded by his religion and his way of life, Thomas McKenny could see nothing but the certainty that in 1826 the Ojibwe had to change everything. They had to discard their language, religion, political system, economics, and their deepest personal identities—everything that made up their world. This is what the Ojibwe met on a beautiful summer's day at Fond du Lac in 1826.

Thomas McKenny was a firm supporter of a removal policy that would have forced Indians to relocate west of the Mississippi. In these new distant lands he was certain they could be converted to Christianity as they became farmers. The underlying reason for the poverty, nakedness and wretchedness of the native people would be corrected by formal education. He was an early supporter of the infamous Indian boarding schools that came after he left office.

McKenny was not alone in his certainties. As a society, America forced its beliefs onto the Indian people. How could they be wrong? They were educated, progressive, and well informed. Besides, it had worked for them. Certainly, it could work for the Indian too. Christianity, schooling and good hard work were the answer.

Thomas McKenny was a tall man who was a colonel in the War of 1812. He is said to have carried a military bearing all his life. Interestingly, it appears that his three favorite adjectives came to live with him the last twenty years of his life. After being removed from office by incoming President Andrew Jackson in 1830, his life was said to be a series of reverses and failures—a time of obscurity and poverty, and yes, perhaps wretchedness. He died alone and penniless in a Brooklyn boarding house in the deep cold of winter, on February 20, 1859.

THE OJIBWE REMOVAL ORDER
OF 1850

March 4, 2007

IT IS JUST OVER ONE HUNDRED AND FIFTY YEARS AGO that a United States president signed an order to move the Ojibwe people from Wisconsin and portions of Upper Michigan to what was then Minnesota Territory. For the last few months I have been studying the documents from that event and they set me to thinking.

The story of the attempt to move the Ojibwe is a complicated one that cannot be told in its entirety in this short piece. It is a fascinating story, both for its attempts by government officials for self-gain, and for its wonderfully human struggles on the part of the Ojibwe to stay in their beloved homeland. They not only stood fast, but they rallied their forces and used their diplomatic skills to defeat those behind the presidential order. Perhaps the story is a prophetic one, telling of how a people felt to be poor, destitute, and destined to give way to a major power like America surprisingly stopped this power in its tracks.

Perhaps it is easy to imagine what life was like for many Americans of the time. The Civil War was only a few years away, but slavery was ongoing as it continued to help reap huge profits for southern landholders. And importantly, the Industrial Revolution was roaring across the continent. America was having its way, and surely a few thousand Indians in the woods of Wisconsin and Upper Michigan would not stop it.

Although we might think that pressure for land was the reason for the order, contemporary historians have concluded that it was planned and orchestrated by a mere handful of businessmen and politicians for their personal gain. In fact, while there probably were several prominent individuals in both the business and governmental communities of the time who were influences behind removal attempts, it seems that only five or so played key roles in bringing the removal order about, and most of them had a connection with the Chequamegon Bay region.

Henry Mower Rice, a founder of Bayfield and the local person with the government contract to oversee the removal of the Ho-Chunk (Winnebago) from Wisconsin and Iowa a few years previous, is not usually said to have been officially involved in the attempts at Ojibwe removal, but it is clear he was part of it. Dr. Charles Borup, a one-time Madeline Island fur trading official and later St. Paul businessman was also involved. Charles H. Oakes, of the prominent Madeline family, was appointed a removal supervisor after the order was issued—an appointment applauded by some government officials because of his familiarity with the Ojibwe people. John Watrous, a former fur trader from Madeline, and a Wisconsin politician, went on to play an infamous role. Minnesota's Henry Sibley was involved as well, but the most prominent was Alexander Ramsey, the first governor of Minnesota Territory.

Today we find a local Bayfield street, an important downtown St. Paul park and probably more named after Henry Rice. Henry Sibley has a large urban Twin Cities high school named after him, and Alexander Ramsey has a major Minnesota county named after him. It seems nothing is named after John Watrous.

Surviving personal letters of Sibley, Ramsey, and Rice show that these three businesspersons wanted to have the Ojibwe moved into Minnesota Territory for financial gain. In those days there was money to be made on Indians. The Indian trade involved annual federal appropriations of thousands of dollars for treaty annuities in the form of material goods and cash. The purchase, shipping and handling of these goods was big business. Minnesota territorial newspapers of the 1840s tell how the economy of the St. Paul area was dependent upon the annual in-flow of this revenue. Sibley, Ramsey, and Rice knew what they were after.

Those who care to be informed about the Ojibwe Removal Order know how Chief Buffalo and other leaders stepped up and resisted the Americans. They know of Buffalo's trip to Washington in 1849, and his second one in 1852. Buffalo is said to have been in his nineties when making these arduous trips. While these were important gestures, there was much more. In these years the Wisconsin Ojibwe pulled together. Runners moved between the several communities carrying messages about the resistance. One story tells how after the order was issued and government officials brought gifts of twists of tobacco to the Ojibwe at La Pointe to win their favor, that these same tobacco twists were used surreptitiously against the Americans as swift runners carried them from village to village with messages encouraging resistance.

We also know how regional non-Ojibwe persons sent letters and petitions to Washington denouncing the removal attempts. American citizens along Lake Superior's south shore rallied with the Indian people and Ojibwe resistance solidified until finally, the order was rescinded.

The Ojibwe Removal Order includes the tragedy at Sandy Lake, Minnesota, in the early winter of 1850 that saw approximately 400 persons die. The bulk of responsibility for this falls at the feet of John Watrous and Alexander Ramsey. The year after Sandy Lake these two men continued to attempt to move the Ojibwe even after Washington sent an initial notice to stop their activities.

It seems important that we learn all we can about the Ojibwe Removal Order of 1850.

WARRIORS OF OLD

August 14, 2002

THE VISIT OF THE US BRIG *NIAGARA* to Chequamegon Bay a few weeks ago set me to thinking. The tall ship is a rebuilt battleship from the War of 1812. That's right—1812. At least a few of its innermost timbers are from the original Niagara that Admiral Perry and his sailors used to fight the English on Lake Erie during that war of nearly two hundred years ago. Today it might seem odd that the British and Americans should have been trying to kill one another since we have been strong allies for a long, long time. But England and the United States once were at each other's throats—in the 1776 Revolution of course, and again in the War of 1812.

Standing on the Bayfield dock, I was struck by the beauty of the ship. It was magnificent. Unfortunately, I was not able to get down to it over the weekend when onlookers were invited to step aboard—after purchasing a ticket—for a much closer look. But I did get to the dock Monday morning to watch it leave port on its way to Duluth. As a veteran of the U.S. Navy—I was on a destroyer in the 1950s—I stood in awe, looking up at the tall wooden masts, the many lines, the old-style wooden pulleys, and the large canvas sails. Instantly, an appreciation for the 1812 sailors (and those aboard today's rebuilt replica as well), swept over me. These people had to know how to handle such a ship, to make it respond to their commands. And I recalled my small destroyer in heavy seas. How the *Niagara* must roll, sway and buck in rough weather!

And I thought of more. This was the ship's first visit to Gichigami and it was nice that it paid a call to Bayfield, especially on the weekend of the annual arts show held in the lakeside park. Streams of visitors flowed through the show and along the dock to visit the ship. It was a festive but almost quiet event, comfortable despite the bright sunshine and heat, and the tall ship fit into the scene quite nicely. Surely the ship's visit helped the town's shop—and innkeepers. This was summertime, a few weeks after the Fourth of July. Patriots probably felt good with the ship's presence, especially when viewing its banners showing the famous quotes by Admiral Perry.

But I felt how nice it would have been for it to have made a stop at Red Cliff as well. Surely more ticket money was made at the Bayfield dock than could have been made at Red Cliff, and if money is what the ship's owners— the State of Pennsylvania—wanted, then to Bayfield it had to go. That's where the crowd was. But isn't the *Niagara* about more than money? Isn't it about seamanship, history, and the passing of time, about community, and how we see ourselves? That's why I think it should have come to the Red Cliff dock.

Such a visit could have been offered as a poignant symbol of reaffirmation of the friendship between the Ojibwe Nation and the United States. You see, during the War of 1812 these two nations were adversaries. Some Ojibwe military men (and perhaps military women as well) from Chequamegon Bay paddled the hundreds of miles to the eastern Great Lakes to join the Redcoats in their war against the United States. That's right. Ojibwe military personnel from LaPointe fought as allies of the British against the Americans in the struggle of these two countries in North America so long ago.

In the early 1800s these long paddles from Madeline Island (and the Red Cliff shoreline) were not unprecedented. The Ojibwe had been paddling from western Lake Superior to the eastern French centers for trading purposes for many decades. Then with the outbreak of hostilities between the French and English in North America in the 1750s, the Ojibwe joined the French in their battles against the British. The early Ojibwe historian, William Warren, says the Ojibwe fought in many battles alongside the French against the British and that Mamongeseda, a famous military leader from LaPointe led a fighting force from Chequamegon Bay on its nearly two thousand mile paddle east to Quebec. It was here in 1759 that these Ojibwe warriors fought on the celebrated Plains of Abraham in the battle that saw the defeat of the French and the death of their famed General Montcalm.

How interesting it would have been to witness today's captain of the *Niagara*—Captain John Beebe-Center, his seventeen officers, (and any of the ship's twenty-five volunteer crew members not busy bringing the ship into port)— standing at ceremonial attention as the gallant ship silently came in and quietly tied up at the old Red Cliff dock. Tribal officials, religious leaders, elders, and others could have likewise been in ceremonial repose, ready to receive them. The drum, tobacco, the pipe, perhaps a welcome prayer from a Catholic priest or two, could have been part of it. And maybe *migizi* might even have paid a lofty call, circling high above, its bright white head and tail glistening in the sunshine as it offered its approval. There could have been food, and the exchange of gifts.

But it did not happen. The *Niagara* made no stop at Red Cliff. Joe Duffy's black-and-white fishing boat would remain alone beside the old dock. It would have no dignified visitor from the east. Instead, the *Niagara* quietly, and beautifully sailed out of Bayfield harbor, past the Red Cliff dock and on along the miles-long reservation shoreline, past Red Cliff Creek with its important Old Pageant Grounds, past Frog Bay with its pristine beach (thank God it is still not developed!), past Raspberry Bay, Eagle Bay, Sand Bay, and past the far western edge of Red Cliff where the Apostle Islands National Lakeshore people now claim ownership.

The tall ship *Niagara* had a chance to visit the Hub of the Ojibwe Nation, but it let this opportunity slip away. Such a visit could have been taken as a ceremonial call to the many Ojibwe communities along Lake Superior's and the other Great Lakes', shores. It would have been a deeply meaningful international visit, one with proper protocol. In it, old friends who once were enemies, would have celebrated their important, long, peaceful relationship.

But finally, in a small way, all was not lost. Luckily, before the beautiful ship quietly slipped away I documented a Red Cliff connection with it. That Monday morning I was able to snap a photo of two Red Cliff tribal members standing beside the ship as its crew drew in the heavy hawsers that secured it to the town dock, pulled up the sails, and set the ship adrift. Seven-year-old Mijen Avery Armstrong and his five-year-old sister, Grace DePerry Armstrong, both with old Red Cliff names, stood beside the ship and helped make that *Niagara*-Red Cliff connection that goes back to 1812. In the photo we might let these kids represent those warriors of old who came from Chequamegon Bay, paddled to Sault Ste. Marie, and on to the eastern Great Lakes to go into battle against the Gichimookomaanag (the Americans)—the United States. Through this snapshot a connection between the *Niagara* and Red Cliff was made after all.

The beautiful reproduction of the old sailing ship was a contrast: with its complex array of ropes hanging from each mast, sail and yardarm, it offered a maze of details that appeared very complicated, while contrariwise it suggested an ancient simplicity. Compared to the tourist cruise boats and the upscale yachts berthed at the city dock, the ship was big, but would have been dwarfed by today's large warships. It was from another era, perhaps a simpler time. And interestingly, being a recent reproduction, the *Niagara* was young but still so very old. The two Red Cliff kids, both so very young and offering the wonderful simplicity of childhood, were the same. They also held something very old. They, like the ancient timbers salvaged from the original *Niagara*—timbers hidden deep in today's ship—held a solid connection with those Ojibwe warriors of nearly two hundred years ago. Like the old wood in the new ship, the old genes in the new youngsters made a wonderful connection between a time so long ago and today. As the ship's salvaged timbers made its link with the original ship of 1812, the youngsters' biology held a tangible connection with those Ojibwe people of 1812. So much time had passed since that early war, but the ship and the kids reached across that gulf of nearly 200 years. They made the connection.

I told the youngsters of the War of 1812 and how their unnamed ancestors stepped into birchbark canoes almost 200 years ago and made that long paddle to the east. I don't know how they felt, exactly what they thought about all this. In the ancient Ojibwe fashion, they were silent, but obviously interested. They looked pensively, at the beautiful ship, then at the big lake. Then their gazes moved north, along the wooded shoreline running out of Bayfield, that in only three miles leads to today's Red Cliff.

LA POINTE IN 1855

T HE YEAR WAS 1855. The place was old La Pointe. It was a few weeks in fall during the time of the annual payment of treaty annuities for the Ojibwe people, and the events are seen through the eyes of a protestant clergyman, Richard Morse. He wrote them in 1857, the year they were published in a collection of historical documents for the still new state of Wisconsin. For the past week or so I have been studying Morse's writings, and they set me to thinking.

In the thirty-one pages Morse left us we begin to see what life was like in western Lake Superior. It was clearly a time of change for the Ojibwe, but also a time of on-going traditions. By then protestant missionaries had been living in their very midst for just over twenty years, insisting that the Ojibwe change their ways, or, as it was phrased back then, that they "become civilized." This, of course, meant that they were to live like the Americans. Actually, the admonition to become civilized had been addressed to the Ojibwe ever since the French Jesuits were in Chequamegon Bay back in the mid-1600s, so by 1855 Ojibwe people had been admonished to change their ways for over two hundred years.

Scheduling such an important event for late August was unfortunate since this was the time for harvesting wild rice and when arriving at Madeline some of the band leaders complained, intimating that Washington officials needed to understand the importance of rice to the people. They could not be called away from this harvest since they needed to lay in a good supply of the grain for winter use. But, history tells that government officials often scheduled the annuity payments sessions right during wild rice time.

Upon Colonel Manypenny's arrival, canoes and runners were sent out to notify the different bands of the annuity payment gathering and eventually some people began to appear. Morse tells how for a few weeks many sittings and councils with chiefs and others were held. We can imagine the scene. By 1855 there were a considerable number of white folk residing on, or at least visiting the island, and these councils soon attracted such people who took seats along the edges of the council ground to observe the colorful proceedings.

Richard Morse tells how one day a large Ojibwe band from Minnesota Territory arrived with eighty to 100 warriors. These men walked tall, and showed a "sprightliness of mind." It is evident that Reverend Morse admired them and their leader who, he said, "was the smartest orator on the ground." Like all warriors, he colored his face with vermillion. When speaking in council this man wore "an elaborate turban of turkey feathers over his head and shoulders," headgear that set him apart from the rest even more.

This leader's daughter was with the group and, even though only about twenty years old, was a renowned warrior. She was said to be the only female allowed to participate in war ceremonies, and to wear a warrior's feathers. A beautiful person, she was also a swift runner, her fame known throughout western Lake Superior country.

The several weeks were a time of the meeting of two different worlds. By 1855 the Ojibwe had made accommodation to the Americans, a fact reflected in the words of Richard Morse. For example, on the first day a particular band chief spoke before the assembly he appeared in his traditional garb—a blanket, leather leggings and shirt, and wearing moccasins. But on another day this man appeared in a suit of blue broadcloth with a vest and "neat blue cap," but still wearing his "elegant finely-wrought moccasins." By 1855 the Ojibwe had become masters of adaptation.

A few thousand people congregated on Madeline Island, and Richard Morse was moved by the event, but perhaps what moved him most was that during these proceedings the aged and venerable Chief Buffalo passed away. It is thought that he may have been ninety-six years old. He suffered from a pulmonary disease for some time and two or three days before his death he prepared his will, gave his pipe and tobacco pouch to Colonel Manypenny, and much more interesting, accepted baptism into the Catholic faith.

Richard Morse did not comment on any particular meaning that might be seen in Buffalo's last act, nor am I familiar with any writer since then who has. Historians have said Buffalo was quite receptive to change, and that his large extended family was among the most "civilized" Ojibwe at La Pointe. I feel a careful reading of the historical literature shows that Chief Buffalo was resisting the Americans and their way of life throughout his later years at La Pointe, and it is very interesting that he refused Christian baptism until his death was imminent. All his life Chief Buffalo was a man of the pipe.

On September 9, 1855, his body was carried in a procession with two American flags at its head, followed by a large company of Ojibwe with rifles, firing volleys at intervals. A long concourse of Indians followed and services were in the nearby Catholic Church. Nothing is said of the pipe or drum but we should assume that they, like their usual companion, tobacco, were never far away.

TREKKING TO SANDY LAKE

September 6, 2005

LATE IN JULY I LEFT THE CREEK to drive to Sandy Lake, Minnesota, for a small gathering at the new monument commemorating what has been called the Ojibwe Death March. This was my second time at these annual meetings, and I hope to go again next year. At least three Red Cliff persons were in attendance, but maybe next year there will be many more.

Over each of the past dozen or so years, more and more people accept the deep importance of Sandy Lake. This is not just an Indian thing. Sandy Lake is about America and the way it used to think, and for some of us the way we still do. It is about truth, knowledge and power. Sandy Lake is about values, certainties, assumptions, religion, and political might. It is about colonialism and how a minority people was, and in some ways, today still is, treated by those who feel they alone hold the truth.

That late July day was sunny and hot and I was glad for our vehicle's air conditioner. As my wife and I moved up the hill in Duluth and found the turnoff at Black Bear we came upon a flat, almost desolate land. It looked like good wild rice country and this was what made Sandy Lake an important place for Ojibwe and Dakota people long ago. This rich history is what helps make it so meaningful today. Some might see it as a sacred place, one filled with the spirits of the past.

Most of us, I suspect, are not familiar with the details of the Sandy Lake story. It is all there in the books and papers of the past, and no doubt, for a few generations it was in the stories that elders at Red Cliff told their young. But I fear there are those today who are not familiar with the importance of Sandy Lake. It is time for them to learn it. A story like this is too important to ignor.

Times were difficult for Chequamegon Bay's Ojibwe people in the early 1800s. The Americans were coming in increasing numbers and food was getting scarce. Trying to help his people in these years, Chief Buffalo accepted the ideas of the Shawnee brothers—Tecumseh and Tenskwatawa (the Prophet)—and according to the historian William Warren, "fervently preached" their message to the LaPointe Ojibwe. Importantly, this was not just a religious message—it was a political call to resist the new Americans. Times must have been tough for Buffalo to take such drastic measures.

By the 1820s the idea of moving the native communities westward was gaining popularity and in 1850 President Zachery Taylor signed an order to move the La Pointe Ojibwe to Minnesota Territory. Behind this were the machinations of local business and political leaders like Henry Mower Rice (Bayfield's Rice Avenue is named after this man) and Alexander Ramsey (another politico and business tycoon). Rice and Ramsey left a legacy of crafty intrigue that lives on today.

If the Ojibwe would be moved large federal appropriations for their administration would go to Minnesota, and enterprising men like Ramsey and Rice wanted their share. Consequently, the treaty annuity payments that for years had been made on Madeline Island were switched in 1850 to Sandy Lake. And importantly, they were set for October in hopes that such a late date would cause the Ojibwe to stay in the region rather than return to Wisconsin and Michigan.

As history tells us, the people came, government food was not only late but was spoiled when dispensed, resulting in the deaths of at least 400 persons, and untold hardship for the survivors. These deaths are the lowpoint of the Sandy Lake Tragedy, but a story just as important is the political, economic and ideological intrigue behind the deaths. This too, is part of the Sandy Lake story.

This story was retold at this year's gathering. The drum, tobacco, and pipe were all there. The rich Ojibwe language was heard throughout the day. Ojibwe people, male and female, young and old, gathered to quietly remember. No missionaries were present. Several canoes of Ojibwe moved across the big lake like those who came to the lake over a century and a half ago, and put in at the very spot used in 1850. A connection was made.

What struck this writer was how non-tribal campers and boaters were in the park that hot day of the gathering, not more than thirty yards from the site of the ceremony, and seemed unaware of what was going on. While the drum and its singers celebrated the memory of 1850 these vacationers backed their showy boats to the landing the people used long ago. While the pipes were passed and the spirits invoked through the Ojibwe language, these vacationers glanced up to where we stood in a circle around the monument. What were they thinking? Did they have any idea about the sacred importance of the place they were using? Their lives of leisure went on. Had they learned about Mr. Rice and Mr. Ramsey and their drive for affluence? Had they even heard of the Ojibwe? And what assumptions do they hold about Native Americans today?

The contrast between the ceremony at the monument at Sandy Lake and the vacationers in that park lingers on in my memory. They ignored the ceremony. For them, it was business as usual.

Farming at Red Cliff—Again

June 6, 2005

By now most community members must know that recently the people of Red Cliff have purchased the Aiken Farm. After many years, this historic parcel of land is back into tribal hands. This past week when I left the creek to run a few errands, I noticed that the garden plots at the farm have been plowed. I hear that the plan is to have those plots made available for community gardens this spring. All this set me to thinking.

Early Ojibwe teachings tell that the people always did a good amount of gardening. The old books support these stories, saying that in the seventeenth and eighteenth centuries when the Europeans arrived they found plots of cultivated plants in Ojibwe communities. On occasion, these early European and Euro-American visitors to Indian Country traded for produce from such plots.

As hunters and gatherers, the earliest Ojibwe people in Lake Superior country harvested many varieties of native food plants—perhaps manoomin being the best known—but gardening also was an important method of getting food. Such gardening was largely the work of the women, but there are accounts of men helping with some of the heavier tasks.

Scholars who study the history of how humans have domesticated plants for food distinguish between gardening, horticulture, and finally, agriculture. Gardening is done with human muscle power, and agriculture often uses animal power or, after the Industrial Revolution, machine power. Horticulture lies between these two extremes. Such classifications of different ways of tilling the soil are abstractions that are useful for analytical purposes, but perhaps they obscure the reality of the major similarity between all three types of growing food crops. All involve the use of the earth for planting seeds, tubers, or roots for human food consumption. Perhaps we might say that all three are types of farming.

Once a culture adds the cultivation of plants to its food-getting practices, it experiences some major changes in its adaptation to the natural environment. World cultures that rely only on hunting, fishing, and the gathering of wild plants for food usually are more mobile than those that add the cultivation of plants to its repertoire of food-getting activities. Gardens require a degree of tending, or at most, once they are planted they must be returned to for harvesting. This ties a people to a geographic place in different ways than non-gardening peoples' experience, and therefore, they begin to relate to their world in a new way. These people begin to settle in to a place with a degree of intensity that may not be found with most non-gardening cultures.

Early Europeans and Euro-Americans never related well to the mobile life style of hunting-and-gathering peoples they encountered in the Americas. Immediately they concluded that such humans "roamed" over the land, meaning they almost mindlessly traveled hither and yon. The newcomers struggled to understand this movement, unable to appreciate the complexities of how the tribesmen were adapted to the resource requirements of the their native land. It did not take long before the newcomers were preaching to the Indian about "settling down" to farm. Agriculture was soon felt to be the way of life the tribesmen had to take up.

In the early 1800s when the Americans came to the midwest and demanded land cession treaties with the Ojibwe, articles for allotments of land for farming were often included. Red Cliff has a long history of such family allotments. In these early decades of the nineteenth century Red Cliff people were told to turn to the land—as tillers of its soil. Later, in 1887, the Dawes Act made such allotments the law of the land. With the passage of this congressional edict, the Indian was to become a farmer. Indian agents at Red Cliff set to work to get this accomplished. People were encouraged to root out tree stumps and to take up the plow. Rods of barbed-wire fence were run.

Today some reservation families remember these old days of farming. The Daley and Basina families quickly come to mind. Never huge operations, these family farms saw the keeping of small herds of dairy cattle, a flock of chickens, and perhaps a horse or two, but in time, it all ended. Soon the small fields were overrun with aspen, birch, maple, and oak, and their fences were swallowed-up by these returning trees. Now, some seventy-five, or so, years later, there is this talk of "farming" returning to Red Cliff.

In the early 1960s when I first came to Red Cliff, there were numerous families who gardened. It was exciting to see these plots of land and how they produced fresh vegetables for local tables, but then something happened. Almost all of these families stopped putting in gardens. I am not sure why, although I have some ideas. I was sorry to see those gardens go. The good, healthy, fresh food they provided was an important part of family menus.

What will come of this latest farming venture? Will we see rows of raspberry and blueberry plants? How about leafy green vegetables? And what about those colorful and nutritious root crops—the potatoes, beets, turnips and sweet jiissan? And the squashes—we cannot forget them! Squashes are soul food at Red Cliff.

So we will be watching the activity at the old Aitkin Farm. There is no doubt that this is an exciting project, one that could have a very positive effect on reservation diets and much more. Gardens can be places for families to renew themselves. Think of the possibilities! They can be places to literally "find your roots." Yes, good things can happen in gardens.

WALKING IN RED CLIFF

January 3, 2006

YESTERDAY I NOTICED A SIGHT MANY folks in Red Cliff see almost every day. I refer to people out for a walk. Perhaps this has become so commonplace that few passers-by give it a second glance, but today it set me to thinking.

I first came to Red Cliff back in 1959 and I noticed folks who walked along the highway at that time. The notion of physical fitness was a long way off, so these were not exercise buffs. No, they were walking to get somewhere. They were headed for a destination. There were few motor vehicles in Red Cliff in 1959 and it was common for people to walk to town, or just up to Pit's. Pit LaPointe and his wife, Lucile, ran a grocery store on the highway just south of the reservation boundary. Back then it seemed there was always someone walking to or from the store.

In the 1950s there was a lot of walking on the Rez. People got their exercise without having to buy those expensive running shoes that most everyone wears today. Very few homes had plumbing so someone had to go to a pump almost every day. Then, of course, most people also had to walk to the woodpile—and the outhouse. Walking was just part of living. Today the neighborhood pumps are gone, and few Red Cliff homes have woodpiles, and I suspect even fewer have outhouses. As Mike Dip used to say, "It's all modern now."

It's good to see today's residents out for a walk. These are people who have been thinking about their health and have decided to do something about it. I suspect everyone in the community is pleased to see Jenny Goslin out on her walks. Grandma Jen is a living treasure. And sometimes I see Jenny with her daughter Diane, walking side-by-side along the roadway. Not only that—they're enjoying a conversation as well as the walk! Yes, they converse with each other. It's a nice sight, seeing a mother and daughter together like that. But I think about how things have changed. Over the almost fifty years since 1959, some people still walk, but for different reasons.

Oh, I still see a few walking to the store now and then—today it is Peterson's instead of Pit's—but most residents drive there. Today motor vehicles can be found in virtually all Red Cliff yards. Some people seem to drive almost everywhere they go. I suspect some of the employees at the main administrative offices drive to work even though they might live only a block or two away. Apparently, for them, driving has replaced walking. With gasoline well over $2.25 a gallon and rising, I wonder how long this will continue.

Back in the fifties and sixties lots of folks used to walk to Bayfield to watch a movie, to roller skate in the pavilion, to visit friends, or for other reasons. And there were those high school students who had to walk home after a basketball game, or other late night event. In those times the school bus would not take them out to their homes, instead it dropped them off at the edge of town at O'Malley's Hill. Those young people had to walk three miles to get home. (That still seems strange to me, given that the school was receiving federal funds to cover expenses for Native American students.)

And I remember how I would lie out on the lawn under the Whitney Crab apple tree with my father-in-law watching the weekend traffic pass the DePerry house on Highway 13. This was forty years ago. There really was not much traffic to watch, but some pretty large boats on trailers went by, especially in early spring and again in fall. Now the vehicular traffic seems endless. Red Cliff has grown since then, and it seems most adult residents have a car. This is what makes today's walking so interesting. Many Rez folks seem to enjoy driving their cars, trucks and what have you, but there are those who still walk. What causes the difference? Why do some find walking meaningful and some not?

There is something special about a long walk. Even when out for a walk that lasts an hour or more, when I begin to feel the legs tell me it is time to go home, and when my body begins to sweat, I still feel an inner peace. Those walkers along Red Cliff's Highway 13 surely must understand this. The traffic that rushes by them must be distracting at times, but even with this, I'll bet they find a good degree of comfort. I think of those early Ojibwe people who either paddled a canoe or walked to wherever they went. The old books sometimes tell of the excellent physical shape of those people! The first English trader to come to Madeline Island—he arrived in 1765—told about the physical beauty of the Ojibwe he found residing there.

When I pass today's walkers out on the highway I sometimes think of Alexander Henry's remarks and I say perhaps little has changed over these approximately 250 years since he was here. Some Ojibwe people are still walking—and still looking good!

THIS SUSTAINABLILTY THING

July 15, 2005

ANYONE WHO PAYS ATTENTION to the local press knows attempts are under-way to make us start thinking about what is called sustainability. For several months now I have been reading articles and letters to the editor on it, and they set me to thinking. I want to be part of this, not just an unknowing bystander who watches it unfold.

If I understand it correctly, sustainability means just what it says: living in a manner that allows us to continue living for generations to come, and beyond. To accomplish this, we must begin changing the way we relate to things around us—to include the natural world and all the forms of life it holds. We must curb our intrusiveness. Our days of raping and pillaging must come to an end. Homo sapiens, as The Great Exploiter, must become The Great Accommodator. We must come into conformance with life's rules—and I mean all of life, not just that of our species. For too long, too many of us really believed we were given a divine mandate to overpower our planet. Those sustainability folks are saying that if we want any kind of future for our species, and the others, we must change our ways. We must begin living with these others, not off of them.

Sustainability is a wonderful concept, but in recent weeks a few letters to the editor have appeared in the local press that warn of its left-wing dangers. Perhaps we should expect these initial, uninformed and unfortunate reactions at the first go-round. As always, when raising questions about the way our species lives, there are those who will feel threatened.

There is no threat in sustainability, other than the fact that if we do not consider what is being suggested, and make appropriate adjustments, our long-term existence will be called into question. It really is that simple. We cannot go on the way we have. To do so will mean eventually there will be no future. Therein lies the threat. Who will deny its importance?

We in Chequamegon Bay are fortunate to be bracketed by two Native American communities that have the potential for playing leading roles in what this sustainability thing is about. Both these communities have been busy with sustainability issues for some time, and one of them has been publishing a newspaper on this. Just in case you have not noticed, pick up a copy of *Mazina'igan*, the newspaper of the Great Lakes Indian Fish and Wildlife Commission (GLIFWC) and start learning about how the regional Ojibwe people are taking action on sustainability issues. Some of the things these folks have been doing are truly amazing. If you want to start feeling good about how some of our local fellow humans are approaching our natural environment, read *Mazina'igan*. It could change the way you think, and live.

However, do not be misled by the emphasis on our natural, non-human environment *Mazina'igan* shows. Sustainability is about more than our natural resources. It is about how we approach all of life—about the way we think, and finally, about what we hold to be true. It is about social, political, economic, and other relationships. It is about life, and this is what intrigues me. As an anthropologist, I have spent several decades studying what some call "the human condition." From my point of view this sustainability initiative is very anthropological. Pushed to its farthest limits, it is a movement about how we relate to people, as well as to our natural surroundings. It is about what anthropologists mean by culture. Culture is a set of rules about how we live. That is how deep sustainability runs.

Native America can teach us about such important things. Ojibwe communities show an understanding of sustainability in matters of relationships with their fellow humans, in their subject matter and teaching methods in schools, in the importance of the Ojibwe language, and of course, in spiritual matters. Indigenous cultures the world over have much to teach the rest of us. Finally, after hundreds of years of arrogant neglect and oppression, we are turning to them with a new appreciation.

How can we live except in any way that is in consort with our natural world and its other forms of life? At one time all of our ancestors lived in a fashion that was compatible with their natural world. We must relearn, and redeem our original relationship with the earth. There is no other way. This is not a retrograde turning back to earlier ways and times. Rather, it is a return to an early and vitally important view of the world and our species' place in it. The religions of indigenous peoples have never given up this view. It is what sustains them. It is time for we others to consider it.

Unfortunately, we humans may sometimes be so entrenched in our ways that many of us will not accept these earliest of sustainability initiatives. We will be overly focused on our present ways, thoughts and perceived needs. This determined focus itself is a human trait, one that has helped us survive for millions of years. However, we are also an adaptive species. We can and do make changes. Change has been part of our life-way.

So, take a look at sustainability. Think about the way you live. Think about how you use the earth.

The Ojibwe Sugarbush—Always a Sweet Place to Be
March 12, 2005

YESTERDAY WHILE ENJOYING a late breakfast and watching the happy flutter of birds at our deck's feeder my wife and I were treated to a sudden inrush of chickadees. Most picked up a single black sunflower seed and quickly flew to the nearby spruce to peck it open, but one little bird paused, cocked her head at the house windows and loudly sang its famed two note-call—the "T-J" chickadee signature song we love to hear. My wife remarked that it was the first such call we heard this season. That short song set me to thinking.

It was a welcome sign that the days are growing longer and in only a few weeks we could be out in the sugarbush. Chickadees in late winter, by singing this simple song foretell of maple syrup time. These little black-capped birds, their two-note call, and Ojibwe sugarbushes go together. They complement each other very well.

Here at Red Cliff sugarbushes go back hundreds of years and maybe even much, much longer. After a winter that saw families off by themselves in their hunting territories, they looked forward to meeting friends in the sugarbush. It was an early spring get-together. There was a time, not so long ago, when most Red Cliff families had sugarbushes. In those years opening up "the bush" was a welcome rite of spring that was filled with hard work, but also with much laughter and pure joy. The event signaled the end of another winter. The long quiet—and sometimes hungry—time was ending. But I must not phrase this in the past tense. Sugarbushes are still an integral part of Ojibwe culture and here at Red Cliff the few remaining ones are very important.

For years I reveled in being able to take part, even if in only a small way, in the Newago Family sugarbush out in the western reaches of the reserve. Mike and Sam Newago always welcomed me and seemed pleased I could spend time with them in the woods. They are both gone now and I miss them immeasurably, but in spring we come together again. Last year I did not make it out to their bush, instead spending time in my son's and his wife's new sugarbush at

La Court Oreilles. One of the Newago boys chastised me for my absence, and this year I fully intend to get out to the bush again. I miss it.

These past several years it has been run by the next Newago generation, the sons of Mike and Sam. They keep the tradition alive. And just like their fathers, they talk of modernizing the bush, but so far I am pleased to know it is only talk. If a new propane gas boiling shed ever appears out there something valuable will be lost. If some spring I find long plastic lines running from tree to tree, bringing sap to a central collection station, I will probably shake my head in sadness. To me, modernity has no place in that camp. If the loud ring of the double bit ax is no longer heard and if the sap is not boiled over a large open fire it will not be the same. Besides, I would miss the sweet wood smoke.

But while I would lament such changes the younger Newago's might welcome them. It is onto the strong shoulders of these fellows that the hard task of working up cords of firewood, tapping the trees, hauling the buckets of heavy sap, and tending the boiling kettles falls. The chain saw eases some of this labor, but the ax and splitting maul still must be lifted high.

In earlier times the sugarbush was the domain of the Ojibwe woman. These days a woman will make it out to the camp now and then, but it really has become a man's place. I have learned that at Red Cliff before World War II, many women had their own camps scattered around the village and in some cases even miles out. The old books tell of Ojibwe women who went out to the camps and got them going each spring. Ojibwe women are known for being hard workers. I've witnessed one close up for over forty years. She is a working machine.

Schoolchildren are sometimes bussed out to the sugarbush for a day of "cultural enrichment." Over the years I watched them spend a few hours in the woods, shouting, running, and working to haul and boil sap. They seemed to belong there. And a few select elders would occasionally walk the mile into camp to sit around the boiling kettles. I used to love to see them coming in on the trail. The quiet joy they showed was obvious. An hour or two on a sunny late winter's day beside that boiling fire must have brought back fond memories. These elders treasured the balsam tea and bean soup we offered them.

The Ojibwe sugarbush is a sacred place. And this is what is so good about seeing new camps being opened up these days. The Lac Court Oreilles camp I frequent is also run the old way. It's a quiet place, filled with life. These camps are small sanctuaries I go to in spring. Tucked away from the rush of the outside

196

world, they are places of renewal. Almost secretive, they are places where Ojibwe people come who understand their deep importance. These groves of stolid maple trees stand in stark contrast to that other place where so many of us reside. Not everyone understands the wonderful meaning of an Ojibwe sugarbush. It is better that way. Let them stay away, and let them buy their artificially flavored corn syrup in the store. Yet, it really is something to think of what all those people are missing!

How Soon We Forget

January 7, 2004

THOSE OF US WHO ARE READERS surely have the experience of finishing a good book, then, holding it in our hands for a few precious moments as we glance up to look for someone to share it with. We yearn to talk about it—to tell how good, or important it is, but if there is no one to share it with we must keep it all inside. Such times can be difficult, and they set me to thinking.

This it what happened the other night when I finished reading a book about John Muir, the famous Scottish-American environmentalist who for a time, lived in southern Wisconsin. The book is *Yearning for the Land*, by John Warfield Simpson, and tells how humans sometimes yearn to relate to a place in a very deep way. Simpson is a landscape architect, teaching in Ohio, who spent a year in Scotland exploring the place of Muir's childhood. Then he came to Wisconsin and did the same here. It is a good book, especially if you like to think about the notion of place and how perhaps it is a common human trait to yearn for a place we can call home. But, Simpson troubles me when he ends the book by quoting the famous American writer, Wallace Stegner, at some length. Stegner wrote much about our West, and how Americans came to it and "made it theirs." I think John Warfield Simpson missed the boat on Wallace Stegner.

All of this called to mind one of the most important books I have recently read, and this is what this essay is about. *Why I Can't Read Wallace Stegner and Other Essays*, by Elizabeth Cook-Lynn, was published by the University of Wisconsin Press in 1996, and among other things, takes on Wallace Stegner, challenging us to rethink our infatuation with this lauded American writer. I have never met Elizabeth Cook-Lynn but I like her. I like the way she speaks up. I like what she says.

She is a Lakota Indian from South Dakota who spent her professional career as a professor of English at Eastern Washington University way out west near the Pacific Ocean. Elizabeth Cook-Lynn sounds like someone who does not abide a fool. It must have been very exciting to take a college course from her! After reading her book on Stegner I tracked down her other publications and found that along with being a first-class essayist she is also an accomplished novelist.

Why does she struggle with Wallace Stegner and why did the Ohio landscape architect apparently have no problem with him? I am not certain on these questions, except that it is a matter of perspective. As a Native American, Cook-Lynn brings something to the table that Simpson cannot. She has a point of view, a sensitivity that he can move toward, but never completely acquire.

Wallace Stegner wrote about the West as if the Native Americans who lived there for hundreds of years are gone. If he were still alive, he would certainly deny this, but I think it is true. Stegner downplayed today's Native American presence in the West, a presence that is still alive and well.

Like others before him, Stegner used the 1890 massacre at Wounded Knee, South Dakota, as a marker for a widely important change in the Old West. To him, it signaled the emergence of a new way of life as the old tribal worlds were put to rest. Elizabeth Cook-Lynn rails at this, arguing that it is an immoral stand, one that, finally, denies the existence of tribal peoples today. She is an astute observer and an even more articulate writer and thinker, and I will not try to describe her argument in any other way except to say it is a no-nonsense statement about one of this country's literary masters of all time.

Elizabeth Cook-Lynn causes me to think of how some non-Native writers have portrayed Ojibwe people in regional histories for our area here in Chequamegon Bay. To be sure, early local writers like Guy Burnham and Walt Harris included the Ojibwe in their histories but it seems to me this was true only for the earliest years their manuscripts speak of. When I read these writers I discover that as their books unfold there is less and less about the Ojibwe people in them, and near the end they are hardly mentioned at all. It is as if through the years in Chequamegon Country they have disappeared.

Perhaps Wallace Stegner would applaud history books written this way, saying that these books show that, indeed, the Americans have come to this big lake and over time made it, and the surrounding forests, theirs. They have truly Americanized this place.

But maybe I am too hard on writers like Guy Burnham, Walt Harris, and Wallace Stegner. Perhaps I had better get on with life and leave it all alone. We have bigger things to think about these days—like Iraq, global warming, and all the rest. But then, I also think of John Hassler, the Minnesota writer who I enjoy, whom when I asked why he included the Ojibwe people in several of his regional novels, told me, "Well, because they are always out there somewhere—they are always around, standing nearby."

CALAMITIES AND ABOMINATIONS: LIFE ON MADELINE ISLAND IN THE 1830S
April 15, 2005

SHERMAN HALL WAS THE FIRST Christian missionary to live permanently on Madeline Island. A protestant, he and his wife arrived in 1831 and stayed twenty-four years, until leaving for a new post in Minnesota. This winter I have been reading the diary and letters he wrote when living here and for a number of reasons they set me to thinking.

A year after their arrival Mrs. Hall gave birth to a daughter said to have been the first white child born on Madeline. This event may be interesting as a bit of historical trivia, but it is not what makes the Hall's so important.

Missionaries always bring more than religion, for religious beliefs can never be meaningfully separated from a social and cultural context. They do not stand alone. It is in this sense that a careful reading of Sherman Hall's writings shows how he worked to bring more than Christianity to the Ojibwe. In his own words, he labored to civilize them, and this meant of course, that he tried to get them to give up their way of life, and adopt his.

It wasn't long before he opened a mission school on Madeline. The Halls worked hard to learn the Ojibwe language so they could translate their religious texts and use them in this school. It appears however, that few Ojibwe youngsters spent much time in that classroom.

By the 1830s, Chequamegon Bay's Ojibwe were experiencing strong pressures to change. By then the French and British had moved on and the Americans were here to stay. With them were the Halls, who said the Ojibwe had it all wrong. They claimed that the peoples' religion was nothing at all, and that they had to change almost everything about their lives. Sherman Hall called them heathens, meaning that they had no religion. Like the Jesuits back in the seventeenth century, he said their religious beliefs and ceremonies were abominations. In more than one letter to relatives back in Vermont he exclaimed, "It is a calamity to be born into heathenism!" He was convinced that his god had sent him to Madeline Island to "save" the Ojibwe people. Imagine how such a scene would play out today—someone publicly calling someone else's religion and its ceremonies abominations. The America Sherman Hall came from was a headstrong place. Woe to the person who did not walk the walk of its mainstream!

Sherman Hall was not successful in converting many native people to his religion. In fact, Hamilton Ross, the early Madeline Island writer, said that during the Hall's long tenure "only seven or eight mixed bloods or Indians joined the church by a confession of faith." We are told they avoided Hall as much as possible. This at least, was an observation by Lieutenant James Allen when he passed through the region in 1832 as a member of the Schoolcraft expedition to the headwaters of the Mississippi. Lieutenant Allen described Sherman Hall as a cold and austere person who did not relate well to the Ojibwe.

The peoples' seasonal movements troubled this missionary. At first he followed them to their rice fields, sugarbushes, gardens, and hunting grounds on the mainland, but soon gave this up. On these trips he would approach a lodge and upon entering preach to its residents. He wrote how sometimes he was rebuffed, but occasionally was allowed to remain while the people sat, politely listening. Deciding that this was not an efficient use of his time, he tried to get some families to stay on the island year around, and in 1835 he helped build a house near his for one of them so he could more easily, as he said, "work on their minds."

Imagine the ramifications of an Ojibwe family staying on the island year around. It would have been pulled from its extended kin network and to a great extent isolated socially, economically and politically, from the rest of the native community. How would this family have survived unless it adopted the way of life of the Halls? And this, finally, was what Sherman Hall was after. He worked to destroy Ojibwe culture.

This winter I often think of those Indian people back in the 1830s. The books show us that they were still moving with the seasons and enjoying their *midewiwin, wabeno,* and other religious institutions with their complex ceremonies. Ojibwe culture, with its rich religion, was ongoing. Euro-American visitors often wrote about the poverty, nakedness and hunger they found among the people in these years, but I wonder about that. What could they see through their biased predispositions?

The contemporary theologian, George E. Tinker, in his important little book entitled *Missionary Conquest,* says that people like Sherman Hall were directly related to community and personal dysfunctions found in Indian Country today. What must it have been like to live in a community all your life and one day have someone move in who said you were doing it all wrong? He would say your ancestors lived lives based on false premises—that they worshipped false gods. He would say that the way you saw yourself deep inside was a calamity and an abomination.

THE IMPORTANCE OF SANDY LAKE

September 16, 2005

TWO WEEKS AGO I ATTENDED a ceremonial gathering that will not leave me. Surely you have had such experiences. What is so special about these sorts of events? Why do they take hold of our hearts and refuse to let go? Sometimes when ritual, the spoken word, music, smells, tastes, and colors come together in just the right mix we can be deeply affected in ways we do not soon forget. All of us must experience these rare times when we are magically transported to a place lying beyond the ordinary. Words fail to capture the importance of such happenings, but I will try to explain what struck me so deeply, and in a very important way, what set me to thinking.

It was in the last week of July when I left the cabin so my wife and I could drive to Sandy Lake, Minnesota. The event was arranged by the good folks from the Great Lakes Indian Fish and Wildlife Commission from Odanah of the Bad River community. Sandy Lake can be easily reached from our home on Chequamegon Bay and as we headed west from the interstate at Duluth, we began to notice how the land leveled out and became what I call low country. It was not good farming land. This is where the Ojibwe people were to live. In my younger days I might have concluded I was entering a desolate land, one of no value at all. Even though the summer has been dry, we saw and felt that we were entering a wet place—a wide country filled with swampland. Bogs and marshes were ubiquitous throughout the entire landscape. My Germanic forbears were certain such land was worthless.

What is so important about Sandy Lake and these annual gatherings? Why has a small group of Ojibwe people and friends come to Sandy Lake each of these last several years? And why do so many other Americans seem not to notice? These are the sorts of questions that visit me almost daily, clamoring for answers. They are not easy questions since they are knocking at doors that, if opened, can lead to the deep recesses of our personal, and very private, lives. They are questions that ask us who we think we are. They are questions that take no prisoners.

Simply put, the reason for my wife's and my trip two weeks ago was something that occurred back in 1850. An event took place that caused the death of approximately 400 human beings, and unfortunately, altered the lives of many more. However, this event was part of something much deeper and widespread. Sandy Lake is not simply important today because of what caused so many deaths. It is important for the assumptions and certainties that brought this event to fruition. The Ojibwe deaths in the winter of 1850-1851 were caused by ideas and "knowledge" prevalent in the Euro-America of the times. Here is the underpinning of the Sandy Lake Tragedy.

Today, it seems that unknowingly to the Ojibwe, they had signed treaties with the United States that divested them of all their lands in what is now the State of Wisconsin. While the people were led to believe they were just selling the pine timber and minerals, the Americans were after the land itself. By 1850 Euro-American politicians and businessmen like Henry Mower Rice and Alexander Ramsey, understood that they could gain significant wealth if they were successful in moving the Michigan and Wisconsin Ojibwe to Minnesota Territory. It was this that was behind the 400 deaths. The machinations of these two prominent politicos and entrepreneurs led to the Removal Order of 1850 signed by President Zachery Taylor. Some would call it greed, but it was more than such a common human characteristic. Rice and Ramsey were certain the Ojibwe were a people destined to give way. They were certain the Ojibwe had to become Christians and adopt the way of life of mainstream America. They were certain the Ojibwe had to change their whole world. Along with the deaths of 400 people, this certainty must be recognized as part of the Sandy Lake tragedy.

That hot day in late July the sacred drum came to the historic landing at Sandy Lake. Tobacco and the pipe were there as well. The rich Ojibwe language was heard throughout the hours-long event. Tribal elders and the very young, were present. Both the male and female voice was heard. The sacred foods of the people—venison, wild rice, blueberries and more—were present as well. And while unknowing tourists and recreational boaters labored to maneuver their showy craft to the nearby docks—just thirty feet or so from the ceremony's site—we formed a circle on the small mound where today's monument honoring those who died now stands. The contrast between the boaters and the people at the ceremony was striking. Two worlds were once again, side by side. Unlike in 1850, this time the people were not at the mercy of the politicos from Washington and St. Paul. No such out-of-town dignitaries presided over this ceremony.

It was an honor to be present at Sandy Lake. The fifty or so of us who came were strong in sentiment and prayer. We remembered the strong people who died over one hundred and fifty years ago.

WRZC-92.3 FM,
HOMETOWN RADIO
November 17, 2007

THURSDAY MORNING I WAS A LITTLE LATE getting to the radio station for the weekly show I have been part of for the last three years and while driving in for the first time I was able to listen to a few minutes of the show live. It was good to hear my friends Jack and Frank open the hour up and after introducing their guest, engage her in a conversation. Their voices came in loud and clear, and they set me to thinking.

Hometown public radio is pretty neat. There are no commercials and for our show at least, the music is most often live, performed right in the studio. We play very few CDs. Our guests are from the community with messages for the people. And in our case there is no fast-talking, loud disc jockey going on about what is happening in Hollywood or New York City. We are homespun, maybe even provincial. Some might even say we are crass amateurs.

When I retired several years ago if anyone would have told me I would soon be part of a weekly radio show in Red Cliff, Wisconsin, I would not have believed it. But here I am, with a handful of good friends, getting onto the airwaves every Thursday morning for an hour, talking about how we see things. In Frank's case he also sings about how he sees things. As a friend of mine used to say, it has been "a hoot."

The show is *The Gitchigami Hour*, and we are on the air from 10:00 a.m. to 11:00 a.m. on Thursday mornings. WRZC is found at 92.3FM and its signal goes out only twenty miles, so we like to think our listeners are a very select group. We know they are out there because they tell us so now and then.

We never know who will come to the station and on a few occasions I have been there alone. But such times are rare. Actually, I suspect all four or five of us really enjoy our weekly time together or we would not keep doing it. Like so much going on in small communities, it is unrehearsed and genuine. We are just regular folks coming together for an hour or so on Thursday mornings to do our thing.

The heart of the hour is Frank's music. He lives on the Rez and brings an instrument or two along each week. He is known for his guitar and wooden flute music, but he plays the accordion, mandolin, and at least a dozen other instruments. We never know what he will bring, and I suspect a few minutes before he leaves his house he does not know either. His abilities and versatilities are truly amazing. For about three years now I have sat right next to him as he plays and sings, and it is done from the heart. There is no sheet music in sight. And the man writes poetry as well.

Another person who has been with us almost from the start is Jack. Living just outside of Bayfield, this fellow writes love poems. He showed up several months after we started the show and has been a mainstay ever since. That first day he brought a folder of poems handwritten on lined yellowed paper and after reading a few, quietly said that was the first time he read his poetry to anyone. "Even my wife has never heard these poems," he claimed. Jack passed a threshold of some sort that day. Now he reads his stuff at the drop of a hat.

Then there is Jeff. This quiet fellow phoned only a few weeks after I began the show, saying he wrote poetry and wondered if he could come to the station and read a few pieces. He was welcomed and stayed with us each week for a year or two before being pulled away by his work. Now he joins us when he can and we miss him when he cannot make it. After some months of being with us he went on to win a major poetry contest. Soon, we hope, his pieces will be in print so more poetry enthusiasts can enjoy his work. It is good stuff.

There are others who are part of *The Gitchigami Hour*. Ted was in it from the start, and although his work pulls him away now and then, he makes it when he can. His immediate wit provides a needed measure of upbeat energy, and his poetry is top-notch. Ted is our weatherman, who at the nod of a head can cut in with the latest on what is really happening in the sky. His spends much time on our big lake so knows the importance of ascending and descending air masses and how they can affect us.

Who else is part of the show? Rob, Rainer, and Laughing Fox come to mind. All of these voices take part when they can, and all bring points of view that are welcomed. Rob continues to win prizes for his poetry and Rainer excels in matters of contemporary political commentary. Laughing Fox combines poetry with native wooden flute music and is excellent at it.

It is low power, community radio. Poetry, music, weather, and news. Local radio for local folks.

PART

IV

PREFACE TO PART IV

THE ESSAYS IN THIS SECTION SUMMARIZE various topics relating to contemporary life at the tip of Wisconsin's Bayfield peninsula. It takes effort to earn one's living in this land, and surely a year-around resident knows of the labor needed to produce our bountiful apple crop, and the sophisticated work-skills called for on the increasing number of our blueberry-growing farms. Strawberries, raspberries, blackberries, and even gooseberries are grown here, and each has its own season as well as set of talents needed to produce and market a bountiful crop. And, of course, the old practice of commercial fishing still goes on. The taking of whitefish, lake trout, and freshwater herring no longer reaches the tonnage of the catches of the past, but in season, fishing tugs still leave Bayfield's docks at dawn to lift and re-set Lake Superior nets. Other skills, however, have had to be developed and honed for the more recent tourist industry.

Pleasure sailboats now dot the channel between Madeline Island and Bayfield on most summer afternoons, and the ubiquitous kayak has come to town bringing new visitors with different needs. Red Cliff and Bayfield have responded to these challenges, and these new industries have found a place at the base of our region's commercial life. But we still are part of a larger world and we inform ourselves of distant events of importance. We are not isolated from this bigger world, and many of these pieces speak to one writer's view of how our chosen place is affected by it.

THE RETURN OF THE TOURISTS

April 17, 2007

Spring is arriving in fits and starts this year. Bayfield has had a downright cool breeze coming off the big lake for what seems like several weeks now and it keeps some of us from putting away our heavy winter coats and caps. But over the past two weekends a good number of out-of-towners have shown up to walk our nearly bare streets—and to take the few precious seats in our main street coffee shop—and these welcome folks are signs that our tourist season is not far away. I watch these early birds, and they set me to thinking.

Where do these people come from and what keeps bringing them here? Some have blue-and-white license plates so I suspect most of these are from the Twin Cities, or possibly Duluth. Others have Wisconsin plates. So far this season only a very few are from Illinois. Last weekend I spotted one from Missouri but that's unusual this early in the year. When I can count a dozen or more plates from states other than Wisconsin and Minnesota is still two months or so away.

The official promotional materials for this town speak to its lakeside quaintness. That might mean a few different things, but mostly I suspect, it suggests that life is slower here, a bit more relaxing than in fast-paced cities. Some visitors tell me Bayfield reminds them of small New England towns they enjoy. They profess to like the architecture of the early styled clapboard houses that still can be found on this hillside.

Some speak of the quiet effect of the ever-present water. They claim not to venture out onto it very often, except for an occasional ferry ride over to Madeline, but they still recognize the importance of this lake. These folks do not own boats, so they are a set of visitors noticeably apart from our sailboat crowd. It is enough for them to enjoy the quietude of this big body of water without challenging it as sail boaters and kayakers might do.

Over the past two months or so some of us who live here all year took our usual late winter vacations to our favorite get-away places. A few went to Branson, others to Vegas, and some to the Caribbean or Mexico. Recently two of these friends remarked about how they noted the large number of people in the distant locales they escaped to. One who went to Palm Beach, Florida, shook his head as he told of the people and traffic he confronted there. Another remarked that after driving to South Carolina with his family for a week of enjoying the seacoast, how upon driving back they struggled with bumper-to-bumper traffic for the first ten hours of the twenty-four-hour trip.

I countered by saying on a recent drive to Hayward, I was a bit put-off by what I felt was its noise and faster pace from what I enjoy here in Bayfield and Red Cliff. They smiled at this, then, remarked that I might need to get off my hillside more often.

What all this tells me is that here in the Northland we really do have something special. And at base, that treasured quality is the result of our lower population level. What makes our place pleasant to so many visitors is that there are less folks here than where they come from. This, coupled with the naturalness of our physical surroundings makes them feel comfortable. They like being in a place with fewer people, not many flashing lights, honking horns and all the rest. This of course applies to times other than our famous Apple Festival, and the usual celebrations like our Fourth of July weekend.

Fewer people also can mean that we do not alter our natural environment as much as is done in areas of high human population concentrations. In this sense, it is not just the big lake that is appealing to visitors, but it also is our relatively untrammeled wooded countryside. We still have a lot of trees on the Bayfield Peninsula, and their presence adds to our enjoyment.

This message about our mere numbers as a prime variable that directly affects our comfort levels is just beginning to reappear in our national dialogue. It can be found in some of the more thoughtful statements on issues like global warming and concerns about peak oil. I recall when human population numbers were a major topic of discussion in this land. Back then—I think it was the late 1960s and early 1970s—I was one of those who pinned a ZPG button on my lapel. Zero Population Growth. As a nation we were to work toward this goal.

To some of us this might sound like a pipe dream, or worse yet, even elitist. They might say it would not be good for business, and our economy is always the bottom line. I don't know. But, I cannot help to wonder that should our human population in this Northland suddenly increase to uncomfortable levels if these annual visitors of ours would keep coming. I think of Lake Geneva, Wisconsin Dells and Door County, and what has occurred in these beautiful places. I sure do not want that to happen here, and I don't think this season's earliest visitors do either.

HEADING INTO SUMMER AGAIN

June 12, 2006

THERE CAN BE NO DOUBT that here in Chequamegon Bay summer has arrived and plans to stay. When the wind comes off the lake we sometimes feel a slight chill, but the big story is still the coming of warm weather. According to the calendar summer does not start until June 21st, but I'd say it arrived about four weeks ago, and its coming sets me to thinking.

Perhaps for some of us, summer is a relief of sorts, since our winter heating bills finally take a welcome plunge, and our concerns about clothing lessen because we need not wear so many layers anymore. My winter cap, for example, is stashed away on the closet shelf along with my warm leather choppers, and their companion, the heavy, lined coat hangs on the hook below. These pieces of clothing served me well since last October or so, and now they can rest for a few months before called into duty again.

But, it is not just our heating bills and clothing that are easier to handle with summer's arrival. All of life seems a bit easier now, and although I love winter, summer brings a refreshing casualness that is downright enjoyable. The old song says this is the time when living is easy, and today I agree. The mosquito population is still low and those terrible biting black flies have not yet arrived. Wood ticks might be a problem, but with proper precaution they can usually be avoided.

This week I broke out a new pair of walking shorts, recently purchased by my wife at some shop up on the hill in Duluth. She likes to take trips over that way to spend hours walking though her favorite stores. She is good at that and I am glad to leave such things to her. I suspect that when she was young about the only clothing store she found herself in with any regularity was Jack Lee's right here in Bayfield. Now, as a grandmother she likes to branch out a bit, in fact, I think that every few weeks she feels the urge to drive somewhere and do a little shopping. It has become a big part of her life.

Last weekend we attended the high school graduation ceremony here in Bayfield and were treated to a lively, fast-moving event. The graduates were all in white gowns and some were wearing shorts. It looked and felt like a light, airy, almost festive time. Unlike other years, the temperature inside the gymnasium was cool, so even though my wife and I were in the bleachers it was a comfortable time. Dr. Jim Pete of Red Cliff was the main speaker and he kept it lively and short. All in all I'd say it was a well-planned and well-executed ceremony.

Upon leaving the high school we drove out to Red Cliff for a few receptions for graduates. These days such open houses have become part of graduation and this year there were a dozen or more to get to. It is always a challenge not to overeat at the first one because there are many tables of food waiting at the next ones. When did these open houses become part of it all? My wife and I do not remember having them—but then, we graduated fifty or more years ago.

Now that school is out our town beach down near the fish docks is getting much use, and one of my brother-in-laws has had at least one cookout. He began collecting dry wood for these famous events a month or so ago. Uncle Ed's Red Cliff cookouts are the real thing—everything prepared over an open wood-fueled fire—and the extended family does not need to be told twice when one is scheduled. These gatherings have become favorites for the nieces and nephews.

Another joy of the coming of summer is the arrival of the earliest fresh fruit and veggies from local gardens and secret wild places. So far I have made and enjoyed two batches of rhubarb sauce and one double-crust pie. Weeks ago the first picking of wild leeks was done. They were sautéed as a side dish to a delicious whitefish supper last week. And we have been picking fistfuls of multiplying onions for some time now. Like the leeks, these stay in the ground over winter and come up early. A few of these tasty gems with a sandwich and a bottle of golden glow out on the deck is a great lunch, especially in late May and early June.

And of course, summer brings out the lawn mowers. Bob King has been busy mowing grass around town for a few weeks. In winter he is hard at work with the snow blower, and in summer it's the lawn mower. He has become a fixture in Bayfield and there are a lot of folks who would be hard pressed to get their lawns cut if it were not for him.

Yes, spring has turned into summer, but I can't help feel that it happened too quickly this year. I don't know—are those folks who like to tell us about climate change right? For now I'll let them worry about such important things. I am too busy getting used to having summer around again. I'm too busy just taking it all in.

ZIINZIBAAKWAD – MAPLE SUGAR

March 6, 2007

W e're heading into mid-March and that means its Sugarbush Time. The month blew in like a lion but now we have a warm spell so very soon some of us will be out there cutting firewood, tapping trees and hauling and boiling sap. Each year at this time sugarbush season sets me to thinking.

Sugaring, as it is sometimes called, is an ancient custom of the Ojibwe. Origin teachings tell how it was brought to the people long ago, and since then has never left. These last several years have witnessed a resurgence of interest in this activity and no wonder. Each spring the sugarbush is a place where special things happen—warm weather returns, and critters that have laid low for the winter begin to stir—as the woods comes back to life. Humans catch the spirit and join the celebration.

Thankfully, that store-bought imitation that tries to pass as maple syrup is no longer part of the menu in our house. For a long time now, we have been privileged to enjoy the real thing: genuine maple syrup made locally. And on occasion, we are also able to use real maple sugar—granulated by family members and friends who take the time and make the effort to produce it. With family and friends like that, you do not need much else.

A question that sometimes rises is whether or not the Native Americans were making maple sugar and syrup before the coming of the Europeans with their metal boiling kettles. Carol Mason, an anthropologist, feels the Europeans taught sugaring to the tribesmen, but others disagree, saying there is ample evidence to refute that Eurocentric notion. To support her contention Mason observes that the absence of any reference to sugaring in the writings of Nicholas Perrot, who was in Lake Superior country in the late seventeenth century, suggests that the tribesmen were not doing it. She opines that Nicholas Perrot did not miss very much that went on in his neighborhood. But, recent Canadian researchers say there is no doubt that maple sugaring is an ancient North American activity, one that flourished long before the coming of the White man—and I agree. Some Ojibwe say their people have always made maple sugar. Why not believe them?

My sugaring days began on a dairy farm in northeastern Wisconsin. My dad would tap the few large trees that stood in a rocky pasture near the house and boil the sap on the kitchen range. We never produced more than a few quarts of syrup this way because we had only a few maples, and my mother soon grew tired of the wallpaper loosening from the abundance of steam. Later, I was able to be part of the sugaring operation in the Newago Family's bush at Red Cliff and it is here where I was introduced to what I call traditional Ojibwe sugarmaking. For many years each spring I was able to come north and join in as the family labored to produce syrup. Mike Newago and his brother Sam were good teachers. And they were patient as this greenhorn struggled to learn their ways.

The weather was always a factor. On occasion sugaring ran into April but usually it was over by then. A few hundred trees would be tapped, some with multiple taps but most only one. An assortment of spiles—some wooden, some metal—were pounded into the drilled openings and three-gallon cans were hung on nails underneath. In the right weather the musical *ping, ping, ping*, of dripping sap hitting the empty can bottoms rang through the woods. That was a welcome sound, but it also foretold of much work. We usually collected sap each afternoon and when we heard the loud pinging early in the morning it spelled a busy day.

Today, in this Red Cliff camp, the sap is still boiled in large metal drums hung over roaring hardwood fires. In good seasons the boiling might go into the night. The fire, with its pungent smoke and loud hissing and crackling is the center of camp. Once the boiling began we gravitated to the kettles as we kept a watch over them. The fire needed almost constant feeding and the sap must be watched lest it boil too hard, spilling onto the fire beneath. To curb over-boiling a small bough of fresh balsam was quickly dipped into the barrel. These *zhingobiig* never failed to do the trick. The syrup produced in this camp has a deep, dark color and a pungent, almost smoky taste. When I use it I am reminded from where it came.

The days I spend in the sugarbush are escapes. I leave the mainstream and walk to another world. Here is a place where Ojibwe people continue a custom their forebears carried out long ago. Despite the passing of time, these camps are like they were a century and more ago. The technology involved has been modified somewhat with the addition of metal tools but little else has been altered. The sky is still above, the earth beneath, and the maple trees are as they have been from the beginning. When the time is right the people come to them, put tobacco down, and ask for their help. And, as has always occurred, the trees respond approvingly.

SWEET, RED STRAWBERRIES

June 22, 2006

THIS WEEK THE LOCAL STRAWBERRIES came in. And they arrived with a wallop! Never before have I witnessed such a crop of bright, sparkling red berries, and their flavor matched their appearance. When popping one into your mouth it is like tasting a great summer day. Surely this year's strawberries set me to thinking.

Perhaps many of us have memories of the strawberries of our childhood. Mine go back to the early days of World War II when I lived with my maternal grandparents on what was left of their 200-acre dairy farm in far southern Milwaukee County. Our fields were alive with activity in summer and we had strawberries on that place, but they were nothing like what are grown on the Bayfield hillsides today. Our berries were smaller, fewer, and their season passed too quickly, but their wonderful memories stay with me.

My grandmother was the gardener. My dad was off in the war, a soldier stationed up in Alaska with its Aleutian Islands. My mother worked as a clerk in a manufacturing plant in town, and my maternal grandfather worked in a wooden crate factory. They all were busy and it was my grandmother who watched my brothers and me once school was out. We played war games with wooden rifles in and around the buildings that made up our farmyard. We were the Americans, and we killed the Germans and Japanese.

Grandma had a few patches of cleared earth beside the house next to one of the apple orchards, and one of them was devoted to strawberries. In those days we enjoyed a few pickings as shortcake, but most were canned and came to the table in wintertime after losing their bright red color. In the heat of the picking season some were decrowned, washed and served in smaller rectangular tins as open-topped custard pies. We were German-Americans and we called such desserts *kuchens*. They were simple—just a quickly made single crust filled with berries and a mixture of beaten eggs, milk, sugar, and cinnamon. It seems we always had a *kuchen* or two on hand from early summer to just after the first killing frost. Strawberries, tart cherries, raspberries, blackberries, apples, currants, gooseberries, plums, ground cherries—all were picked on the farm and went

218

into *kuchens*. One year we had a peach *kuchen* when my grandmother's two peach trees produced their one and only crop. I still have one of those old rectangular tins, a family relic kept on a shelf in our Bayfield basement.

Straw-berries. Sometimes my grandmother would place yellow oat straw between the beds of berries to keep the weeds down and provide a nice clean base for the ripening fruit at the edges of the rows. The straw came from our strawstack in the farmyard beside the diary barn. In those years we made a new stack each summer when the oats was harvested. I remember those times with some joy. Each August we had an old-fashioned threshing bee, complete with several neighboring families who came together to help each other bring in the grain. Sometimes when I start thinking of strawberries I recall those threshing bees.

Although so much of my life has changed, strawberries remain. Their presence is a constant. Like so many of those quiet celebrations in our lives, strawberry season comes each year. Many years ago, before the Bayfield Apple Festival took over, we had a Strawberry Festival in town. I recall a few of these from the very early 1960s—small gatherings when fruit growers set up their little stands on Rittenhouse Avenue and a few tourists came to purchase berries. No doubt my memory of those events lacks important details, but I still recall those little festivals. They were good times. Going to the Rebekah Lodge for shortcake was a must.

These days here in Bayfield it is the apple crop that gets the most attention, but our strawberries have their own allure. To be sure, like the McIntoshes, Cortlands, and other apples, strawberries are an important source of income for the farmers who grow them, so money is involved with this sweet red fruit, but I want to think there's more. Even though strawberries arrive along with the Fourth of July when there can be some noise around town, the loud hoopla of the apple harvest is missing. The strawberry is celebrated in a quieter way. Those folks who drive a considerable distance to come and pick them each season, and carry away the waxy brown cardboard trays heaped with their sweet, red treasure, have a look of quiet pleasure in their calm faces. As they place their berries into their automobiles to return home no loud marching bands parade down our streets.

Sometimes I think my German-Lutheran grandmother would agree. She was a quiet person and when in her strawberry patch she grew even quieter. Perhaps this is one of her lasting teachings. The strawberry is a lowly fruit, causing you to get close to the earth to harvest it, and in the fast-paced world we live in today, it is a reminder that some of the old, simpler pleasures are still the best.

ANOTHER SPRING!

March 28, 2006

THIS WEEK OUR WINTER ICE covering the channel between Bayfield and Madeline Island is leaving us. Sunday morning the wind sled made its last trip and that afternoon the ferry was pressed back into service. Then, yesterday I paused to watch one of our black-and-white commercial fishing boats break through the weakening ice as it ever so slowly headed to open water beyond Basswood Island. As I view this from my study windows at my home on this Bayfield hillside, I am set to thinking.

Here in Chequamegon Bay Spring is slowly arriving, and once again it is a beautiful sight. The joy of the bright green of our lawns and the rainbow of colors from our earliest flowers is only starting to arrive, but we still have a very colorful world. Some of us have witnessed all this before—and many more than just a few times—but it never grows old. Day after day, season after season, nature just keeps doing its thing and we stand in awe.

The change of seasons has always caught my attention, although there were times when I was preoccupied with other things and in those days I might have given it only a fleeting glance. My hormone-laden high school years, for instance, and those when I lived on a deck-gray navy vessel on the Atlantic Ocean come to mind, but even then I kept an eye on the natural world. It was impossible not to do so. My youth was spent on a series of northern Wisconsin farms where daily I confronted nature. There was little concrete and asphalt in my life in those years, and each day my family and I not only smelled the earth and felt its soft presence beneath our feet, but sensually knew it at our fingertips.

This morning my daily walk was extended out into the nearby orchard country and at one point I stepped through the ditch to snip a small bouquet of pussy willows my wife asked me to bring home. Not many of these spring delights are out yet—apparently the roadside willow brush is only now beginning to move its sap. Pussy willows are one of those quiet little joys that ride in on the earliest warm breezes of the season. Some years I would cut a few sprigs a few weeks before they showed any signs of budding, bring them indoors and force their early bloom, but now that I am retired such an act seems out of place. Now I have the patience to wait for nature to open the buds. I do not desire to force much of anything anymore. My days of hurrying things are over.

The last few mornings, robins have been wonderfully loud just outside our bedroom window. And yesterday I heard the first rippling notes of music from song sparrows. These brown birds rank among the best of our spring musicians and their arrival tells of the end of winter. Their singing is truly a very fine way to be wakened after a refreshing night of sleep.

But what really strikes me this week is the color of our world. We still have the grays, browns, deep emerald greens and blacks of winter that predominated these last few months, and due to rains and warm temperatures our whites have almost completely departed, so the subtle color change of early spring is yet to come. The light, fluorescent greens and pinks of the new leaf and flower buds is still a way off. Given our drab colors of the last week or so, we might be reminded of the early hues of November, but this spring I feel differently about all this. This year these normally dull and drab tints seem endlessly bright and full of expectation. The heavy fog we experienced last week surprisingly failed to feel depressing and glum. I enjoyed it, even might have been said to revel in it on my early morning walks.

This morning's pussy willows with their soft, gray catkins blended into this mix of darker hues. The deep oxblood-red of the willow sprigs that held them added a nice earthy appearance to their silky steel-gray blossoms. These pussy willows made a welcome complement to Lake Superior's gray ice and last week's fog.

Into this mix of colors we could add the deep browns of maple syrup I worked to boil in my son's Lac Courte Oreilles sugarbush last week. The tawny brown of that sweet syrup appeared after a few hours of steady boiling—another welcome addition to our spring palette of colors.

Perhaps some of us might say, "So, what's newsworthy about this? It is still a very gray time." Well, I like these early April colors of brown, black and gray. Spring is still a way off, and its telltale signs of change are slow in coming, but something is up. Geese have been heard overhead, and last week I thrilled with the hauntingly high calls from sandhill cranes as they headed north. Edna St. Vincent Millay's old poem ("Spring Song") in which she told of an April when spring forgot to arrive might be called to mind this year, but I think not. We have made it through another winter, and even though the air is still chilly and we have had weeks of overcast skies, I say, get ready. Spring is on the way.

SNOWBIRDS

May 24, 2008

Now that Memorial Day Weekend has come and gone, we can get serious about the new warm season. Summer will not officially arrive for a few weeks but around Red Cliff and Bayfield it has already begun. Things are picking up after our quiet winter. For many of us it is time to get back to work.

Local snowbirds have mostly all returned, eager to tell about their winters spent in Arizona, Florida, or similar places. These folks still interest me. Jetting, or driving off to warmer climes for the winter never has been part of my personal world, and even though I am no longer in harness I still do not feel the urge to go south for the cold time. Perhaps it is my upbringing—driven by things like the Protestant Ethic—that causes me to stick around during winter. Wintering in places like Arizona seems like eating cake and ice cream three times a day, or like going to school and having recess all day long. I think I would soon tire of it. Except for a few years spent in Uncle Sam's military when I was still a teenager, the rhythm of the cycle of the seasons has always been part of my life and I suspect I would miss it if I suddenly had to give it up. Maybe I am just a creature of habit, but this morning that seems all right, too.

These songbirds in our backyard are like our neighbors who disappear with the onset of cold weather. They pack up and head south with summer. Maybe that is why I feel a certain affinity with our year-round birds: the crows, ravens, chickadees, blue jays, and the like. There is nothing fancy about us. We are just the common folk who tough it out all year long, doing our "singing" in one place.

Some of these folks who winter in southern climes come home in spring and seem to enjoy telling us about how nice it was "down there." They must think we actually are interested in hearing all that, as if we really want to go south too, but for whatever reasons must stay home and freeze. You'd think they would realize that if we wanted to hear about Arizona we would go there and see it for ourselves.

But, perhaps we all do what these snowbirds do. Now and then we might travel and come home to tell our friends where we have been, perhaps implying that they have missed something. Sometimes we are showered with photos of these warm places, and maybe we old stay-at-homes must shoulder such burdens. Maybe it is just part of the lot we were cast.

All of this reminds me of the times when I would bring city friends out to the family cabin at Red Cliff and it seemed like the topics of conversation for the two days focused on life back in the city, not on the place where we were spending our weekend. We left the city to go to the woods where we talked about the city. Those weekends were like working retreats and I soon tired of them.

Anthropologists call most human behaviors adaptations, meaning they are ways of doing things that are useful for our long-term survival. But what can the custom of wintering in southern places and coming home to tell your friends and neighbors about it do for us? How is our species' survival enhanced by such behavior? Try as I might to understand this I still come up empty handed.

Someone once explained this to me by saying our social class system is legitimated by such a custom. The point is that traveling costs money; discretionary cash that not everyone has. So when a friend comes back in May and drops a stack of snapshots on your table—or, perhaps more correctly today—emails you a slew of colored digital photos about how they spent their winter down there, you are supposed to decide then and there to earn more money so you can do the same next year. I guess it is all about being upwardly mobile. I guess it is all about boosting our economy, something that is supposed to be good for all of us.

This argument claims that all this is about what the textbook calls manifest and latent functions. The obvious reason folks go south in winter (the manifest, or visible reason) is to get away from the cold, but the underlying reason (the latent, or hidden reason) is to shore up our stratified class system. Our snowbirds are signaling the rest of us to work harder—I guess.

Well, be that as it may. All I really know is that Memorial Day came again and once more a lot of new folks were walking Bayfield's streets, and were seen in Red Cliff's casino at night. The warm weather is back in these parts and it brought new faces. This is what we want to happen, for without these faces most of us could not live here, year-round or not. We would have to fold our tents and move to greener pastures—or something. Of course, we oldsters who paid our dues long ago could possibly still hang on to tough out our long, cold winters with the other common birds shivering at the feeder.

KILLING SADDAM

January 2, 2007

OUR WAR IN IRAQ HAS BEEN GOING ON so long that we might be growing tired of it. But then, our war in Afghanistan has been going on even longer so we must be even more tired of that one. Two simultaneous wars. Two simultaneous feelings of exhaustion. As of the moment I have lost no relatives or friends in these battles—nor had any wounded—but the death and destruction is still getting harder to bear. Each time I learn of another Wisconsin, Minnesota or Michigan soldier being killed I feel that old heaviness again. And when watching that honor roll of the dead on that public television news show I grow silent. Those faces linger in my mind. When will these wars stop? Those poor grieving families! Those poor dead soldiers, and those poor Afghan and Iraqi civilians!

The morning of 9-11, I was enjoying a late breakfast with two friends at a Twin Cities VFW Club. We were surrounded by framed portraits of past post commanders, and sets of American flags hung loosely draped beside glass cases of World War II wood stocked rifles. Everything around us told of the military. Then suddenly the morning television news show piped into the small veterans' club was interrupted as we learned of the Trade Center attack. For a half hour or more we watched the reruns of that tape of the Twin Towers almost in silence as we mouthed our hash browns, scrambled eggs, and buttered toast, washed down with coffee. It was all so American. My two friends and I served in the military, and suddenly here it was again—people trying to kill us. We were stunned and left that club with feelings of uncertainty. What would happen now?

What had we done to make them hate us so? Surely my friends and I had not done anything to hurt those men who took over the planes that morning. We lived here in the innocuous Midwest—the land that hurts no one. We are the plain folks, those who produce milk and grains—well, and maybe a little beer. We feed the world, not try to destroy it.

But to those middle-eastern men on those crowded planes the three of us were just as guilty as all Americans. It was as if all of us wore uniforms made from Old Glory. We were Americans and part of a way of life that upset them.

224

I recall students who struggled with the aftereffects of the Vietnam War. A few eventually killed themselves. Were my two friends and I part of that, too?

And now we must confront those cell phone pictures of a huge knotted rope being draped over Saddam's head, while a few voices shout hatred at him as they praise their god. Saddam responds in kind, praising his. This man probably killed thousands of people without batting an eye. Now it was his turn to die.

We don't hear much about weapons of mass destruction anymore. Where did Condi Rice go? And even that scare of a nuclear bomb in North Korea and Iran might not have the chilling, fearful effect such weapons once did. Have we become hardened? Sometimes when I cruise the channels I come upon what seems like untold numbers of high-tech crime fighting shows that have proliferated like viruses these past years. Most of the actors in these things are handsome, healthy and at the top of their lives' game. Like those football players we watch on weekends (and Monday nights), they are athletic and even downright sexy. These shows are as physical as a James Bond movie. They thrive on violence and deep, raw emotion. What happens to us when we watch such things? Do they steel our psyches so that we are no longer shocked at scenes of Baghdad bombings?

Somewhere in the world little children still run in green meadows, laughing and chasing butterflies. Why do we turn these great kids into soldiers? Were there Gold Star Mothers in Ancient Rome who grieved sons who were slaughtered in the loud battles of the famous Roman Legions? When I was seventeen I wore my uniform with pride. I spit-shined my shoes.

But there is another side of war. It involves the silence of cemeteries and empty chairs at family dinners. It involves faded photographs of men and women in uniforms—faces that once looked at blue skies and marveled at butterflies. We humans must enjoy killing because we keep doing it. Why do we defend ourselves by violent acts? Why do we act in ways that upset others? If we hate each other do our different gods hate each other, too?

And when our current leader dies will commentators call him a great American? Or, as was done with Gerald Ford this week, will we praise him for being a Common Man? Is our current leader's propensity to call out the troops a common characteristic for humanity?

Perhaps these are just ramblings of a tired old man who once marched to a martial drumbeat. But, it's no fun anymore. I laid my weapons down long ago. Now it is time to live differently. Besides, why spend our energies on warfare when the earth's glaciers are melting? It's all so foolish. What are we doing anyway?

ROSA PARKS AND
CHEQUAMEGON COUNTRY
November 13, 2005

By now the death of Rosa Parks is old news. Some might say it needs little comment from we common folk since so many of our national leaders have already given their expected laudatory eulogies. The senators, news commentators, and social activists have spoken. Furthermore, some might say, so much praise would have been embarrassing to this humble woman and now it is time for the finality of her passing to be left to settle into our country's history to take its justified place of importance. A few weeks ago when I heard she died I immediately pondered our great loss and now that some time has passed I have gathered my thoughts and feel the need to put them into print. There is no doubt about it—this quiet Black seamstress has set me to thinking.

Fifty-one years ago I was serving aboard a naval warship whose homeport was Norfolk, Virginia. One day after work I left the ship to take a bus downtown for dinner and a movie. As I did so often then, I joined the small crowd of civilian workers standing curbside—who had also finished another work day—as they waited to catch a city bus to take them home. Most of these workers were Black.

Upon stepping up into the bus, dropping my coins into the slot, and greeting the White driver, I did what I usually did on those Norfolk buses: I moved to the rear and took a seat. A middle-aged black woman was behind me but she chose a seat further to the front. After everyone boarded and was seated I waited for the driver to move on but to my surprise, we remained stopped at the curb. A minute passed, then another. A minute can be an eternity for a city bus to sit beside a curb. No one said anything, and then I noticed how the driver was peering into the large rearview mirror above his windshield. He silently stared at the woman. Finally, after what seemed like an awfully long time, she rose and came back to join us in the rear of the bus. Only then did we pull out into the traffic.

This happened in 1954. A year later, in Montgomery, Alabama, Rosa Parks also finished a day of work and boarded a bus for the trip home, and like the woman on my bus she took a seat in the White section, but she refused to move. You know the rest. After much litigation, the country's Supreme Court decided the old southern Jim Crow laws were unconstitutional. Racial segregation had become illegal.

National figures like Rosa Parks have a way of touching all of us. Although no one I spend time with here in the Red Cliff and Bayfield areas has yet to say anything to me about her death, I think even if they did not notice it, Rosa Park's life somehow impinged upon theirs. This northern land is not the southern Bible belt, but surely its past was marked with racial prejudice, discrimination, and segregation. We quickly recall the 1920 lynchings that took place in Duluth only seventy or so miles to our west. Lately I have been attempting to understand what went on in Chequamegon Country between people of different races and cultures in the past—as far back as the seventeenth century—and I am concluding that even though race and cultural relations were often subtle, and always very complex—prejudice, discrimination, segregation, and all the rest were rampant in these northern woods. This sort of behavior occurred long before Rosa Parks' time, but it is not unrelated to her efforts to bring change.

Obviously, Rosa Parks helped us to change the way we relate to each other. Initially, her act on that Montgomery bus was simple. She just wanted a physical change. But, what she and the organization of civil rights workers she was a part of really wanted was an ideological change. She and her co-activists wanted Whites to change the way they saw Blacks, but just as importantly, the way they saw themselves. She wanted them to stop feeling superior to people of color.

And herein lies her contribution to life in Chequamegon Bay. Because of what occurred in Alabama on that bus in 1955, White people throughout the country were forced to look at themselves differently.

This brings to mind a bumper sticker I saw in Bayfield last week. It quietly, but determinedly, said, "America—start seeing other people." That is all it said. I stood and studied its short message for a few moments, thinking immediately of Iraq and the entire Muslim world, and then, since I had just read of the death of Rosa Parks, I thought of how this sticker was repeating her message. But soon my mind focused on this place—this big lake, this shoreline and its long, colorful history, and I called to mind the Jesuits who were here in the 1600s and how they did not see the native tribesmen who were their hosts. And, like a fast-moving video clip, my mind streamed over the nearly four hundred years since the Jesuits were here—nearly four hundred years during which people of different races and cultures lived in this northern land. I wondered about their, and our, struggles to see each other.

ROBERT BLY IN
CHEQUAMEGON BAY

July 1, 2007

IT IS MID-JULY ALREADY AND THE FASTER pace of summer is felt each day. Folks scurry about in both Red Cliff and Bayfield as if they are on a mission—as if they have things needing to be done. Strawberry season is waning and raspberry time is rushing upon us. These precious berries must be taken when they are ready, and in a few days I expect to be out there in Allan Rabideaux's raspberry patch. All this activity in the heat of summer sets me to thinking.

About two weeks ago on a cool Friday evening some of us took a breather from this fast-paced season. That night we drove up Ski Hill Road south of town and quietly took our seats under the blue canvas tent to spend an hour or so with Robert Bly. It was a nice change, and yes, this internationally renowned poet came to the northwoods and willingly spent time with a good-sized crowd of his followers. It was time well spent.

I think of the contrast in tempo between our busy tourist season and a few quiet hours with an eighty-one-year-old poet like Robert Bly. What kinds of people are drawn to writers like him? From my take on the crowd that night, it was composed mostly of local folks. Surely some of them were from distant places, but I suspect most were not. By and large, these were year around northern Wisconsin residents who drove up steep Ski Hill Road to hear some poetry. They seemed not to have come from downstate cities, or as so many of our visitors do, from the Land of Sky-Blue Waters. Perhaps, as was the case with me, these fans of Bly needed a respite from our busy summer.

Poetry is not everyone's bag, but I never fail to be at least a bit amazed at how important it is to many of us. Just as each species of songbird has its own unique song, poetry might be the "song" of the human species. Recently an Ojibwe friend of mine who was invited to read his verses at a major international poetry meeting in a large South American city known for its crime told how really huge throngs gathered for the poetry readings. He claimed that during the several days of the conference the city's crime rate fell to a significant low. Apparently even criminals take time for poetry.

I suspect that the pleasures of a well-turned phrase might be integral to what it is to be human. For, after all, humans think in words, and we take joy in how a good poet can make words appear magical. Like a good song, a good poem can reach deep inside us.

That evening under the tent we were treated to the art of a true wordsmith. Robert Bly has been sharing his carefully chosen words with us for a long time, and for those of us who have been listening, we have been bettered by them.

But, Robert Bly is not for everyone. For example, there are those who do not applaud his involvement in what is called the Men's Movement. A friend of mine scoffs at what he says is "this business of taking a group of guys out into the woods and beating drums while they chant the deep joy of their maleness." In a similar fashion some of my feminist friends do not enjoy him either. They say he cannot appreciate what womanhood is really about. To these two groups of critics, I say, "A pox on both your houses."

For some reason I enjoy the poetry of Robert Bly, and as he moves into his eighth decade I wish him well. I am not sure, but perhaps my attraction to him is because of his strong anti-war stance. He was against the Vietnam War, and now speaks out against our two Bush Wars. Over the years Bly has not been hesitant to express his firm anti-war passions. But there is much more to Bly than his political activism. Robert Bly ponders about the human condition, and if anything, his poetry causes us to think.

Along with his inherent thoughtfulness, Robert Bly appeals to me for another reason. He comes from a rural life, and, I suspect, never really has left the countryside. His early poems are replete with a farm-based imagery that is familiar to me. Its earthy plainness cuts through so much of what we moderns have become. I find it interesting how Bly has written meaningful poems about weathered barnyard boards and grassy rural roadside ditches, two insignificant elements of my past.

Under the blue tent that night he was joined by a violinist, a cellist and a percussionist as these four artists shared music and the spoken word. We were treated to a wonderful session during which Bly recited passages from his recent poetry and the musicians joined in with their great music. At times it was spellbinding.

But, maybe I just go for this sort of thing. The next morning I was down on Bayfield's Rittenhouse Avenue, rushing to the post office, purchasing a gallon of two percent and a loaf of bread at the IGA, and making a fast stop at the bank. It was back to the usual haste of summer.

A POET'S EYE

August 20, 2006

IT IS ANOTHER SUNNY AND COMFORTABLE Sunday morning in Bayfield and the town is extraordinarily quiet. When on my early morning walk I saw nary a person or motor vehicle moving anywhere. As I strolled along block after block I allowed myself to pretend I was a poet, assigned to overlook the sleeping town and take stock of things. This is late summer and most houses are occupied, but in only two weeks or so that will change. With the coming of Labor Day many of our summer folk will depart, as schools open. The multitude of vehicles with kayaks clamped onto their tops will thin out and reappear mostly on weekends, and that ice cream cone-loving crowd at our great downtown ice cream and candy shop will scale down as the rhythm of our town's activity changes. Another summer in Chequamegon Country is coming to an end, and it sets me to thinking.

While war rages on in other parts of the world, here on the tip of the Bayfield Peninsula it is business as usual. Some of our loved ones may be in those distant lands of strife, walking in harms way, but here I walk in peace—a peace, some say, that is provided by those wearing desert-camo over there.

In stark contrast to what is happening in the Middle East, yesterday the town seemed filled with people in convertibles. These clean, shiny and fun-giving automobiles moved around the streets easily, catching the attention of passers-by. In an earlier America these ragtops and summer went together. Folks put on their lighter finery—might have worn straw hats and long silky scarves that trailed in the wind—while speeding along our roadways. Decades ago our mass media often showed them holding cigarettes that had their own wispy plumes behind. And there has to be light, gay, laughter—young, beautiful people with mouths wide open as they move like winged beings, easily through life.

But, most of the folks I saw in yesterday's convertibles were older, white-haired, and with telltale wrinkles by the eyes. These were seasoned veterans of frivolity that, I suspect, paid their dues long ago.

Such fun-seekers come and go all summer long. Usually they drive large motorized vehicles—some of them oversized—that take the prized parking spots on Rittenhouse Avenue, and those in that prime block on Broad Street where the Post Office stands. But soon, they too, will depart for home. Soon we will have our town back again.

My morning walk allows me time to consider how I fit into all this. It affords the opportunity to ponder my place, and ask just what my story is. We all have stories, of course, and surely mine is of no interest to most. This point came to me the other day as I helped-out at the recent fund-raiser for our downtown recreation center and pool. I was asked to volunteer some time at the registration table for the swim to La Pointe, and once again I witnessed a select group of community-minded folk who came forth when called. Over twenty swimmers, each with necessary escorts in boats or kayaks, stepped up, donned wet suits and slid into Lake Superior. It was a special time to witness these wonderful people who enthusiastically showed what community spirit is about.

While I stood by handing out t-shirts to these swimmers and their attendants, I was quietly awestruck by their energetic enthusiasm. They swam and I watched, and now, like an appreciative bard, I sing their praises.

Another thoughtful time occurred the other evening when my wife and I attended the concert of R. Carlos Nakai at the Big Top just south of town. His show was opened by a Red Cliff drum, led by Frank Montano and family members with the help of Michael Charette. These excellent musicians also stepped up as they offered a very apt welcome to Nakai. Here was community again, although this time many attendees came from miles around. Not every American knows who R. Carlos Nakai is, and although drawing a nice-sized crowd, his concert did not fill the tent. The famous Navajo-Ute wooden flute player is world-renowned for his music, but there is more. That evening I saw Carlos Nakai as a prophet in a time of a troubled world. He spoke quietly, yet solidly and confidently of the deep value and, I feel, the lasting truth of Indigenous America. That evening under the tent, R. Carlos Nakai became part of the small town I live in. As when watching those who swam to the island, it was another rare treat merely to be present, standing by, while others stepped up.

This morning as I moved up and down these hilly streets I reflected on what kind of summer we have had here in Bayfield. The oppressive heat, the hard-hitting storm, the steady stream of visitors despite our high gasoline prices, and the ever-present reminders that we are a country at war all have been part of it. We do not ponder these varied things every day of our lives, but somehow these disparate realities come together in the drama that is our life. On these quiet Sunday morning walks this peaceful town becomes my temple.

THE HARD REALITY OF
GROWING OLD

May 16, 2006

S PRING IS ALWAYS A GLORIOUS TIME in our Northland and this year it is no exception. Lately it occurs to me that my family is like the grass, bushes, and trees on this Bayfield hillside that have hurried to push their new blades, buds and blossoms up and out into our warming air. Over the last two weeks or so we have become almost frenetic in our activity as we hurry here and hurry there with all sorts of what must be important things to do. After another quiet and wonderful winter, this scurrying about sets me to thinking.

I must be getting old because at times I simply could not keep up with everything going on. Occasionally I found myself withdrawing from it to take a nearby seat and just watch it all. I started to think I might have become one of those oldsters on the front porch who silently watch the passers-by out in the street. What causes me to think about this is not really the fact of my sitting and watching, but the possibility that I might be beginning to enjoy being an elderly bystander. Maybe that should be a bit scary to me, but I must admit that I do not think it is. I think I am enjoying my rocker time as I watch the younger folk go about their hurried business.

As I write this we are just entering the annual Memorial Day Weekend. That means a few things, but perhaps most importantly, it means that although summer officially does not arrive for a few more weeks, it really is only a day or two away. Visitors to Rittenhouse Avenue in Downtown Bayfield seem to be increasing each day, and the shopkeepers are beginning to take on that "the season has started" look. If it is not a little quiet desperation I see in their faces, it most certainly is a bit of anxious anticipation. The product had better be on the shop shelves by now because "the push" is almost here.

Another sign of the on-coming summer season is the almost relaxed look in the faces of the school teachers I come upon some mornings in the coffee shop just before they head uphill to begin their working day. They smile and nod when I greet them with, "Counting the days?" I recall my over thirty years of being in that harness.

And my grandchildren are also counting. They know exactly how many days are left before summer vacation begins. It might still be too early to hit the local swimming beaches but surely they are thinking about such things.

Last Wednesday my wife and I were among that beaming crowd that filled the pews at the local Lutheran Church for the spring piano recital of Abby Goodier's piano students. A dozen or more youngsters introduced themselves and told us what pieces they would play, then, we had the distinct pleasure of watching and listening as they showed their stuff. How they have improved after another year of study! Abby is rightfully proud of her students, and we community members are fortunate to have her amongst us.

Another sign of spring—and my growing old—was the Bayfield Library's Apple Blossom Run. This year I did the long walk with a few friends and was pleased to finish it without too much difficulty. Many years ago I ran several ten-k's throughout the summer and enjoyed them all, but now my running days are over, and I was happy to be able to walk those 6.3 miles. Although I did all right, once again I was reminded that I am no longer young.

The serious matter of my personal mortality also came to me over the last week or two when I took part in our recent run of funerals. A week or more ago I attended a wake at the packed Elderly Feeding Center at Red Cliff, and after that it was a few visitations and funerals at Bayfield's Presbyterian and Catholic Churches. Always sobering, these ceremonies recur no matter what the season, and among their many messages is the reminder that our days are numbered.

Perhaps one of this spring's signs of my aging that is a bit difficult to accept is that now I no longer cut my own lawn. After what seems like a lifetime of tending a lawn and garden, such enjoyable activity might be coming to an end. This year Bob King is cutting our grass, and like last year our large garden and perennial beds at the bottom of the hill that is our yard stand in weedy neglect. Maybe I should feel a bit uneasy about Mr. King's coming every week or so to cut the grass, but I think I don't. He does an excellent job and I must come to grips with the fact that at some point in our lives someone else will take over our yard work. For an old farmer like me, this is a fact that can call for deep contemplation.

This sunny morning a cool breeze comes up the hill from the lake and it moves the leaves and deep green conifer needles in our yard. That breeze is busily going about its business. I think I will just sit here and watch it for a while.

OF WOLVES AND MEN

March 14, 2006

PERHAPS THOSE OF US WHO READ newspapers and watch TV news shows have been thinking about wolves these days. So far my limited attempts to share my thoughts about *Canis occidentalis* (timber wolves) with friends down at the coffee shop have gone nowhere, but I cannot keep still anymore. The recent news that timber wolves are no longer on the endangered species list has set me to thinking.

In my childhood years the closest I ever came to wolves were those in books written by the Brothers Grimm. Much later when I began to spend weekends and vacations in the Red Cliff woods, even though closer to wolves, they were still something I saw only on paper, television, or film. At the cabin I often kept a lookout for them, but never saw or heard one. Coyotes and black bears yes, but not wolves. Over the last forty years there were a few exceptions, but those wolves were in the Twin Cities and always safely behind chain link fences at the Minnesota Zoo.

But, suddenly, all that has changed. Now I am living in wolf country and when out in the woods I usually think about that. Something is different. My place in this northern forest has somehow been altered. In some ways it is like camping in the Boundary Waters Canoe and Wilderness Area. When out there I am aware that I am a visitor in wolf, black bear and cougar country and even though I feel comfortable I know these critters are around.

Timber wolves have made their way back. We can read about past days in Wisconsin when it was always open season on them and they were destroyed at will. A year ago my wife had a sighting of what she insists was a wolf only a few blocks from our Bayfield home. We are very close to a large wooded tract that could certainly be used as cover when wolves move through the region. They are reported to be working the county forest only a few miles from here so we should expect that at times they might come by our neighborhood. Surely, they cruise close to our isolated cabin at Red Cliff.

What is the implication of this for those of us who choose to make periodic solitary retreats to the woods? Do we carry guns when out there? I do not have an answer, at least not yet. What I do feel is that the return of the wolves is a positive thing. As is the case with bald eagles, whooping cranes, elk, pine martens, and the fisher, when these fellow earth-travelers came back to this region, we were made better by their presence. And the same for plant species that once were endangered but then made a comeback. These life forms are like the original inhabitants of a land who have been in exile but all the time were still holding settlement rights, and we were somehow diminished by their long absences.

Now that wolves are officially here, I do not want to be fearful when alone in the woods. Perhaps carrying a weapon of some sort would solve that problem, but then, I do not really enjoy carrying weapons. Do I want it both ways? Do I want to keep the cake uncut, but still hope to enjoy its taste?

What is happening is that I am working to accept my more truthful place in all this and *Canis occidentalis* is helping with this struggle. We have the opportunity to assume a more compatible place in the web of life here by this big lake. It is like coming home after a long time of searching. Yes, perhaps both the wolves and we humans who live in this wonderful northland are experiencing a kind of home-coming. Maybe we have come home to the acceptance of the understanding that we both belong here and must get along. We must cut each other some slack.

If I were a farmer in these north woods I might feel differently. For me it is too late to take up farming here, but then, these are the North Woods. Is this really the right place to attempt such an endeavor? These woods seem better suited for timber wolves than cows or sheep.

We are not harmed by the presence of these fellow life forms. Instead, we are enriched. If we are wise, now, whenever we enter locales where wolves are known to frequent we must be prepared and not put ourselves in compromising situations. Prudence, foresight, and finally, acceptance are called for.

It might well be that this delisting of the timber wolf is part of a larger pattern of similar events, all speaking to the way a particular eco-system works. Our growing acceptance of climate change and our role of stewards of this land could be linked to the return of the large and potentially dangerous (to us) predators. The natural world has always been a place of both life and death, and our timber wolves can serve to remind us of that. Perhaps for some of us, we have been for much too long, sheltered from the reality of how nature works. This might be the underlying message of the wolves: we humans are not above or beyond nature. We are still part of it.

On Being Obese

January 14, 2008

Perhaps we all are having repeated wake-up calls these days, but last week when I signed up for the latest exercise initiative in the Chequamegon Bay region I was stopped in my tracks. The Body Mass Index chart that folks at the Walk the Talk Today campaign are using told me there was no doubt about it. I was not even marginal, no; my BMI put me solidly in the middle of the obese category. This fact certainly set me to thinking.

Me, obese? I have always considered myself to be thin. What happened? Have I succumbed to that lackadaisical way of life that we Americans are sometimes said to have when it comes to food and exercise? Am I living for the moment, falling victim to base human impulses? Does hedonism have me in its grasp?

Except for a few weeks during my military basic training back in the early 1950s when I and my company of recruits spent most of our days carrying rifles out on asphalt grinders marching 'round and 'round and stopping to do all sorts of calisthenics until we could barely stand, followed by huge meals of—yes— meat-n-taters, I was the slim one. And then, during those few hot summer weeks of drilling and more drilling, my added weight was on my lower limbs, not around my stomach. Besides, when finishing basic I was lean and maybe even a bit hard. When it came to my physical body, at least, basic training had done what it was supposed to do. (Its effect on my mind, however, was another thing.)

While obesity goes way back in my family it always seemed to end with the dissolution of baby fat. Some of us carried extra weight in our childhood years but this invariably disappeared as we went off the bottle and closed in on puberty. We all were on that well-known German-American meat and potatoes diet, and there never was a lack of fat-laden pastries and other desserts in our kitchens, but apparently it eventually worked out. We were busy people, physically active each day and through the entire year. We had no couch potatoes in our midst. Furthermore, the word obesity was an unknown to us. If we used it at all, we did so in mockery of the upper classes with their wealth-derived arrogance.

My older brother may have been an exception when he held onto some excess poundage through his first few years of grade school. I recall that his nickname was "Fat," short for Fatso. Yes we called him that for a few years and he took it in stride. He soon shed the pounds and in high school had a Hollywood physique as he starred on the school sports fields and gym floors. This makes me see how times have changed. We do not openly call anyone "Fatso" anymore, the taboo against this label coming in sometime in the last few decades when being overweight became almost endemic and any commentary on it might have been seen as an infringement of individual rights.

Anthropologically, obesity is always interesting. Physiologically, it is said to be an adaptation for the storage of energy to be used when there might be a lack of food. A society might depend on periodic obesity for survival. We can understand how this would work in societies in which food is not always readily available; when there might be times of hardship before the next season of abundance arrives. In those cases the "fat" people were the fortunate ones, and more than likely, they were the ones to have offspring while the others did not. Thanks to the obese, the community would go on to survive for another year.

There are Pacific Island cultures in which such storage of energy is looked upon not just positively, but as a mark of beauty. This is the way it works—adaptive traits can become normal, even prized. They are signs of success and become goals the masses strive to achieve. We might conclude that a culture's aesthetics is derived from its economic success. (In this sense, maybe Marx was right after all.)

But that was then, this is now. Today, in America, obesity has become a maladaptation. In other words, it signifies a lack of success instead of the opposite. It says something is not going right.

Well, enough preaching. What I am left with is the realization that I must get back to a correct diet and a lively exercise regimen. My life depends on it. But I ponder the extremes in our society. There are the homeless and those who are continually scrambling for food on a daily basis, and there are those who are obese. Our soda pop, beer, and sugar industries keep cranking out product, and we keep consuming it. We even have a food channel on the box that parades all sorts of fat-laden foods before our hungry eyes. Yet our New York models are still those lean and hard persons who walk like flowing chocolate, all the time telling us to be like them.

I am obese and I don't like it. Some of our politicians say this is the year of change. It is time to Walk the Talk Today.

MUSEUM GHOSTS

July 19, 2007

A FEW MONTHS AGO I COULD not say no when asked to serve on a committee at our local Bayfield Heritage Association museum. Our neighbor right across the street here on our hillside is the current president of this organization and he is the person who asked me. How can you turn down your neighbor? Didn't Mr. Rogers say we were to keep the peace in our neighborhood?

Well, it has been a few months now, and I have been putting regular weekly shifts in down in the museum basement, working at accessioning items and generally attempting to help "take control of the collection" as museum folks say. This work is new to me, and it surely sets me to thinking.

Museums were part of my life from the get-go. As a youngster in southern Wisconsin I sometimes was included in a Saturday trip into Milwaukee with my brothers and parents when we would visit the Milwaukee Public Museum. That was in the 1940s. Since then I've seen many museums, in many different places.

When I was a child museums were the repositories for things from the past, or what I sometimes called "old stuff." At first I enjoyed them, but after a few years of college, and after becoming sensitized to things like cultural diversity, ethnic identities, and the like, I changed my view of museums, and consequently there were several years when they lost their luster for me. At that time I viewed them as institutions of the establishment, and this meant that they often were places for the enshrinement of artifacts representing the values and beliefs of those in power. If the downtrodden and colonized appeared in museum display cases they were as dim shadows in the background.

Thankfully, this has changed in America, and other parts of the world. Now we have a holocaust museum, a slavery museum, a Japanese-American relocation camp museum, an American Indian museum, and much more.

One of the most impressive museums for me is that of the Mille Lacs Ojibwe community in central Minnesota. They put "old stuff" in their museum, but they bring things up to date, showing aspects of their life-ways found today. That museum leaves the viewer with the positive message that the Mille Lacs people are not simply from the past, but are here today. This is what a good museum can do.

In our Bayfield museum I have been discovering objects from our town's past that cause me to pause and reflect a bit. We have the large wooden encased telephone switchboard from the old telephone office. How different from our present telephone industry with its cell phones, BlackBerries, and other gadgetry. The huge barber chair and the mirrored "alter" from Ray Cahill's barbershop are also in storage, hopefully soon to be set up in a new exhibit. And, of course, the usual industries like logging, fishing and the orchards are represented, and increasingly, our collections are receiving items from the tourism trade.

Last week, after a few hours of work, I came upon two large black-and-white photographs. One was of a big white clapboard store standing on the corner of Manypenny and Broad streets, where the smaller Chamber of Commerce offices are located today. Two little girls, dressed in their Sunday best, stood before the huge white structure—it burned down sometime after World War II—and it appeared to me that the corner of Manypenny and Broad used to hold its share of busy stores. Melde's Grocery was across the street, and the town train depot was nearby. That intersection was a busy place, with people coming and going.

Another photo was of Ole Englund's Hardware Store. It was a classic inside shot that showed the neatly placed scoop shovels, child's sleds, and other items one would have found back in 1898 in a town like Bayfield. The numerous hand tools in that photo occupied the most important spots in that store, and in doing so told of life in Bayfield back then. And behind a neat, stone-topped counter stood a man and woman, presumably Mr. and Mrs. Ole Englund, prepared to serve their customers. How unlike what our local ACE Hardware store looks like, but yet how similar! Today Bob Buffalo and Jack Quamme, like the Englund's did, stand ready to serve us. In some ways little has changed.

The Bayfield Heritage Museum holds many photographs and written documents from the town's past. Yellowed copies of regional newspapers are stacked on shelves, and storage boxes of personal items from various families rest nearby. Ivory hair combs, doll clothing, an immigrant woodworker's still sharp gouges, chisels and other tools rest nearby. All this is interesting, but it is the photographs that hold me. I look upon the faces of those who lived here before I arrived. They walked the same streets I do, climbed these Bayfield hills like I do, and went Downtown for a cup of coffee. They picked up their mail at the post office and visited friends in the process. And they stepped into a grocery store just like so many of us step into Andy's, for bread and milk – and a bit of news.

In interesting ways, Old Bayfield is still here.

LOVING USED BOOKS

August 12, 2007

THIS MORNING I AM SITTING AMIDST PILES, stacks, and shelves of used books. When I care to admit it, this is where I belong. I am in my study in my Bayfield home, its windows allowing a wide view of our green back yard, and in the distance a blue Lake Superior and dark Madeline Island. This setting and the overwhelming presence of books sets me to thinking.

New books are wonderful, and at times I open them and raise their freshly printed pages to breath in their crisp paper and ink perfume, but used books are enjoyed in a different way. They have their own smell and try as I might I have not yet come up with a description that pleases me. Is it the scent of yellowed paper made from the cooked pulp of aspen trees? Is it still the smell of ink, lingering after years of being pressed onto each page? Or is it the human scent of fingers that have long ago carefully worked their way from cover to cover? Do the oils of our hands soak into the pages to blend with the paper and ink smells? Whatever it is, the smell of used books is inviting.

In the peak of the summer season I sometimes find myself running Bayfield's used book shop a few evenings a week and time after time when I hear the footfalls of someone entering the store there is a pause, and after a moment or two, I am treated to the exclamation, "Ummm–the smell of used books!" This happens at least once a week and I never grow tired of hearing it. "Here comes a book lover," I say to myself. "Here comes the kind of person this shop was made for!"

We know that books are not for everyone, and sometimes a used book can emit an offensive smell—like that of mold, smoke, or other unpleasant odors—but when a serious reader steps into a used bookstore and remarks about the good smell of used books, magic occurs. That person moves from section to section until finding that special area of interest that intrigues them. Then, they settle down and spend a long, quiet time letting their eyes and fingers move over the shelves with their stash of treasures. Usually the customer comes to the counter with whatever they found, and the sale is consummated. Another used book has found a home!

We're not talking about pulpy romance novels, or even popular mysteries here. We do sell these, but our bread and butter comes from other sorts of books. As a retired academician I am uplifted when I see what most of our customers buy. Bayfield attracts folks from numerous walks of life and for those that find their way into the bookstore it is endlessly interesting to see what books they purchase. Each summer some are sold from what I see as the most esoteric of subject areas. But, fiction is perennially popular. Last week, and again just yesterday, someone with what I took to be an English accent came to the counter and quietly asked for an obscure author that I did not recognize. All I could do was point them to the section of shelves where that writer's work should have been if we had it. Both times the customer came back, beaming with what they found. Paydirt! They were pleased and so was I. You never know who is going to walk into that shop, and what their interests might be.

One of my joys is to go to an estate sale and see what sort of library the deceased person left. Sometimes it is already picked over, but usually I still can get a feeling for what the former owner was reading. To me, the books they leave behind are an indication of where their head was when they were alive. Sometimes, however, there is no library for me to peruse. That person, I conclude, lived a life without books, and I am forced to remember that such a life can be as rich and as valid as one filled with books. There are many ways to be human.

But, books are a bias of mine. How could it be any other way? They were with me from the beginning and have stayed all these seventy-some years. While my grandparents and parents were really not avid readers, there still were a few books around the several houses I lived in when young. When deciding to enroll in college, books became even more of a presence in my life. And I still have a shelf of my childhood books. They are part of who I am.

Used books. It pleases me to occasionally pick up a book that a grandparent, or my mother, for instance, owned. I see their quickly penciled marginal notes and think about what caught their eye. It is like taking a stroll down a path they walked long ago. Simple nostalgia? Maybe, but it is something I enjoy.

The pleasant scent of a used book can waft out to a passerby, who, if he, or she, pauses to pick it up and open its cover, might be led into a place they never knew existed. If we are open and receptive, an old, used book can take us to new, interesting places.

ON THE JOYS OF INSULARITY

March 5, 2008

IT HAS BEEN AN OLD-FASHIONED WINTER here in the Northland, but now with the coming of March and daylight savings time our cold days are numbered. This week a few friends casually mentioned it was time for spring, although they were really not complaining; they just have had enough of winter. I think I understand what they mean, but I no longer yearn for much—even for the coming of spring. I know, sure as the earth still spins, it will eventually come, and, meanwhile, I try to enjoy what little time I have left. I like it here and have no yearnings to be any- where else, even in these last, waning weeks of winter. But a week or so ago I spot- ted a letter in the Duluth paper that set me to thinking.

The writer was chastising the newspaper for no longer carrying the *New York Times* list of best-selling books. This person noted how instead of this pres- tigious listing, the Duluth newspaper was offering lists of best-selling books from our region, and she exclaimed that such a list "means nothing to me." I wondered about that—if the writer really meant what she so proudly pro- claimed. Did she truthfully mean that what books folks in this part of the woods are reading means nothing to her? And by extension, is she saying likewise for those regional scribes who write about life in these northwoods?

There was a time when I too, kept an eye on the best-sellers list from New York. I must have wanted to be kept abreast of what world-class writers were up to, and what readers were reading "out there." Maybe I desired to be kept informed of what was going on in the "bigger world."

Perhaps those of us who hunker down in these woods during winter instead of jetting off to warmer climates have met folks who spend time here but somehow never seem to really get to know this place. Even though they might live here for extended periods of time, their point of reference still stems from the Twin Cities, Milwaukee, Chicago, or New York City. I don't know, but I wonder, even though these people are here, are they still living in a world far distant from mine?

The implication I pick up from them is that "everybody" should travel and everybody should be interested in these thick newspapers. Maybe I am wrong,

242

but sometimes I suspect that paradoxically, all that traveling and reading of news from "the big world out there" is a narrowing device. Somehow it might preclude our ability to pay attention to where we really are at the moment. Could that be possible, or am I not getting the picture?

It might be trite to mention Henry David Thoreau at this point, when he proudly announced that he did his traveling "all in one place." He meant, of course, that he found enough to contemplate in the pathways, streams, ponds, and woods surrounding Concord, Massachusetts, the place where he lived. Today Henry David Thoreau is read worldwide.

Long ago my teachers taught me to avoid provincialism and parochialism, to expand my horizons and get out there and become part of our big, challenging world. I soon learned to read the classics and sprinkle my essays and term papers with quotes from world-writers. I struggled with Latin and studied Plato and Socrates.

So I dabbled in a few foreign languages, learned enough to pass important exams–but today I can speak none of them. And interestingly, today I am working to pick up a few phrases of Ojibwe, our region's native tongue. I would like for my Ojibwe vocabulary to grow. Finally, it has come to that.

Through all those years of being taught what was really important, I was being told to pay attention to what I now see as the Western Tradition. My education had an acute European bias, and today I realize that when I was told to expand my horizons, I was being admonished to keep my knowledge within a Western Judeo-Christian framework.

If we don't pay attention to what is being written by our local scribes, and if we don't notice what is being read in our neighborhood, what else are we missing? Have we bothered to immerse ourselves in the history of our region, and especially that history that goes back hundreds, and even thousands, of years? Or are we too busy for that and what it might do to our minds? Are we like those fun-seekers who drive the scenic highways of life, not stopping to step from our vehicles to get any local mud on our boots?

The New York Times list of best-selling books? Yes, it is important, but if we fixate our attention on this list and if the local literary scene is meaningless to us then we are at risk of being a stranger in the land in which we reside. We are like those invasive species that live here but are not of this place. If that reader of the Duluth paper would read a local author she might embark on a real adventure. Like Thoreau, she might travel far by discovering the wonder of the community she calls home.

Hummus, Anyone?

July 11, 2006

A QUIET REVOLUTION IS OCCURRING right under our noses, and it has to do with the foods we eat, the cars we drive, and in general, with much else of what some call the American Way. Things are a'changin'—and it sure sets me to thinking.

More news of this change came yesterday from some Lac Courte Oreilles friends who drove up to Bayfield to pick a crate of raspberries, and to sit on our deck for a few minutes. They quietly mentioned that two new organic food stores were opening in their area. That makes three such stores in the Lac Courte Oreilles region, a number that might seem a bit high. It is not big news and these good friends did not present it that way, but it is typical of what is occurring in today's America. Something is happening to our food preferences.

Here in Bayfield we have been watching this change for a year or two. Our main street coffee shop offers a menu with many vegetarian entrees and is doing well, and across the street that kind woman with the natural food shop seems to be doing alright, too. And of course, Tom Galazen's North Wind Organic Farm is still operating. Then, several months ago the good folks at the IGA added an organic food section that keeps getting larger. Someone is buying that stuff.

Unless you grow it yourself, organic food usually costs a bit more than the other kind, and you know what the other kind is. We have been eating that for most of our lives—the food submitted to numerous sorts of sprays, powders, and what not to keep the bugs and weeds away, and in the case of meat, to make the cow, pig, chicken or whatever, grow bigger and faster. Our food-growers are business people and for generations they have done a good job.

Social and cultural changes can be sneaky. Sometimes they creep up on us and before long we are like everyone else, doing, and in the case of foods, eating these new things and not thinking twice about how we have changed. Look how black beans and rice have caught on for some of us! Today I love the stuff. Then there are those new fan-dangled sandwiches they call wraps. Even the fast-food burger places are serving them. And a few years ago I had no idea what hummus was. I did not know how to pronounce the word. And some folks

I know say they are trying to cut down on eating chicken. They call it The Dirty Bird and are troubled about how those factory chicken farms operate.

Just last week a nephew of mine who we rarely see came for a visit and I learned he has not eaten red meat for over fifteen years. This young man is a schoolteacher in Milwaukee and he easily blends into a crowd. In fact, some might say he is as American as apple pie. He, his wife, and their two young daughters are quiet folk—but they are thinking about the foods they eat, and how they can improve their diet.

Most of us still love their meat-n-taters, and I see folks turning into those fast-food chains over in Ashland, yet, I sense a change. Last winter at one of those great Friday night fish fries at the Bayfield Catholic church I was surprised to see bowls of rice and black beans on the food table. For a moment I thought they looked downright odd, sitting there amidst the usual heavy fare of boiled red potatoes, pats of butter, mayo-laden coleslaw and deep-fried fish, but folks did not bat an eye. To me, on that table black beans and rice were like a foreign exchange student from Timbuktu.

I still see lots of local folks pushing down those big breakfasts of fried eggs, bacon, sausages, and oily hashbrowns, but I also see friends eating more pancakes, oatmeal, fruit and other lighter fare. And those egg substitutes suit me just fine, in fact, when I serve them to my grandchildren they cannot tell the difference. Those kids are something else. This summer the older ones announced that they were going to try to stay away from meat three days a week. Their mother and dad are almost complete vegetarians and these kids are old enough to understand the argument for that.

In some ways it is a new world for me. In my youth we never talked about organic food, and my mother built each meal around a chunk of meat. Breakfast, dinner and supper (yes, that is what we called them) all started with the flesh of some animal. The rest was ancillary—like something added on as an afterthought. Now most of my meals have no meat at all. For some of us what we used to call a side dish has become the main dish. My diet has turned upside down, and I like it.

There still seems to be lots of folks who have not changed the way they live, but this summer I see more and more hybrid cars in town, and that organic food cooler at the IGA keeps needing to be refilled. And each morning that kind woman in the natural food shop makes a fresh batch of those great veggie-hummus sandwiches. They're gone by noon.

Four Bucks a Gallon

June 16, 2008

No matter how I try, I can't ignore the high price of gasoline. Four dollars a gallon, and rising! This is the most I ever had to pay. A few weeks ago I was over in Ironwood and the price range ran from $3.97 to $4.20 a gallon. Good lord, but that is a lot of money! This business of gasoline sets me to thinking.

Those of us who are old enough to remember the days of gasoline wars recall how at times local stations would compete with each other—something that could drive prices down. I recall how back in the 1960s such a "war" between gas stations on the south side of Milwaukee brought the price down to as little as seventeen and eighteen cents a gallon. In those years I was driving a Volkswagon bug so it did not matter much to me what the price was because I was using so little of it, but today it seems impossible that gas could go so cheaply. Now when we talk of gasoline wars we probably think of what is going on in Iraq where bullets are flying and people are dying. Our latest gasoline war has been raging for over five years and some folks are talking of how it might have to go on for years and years longer. Maybe we had better accept the reality of these bullet-laden perpetual gasoline wars. How awful would that be?

When we think about it, at base, our consumption of gasoline is directly related to movement. It is burned in internal combustion engines that, through a system of gears and rods, cause wheels to turn. Gasoline powers much of commerce, and in this way allows us to use commodities that were not readily produced in our home areas. Gasoline—and diesel fuel—allows us to drink Australian wine without having to go down under. It also brings us fruits from California, Florida, and increasingly, points south of the border. Those yellow bananas that have become staples for some of us are brought to our local grocery stores by gasoline. These days how could we live without bananas?

Gasoline is not one of my favorite subjects, yet here I am going on and on about it. That's how troubling it has become. As a youngster I recall how one of my grandfathers had a real gasoline pump standing prominently in his farmyard right outside a large machine shed. The tank was hidden underground and the tall orange pump had a shiny glass globe atop on which the Phillips 66 logo was proudly displayed. There even was a light bulb inside this globe, operated by a switch from the garage. Sometimes on summer evenings when my brothers and I played in the farmyard we turned on the light to enjoy the globe's soft orange glow. The farm's several trucks and tractors would periodically pull up to the pump and be filled with fuel through its long, black, rubber hose and commercial-styled nozzle. I recall how from inside this mechanical contraption a bell would ring each time another gallon was dispensed. That orange gasoline pump was a conspicuous part of the farm's daily operations, and once a month or so a Phillips 66 tank truck came to fill its buried tank. The whole thing was an integral part of our lives back then, never questioned, and I suspect, proudly accepted as part of the status quo. We were modern, and our own private gas pump helped prove it.

Ever since those early memories, gasoline has been part of my life. Daily I come in contact with things brought to me by the burning of gasoline. How dependent I am on this inflammable fuel! Even when I pull a fresh, tasty organically grown carrot from my garden I am forced to recall that the seed I planted for that wholesome vegetable was brought to me by some sort of oil derived fuel. The insidiousness of gasoline in our lives is deep and widely evident, and I doubt that today any Americans live untouched by this dependency. As we drink water, our machines "drink" gasoline. Neither of us could go without our liquid "fixes."

There is a deep paradox here. We humans pride ourselves in our freedom and independence yet, how dependent we are on gasoline! Who are we kidding? We may be the "big-brained one" but our superior intelligence has led to dependency when it comes to our self-derived need for this commodity. From outer space our cueing up to gasoline pumps could look downright unusual. Martians might wonder what it was we were receiving from these god-like altars. Gasoline might appear to be manna for our hungry souls.

Well, if we are troubled by our need for gasoline, we might try to break this dependency. We could reduce our consumption of products that were transported from distant places. Today the call to use locally produced items is heard by all of us, but who is willing to give up bananas? Then, how about those beautiful grapes from Chile? And how could we do without that cheap Australian wine or those inexpensive Chinese textiles?

How much global movement do we want? How much do we really need? What have we done to ourselves?

AUTUMNAL THOUGHTS

October 9, 2008

So far our fall has been glorious. As usual, this morning I was out in Orchard Country with Rosie, the aging chocolate Labrador for our daily constitutional, and it was another good romp. The dog must smell the pungent odor of black bears that come to feed on ripening apples at night, for a few times along the walk she went into her offensive posture complete with hair standing up on her neck and shoulders as she put her nose to the ground and followed the scent. When on these walks we come upon fresh bear scat almost daily. She probably smells coyotes too, because along with bears we have seen them on our paths these last few years.

These morning walks have become important for both of us, and coupled with autumn, are always enjoyable. But, as wonderful as it is, the coming of fall brings a feeling of sadness. Another summer has passed, and even though fall is a wonderful time it is also a harbinger of the end of things. For me, it is a nostalgic time. For several years now, the first clear days of this great season bring back memories of years and years ago when my family began its annual routine of preparing our farms for the challenging times of winter. There were silos to fill, several cords of firewood to cut and bring in, and poultry coops and youngstock barns to prepare for the cold days ahead. Fall was wonderful but it had its share of urgent chores.

This fall I realize that I am not seeing my grandchildren as often as I did when they were younger. In the earlier days they came around more. At those times they welcomed my company and I eagerly awaited their next visit. But now they are like bolting radishes: stretching out much too quickly. That fact was brought home recently when I watched two of the girls playing soccer. Each was out there with their teammates—running, shouting, and giving it their best. My, but those kids' legs are long! Those beautiful granddaughters are nearly teenagers!

Lately it occurs to me that these kids are living in a world distant from mine. The earth, the sky, the trees and waters look the same as when I was young, but all the rest has changed.

Fall can bring thoughts of how fortunate we are to enjoy good health. Just this morning a friend stopped his pickup truck, pushed the button that allowed his window to go down—we don't roll windows down anymore—and greeted me as Rosie and I moved along the roadway. When I asked how his day was going he replied by saying very well. He said he got out of bed, had breakfast, and that was enough right there. Anything else was extra. After open-heart surgery he knows the value of rising on a beautiful fall morning and enjoying a good breakfast before stepping outdoors to meet another day. Open-heart surgery can do that to you.

But it is another good friend that concerns me. Faced with months of medical treatment, he too rises on these great fall mornings to greet another glorious day and to step outdoors as he tries to recapture his life's routines. An inspiration for all who know him, over the next several months this man will have a hard row to hoe. We will walk the row with him and help when we can, but we can do so little. This one is his battle, and we wish him well.

But fall need not be talked about so heavily. I like to recall that it is not a season just for us. As one of our four seasons it knows nothing of human travail. There were many falls on planet earth long before we humans arrived and the multitude of those earlier autumns doubtlessly, were as wonder-filled as ours are today. Our time here is miniscule compared to what came before.

Recently, schools opened and the apples ripened. The local apple festival came and went with its happy crowds. Apparently, driving to Bayfield for this gathering is still popular with many. Then, only a few days ago a handful of large orange pumpkins appeared on the steps of some neighborhood houses, so Halloween must be around the corner. Unlike in days gone by, we do not eat our pumpkins. Like so much of our world today, they have evolved into decorations, meant for show. The very substance of their meaning, it seems, has become cosmetic.

This year, soon after the time of ghosts and goblins comes our national presidential election, and like our pumpkins, its partisan yard signs are out, shouting for our attention. They stand like identity badges on the proud chests of the public. Interestingly, we must have a two-party system because I see barely any third or fourth party signs at all, and when I do see one it seems like a voice in the wilderness.

So, fall is upon us, and one of these nights a killing frost will hit those colorful flowers lighting up our gardens and window boxes, and they will hang their tired heads never to rise again. They will have had their day in the sun; another example of the end of things. Cold winter is on its way.

Ralph Waldo Emerson and Wisconsin

January 16, 2006

A WEEK OR SO AGO I READ WITH SOME interest that in 1856 Ralph Waldo Emerson purchased 129 acres of forested and lakeshore land in northwestern Wisconsin and that recently an Illinois couple decided to secure the land in a trust so some of it will stay undeveloped. 1856? Ralph Waldo Emerson? The year and the name go back a long way. They both set me to thinking.

The writer of the newspaper piece that told of this went on to speculate that Emerson probably "hoped to cash in on the lucrative logging of Wisconsin's timberland." Ralph Waldo Emerson is one of America's premier thinkers and writers of all time. A neighbor and close friend of Henry David Thoreau, he was among other things, a philosopher, poet, essayist, and transcendentalist. Like Thoreau, he wrote at length of his reverence for nature.

Transcendentalism has been called a lot of things—to include a religion —but it essentially argued that the physical, i.e., material existence, is transcended by something else. Emerson felt Nature was the seat of this transcendent essence.

I recall how all this turned me on when I discovered the writings of Emerson and Thoreau back in the 1950s and later still, when I did some heavy reading as an undergraduate at the University of Wisconsin at Madison. I loved it all, and at that time in my life I could not get enough.

Some thirty years after my late discovery of Emerson and Thoreau, my wife, a son, and I walked the pathway beside Walden Pond at Concord, Massachusetts, on land that also once belonged to Ralph Waldo Emerson and was used by Thoreau as the site for his cabin when he lived beside the pond and began his most important thinking. For me, it was a heady experience to walk that path and stand where Thoreau's cabin once stood.

Now we Wisconsinites have an even closer connection to these Transcendentalists with this story of Emerson's mid-western land. Neither Emerson or Thoreau did much traveling, although near the end of his short life Thoreau came to the Midwest and did some sight seeing in southeastern Minnesota.

(Interestingly, he may have met Little Crow, the prominent Dakota leader just before the outbreak of the Dakota Conflict of the 1860s.) It is likely Emerson never saw his Wisconsin land and it seems he never wrote of it either. Apparently it was just another investment, to be sold after it was logged, but it seems he never made the cash windfall from it that he probably anticipated. He held the property for twenty-six years, selling it just prior to his death in 1882.

This Burnett County land was once owned by the Ojibwe people and sold by their leaders to the United States through the treaty of 1837. Emerson purchased it nineteen years after the signing of that treaty and only two years after the famous LaPointe Treaty of 1854 between the Ojibwe and the United States. There are said to have been many wealthy eastern folk like Emerson who speculated in land in those years and who may never have thought twice about it. They were doing what the country expected its wealthy persons to do: invest in the West and help it "grow" as the nation's western border was pushed clear to the Pacific.

Doubtless, Ralph Waldo Emerson saw no moral conflict in his being a transcendentalist who (according to the newspaper writer) "gave nature an exalted, almost religious status" and how contrariwise, he seemingly expected to cash in on this logging venture as well as "profit from the development from the lakefront property." He did what wealthy people do—invest their capital in order to make it grow.

We might call to mind other famous American names with this Ralph Waldo Emerson story. In Wisconsin we have counties, towns and more named after these sorts of speculators. Closer to home we have the lumber barons who set up and ran the loud mills that reduced the logs to boards used to build houses and other structures in distant cities. Today their family names dot our maps. Their stern faces can still be seen in murals, framed photos, and portraits hanging prominently in public buildings, and even carved in stone on monuments in our parks.

But, these were business people. They were entrepreneurs who did these things. They lived in the big houses on the hill overlooking the town below. Perhaps we expected them to do financial speculating. They were the movers and shakers.

Was Ralph Waldo Emerson any different? If we can agree that he was an environmentalist then his investment in Wisconsin land becomes perhaps, more interesting. Today some of our most prominent environmental benefactors might be people who in diverse ways made their wealth by producing products that harm the environment, or at least by being involved in business practices that seem not to have put environmental awareness in the forefront of their concerns.

One of my favorite environmental writers of our time is William Kittredge who once owned hundreds of acres in the west, but had a change of heart and now prides himself in not owning a single square inch of land.

Well, I need to do more thinking about Ralph Waldo Emerson and his interesting Wisconsin investment.

The Beauty All Around Us

May 16, 2006

Y ESTERDAY A FRIEND REMARKED that last week he had out-of-town visitors from North Carolina who had never been to Northern Wisconsin before. They were interested in seeing Chequamegon Bay and its sites, but did not want the usual. No hype, no crowds, no fabricated tourist sites—just the big lake, the woods and the countryside. My friend's words set me to thinking.

He said he decided to take his visitors on a few day trips to places he had not been for some time, and, he went on, "to places that were some of my favorites." This got me interested and I could not resist asking where he took them. I think the question is a good one—where do you take out-of-town friends when they ask to see where you live? It seems to me, for most of us, such a task could be a very revealing one. It might cause us to pause and do some thinking about where we spend our lives, and what attracts us to this place. Perhaps most of us still have to live where the work is, but maybe it is not out of place to suggest that we do not really have to live where we do. After all, if we were willing to make the effort, most of us could probably live somewhere else.

For those of us in The Northland, this is a good time to show off where we live. Spring is always something special for us, but this particular spring is extraordinary. Due to our early rains we have been enjoying deep colors of green, yellow—and in recent roadside blossoms—all shades of whites. A week or two ago the drive north of Washburn on Highway 13 that affords a distant view of the hills at the tip of the Bayfield Peninsula was nothing short of spectacular. The varied hues of light greens and early deep maroons was a sight for our winter-weary eyes. It told of rich summer foliage that was on the way.

So where did my friend take his out-of-town guests? One place was Mellen's Copper Falls. Another was Michigan's Little Girl Point, just north of Ironwood. These places, my friend said, have always attracted him. It does not take long for him to make the point that they have special meaning. Their natural beauty, their quietude, and their relative solitude are what are important.

253

When mentioning these places he said simply, "They please me." A third place was the loop from Ashland up to Herbster along the lakeshore. Here it was the starkness of the forests and the old grassy farm fields at Oulu that occasionally broke the tree line. And importantly, the overwhelming presence of the big lake visible here and there along Highway 13 was a given. Not surprisingly, a fourth place was a morning stroll on Ashland's Mainstreet to peruse the shops, view the murals, and have a quiet lunch. I could not resist telling my friend that a stroll on Ashland's Mainstreet is one of my personal pleasures as well.

After disclosing his special places, my friend said, "Last week I saw what a beautiful land we live in." Perhaps such a statement is not unusual to those of us who spend our days here in Chequamegon Country, but I think my friend was remarking about something more than our land's beauty. I think he was suggesting that too often we get caught up in our day-by-day work routine and loose sight of the beauty of our surroundings. It might be trite, but "taking time to smell the roses" is still one of the really important things in life. These old sayings must have worth, or they would not be repeated generation after generation.

After the meeting with my friend yesterday I thought about where I would take guests who had never been here before. Where would you take first-time visitors who wanted to see where you live? It would depend on what kind of people the visitors were, of course, but if they asked to see the really beautiful places where would you go? The ferry ride to Madeline Island? A cruise out to several of the islands? A canoe paddle on one of several of our local scenic rivers? The Kakagon Sloughs? A walk through Prentice Park?

We all must have our special places that we go to now and then. And hopefully, we all have those friends who challenge us to decide on which are the most noteworthy of the lot. One thing is certain: this spring is a wonderful time to take friends to such places. It is a great time to show off this beautiful land we live in.

THE CHRISTMAS TREE

December 18, 2005

I CANNOT RECALL A DECEMBER 25TH without an evergreen tree sitting in our living room. This European custom has been thoroughly taken over by we Americans, at least those like my family. Back in the 1600s in Puritan times displaying garlands of pine boughs and setting an evergreen tree up in your house could bring a jail sentence for what was a serious religious offense. Christmas trees were considered pagan symbols that belittled the deep solemnity of the time. Not until the 1830s or so when large numbers of German immigrants arrived did the Christmas tree become accepted here. Interesting. You can see why Christmas trees set me to thinking.

My first memory of a Christmas tree goes back to the very late 1930s. I suppose my dad purchased it from a lot and set it up in our living room. Every year since then we have had one. These evergreens with their roots cut off can be very important symbols of life. A dead tree holding its color for weeks brought right into our living rooms might seem strange to some of us, but to others it is as common as snow in winter. This is no little ritual.

Some of my favorite memories of Christmas trees come from my earlier years when I lived on a series of small dairy farms in northeastern Wisconsin. Our farms were set among the rocky lowlands of Shawano County and we had a plethora of evergreens to choose from. Christmas tree scouting expeditions began soon after Thanksgiving when my dad, brothers and I would hike out to the woods to search for just the right tree. It was always a balsam and it had to be full of branches. Sometimes we needed to drill a few holes in its trunk and rig a branch here or there to help fill it out. We were determined about such things. Neighbors who accepted thin, scraggly trees were talked about. No Charlie Brown trees for us.

The decorations were an eclectic collection of the old, the new and the homemade. For years we had several real wax candles with tin bases that came from a line of grandmothers. Rumor was that long ago they were brought over from The Old Country. Then, there were those post-WWII ornaments from

255

occupied Japan. We belittled these, saying that the Japanese made cheap things, usually of plastic or white metal that just did not last. We were proud Americans and wanted nothing from Japan.

I guess our grade school teachers did not have us make Christmas tree ornaments to take home and be hung on the family tree year after year, or else if I did make any they did not hold up. My wife and I still have such ornaments our youngsters made and proudly brought home. Today they are the centerpieces of our decorated tree. We still love them and after Christmas they are carefully wrapped in tissue paper and placed safely into their own box for storage. Homespun heirlooms.

Now we try to have our grandchildren decorate our tree while they are still young enough to find joy in the chore. My joy is to sit and watch them and wonder what some people do without the laughter of grandchildren at year's end.

Many years ago at Red Cliff I witnessed artificial Christmas trees make their quiet entries into the season. My mother-in-law's tree has been coming out of a cardboard box for years. She wanted it that way, and she was not alone. Many reservation families have artificial trees these days, but if I must put a tree up I want it to be the real thing. I'm not sure why, especially since over the years I have adapted to having many artificial things. They're hard to avoid these days.

But I still wonder about this ritual. A dead tree as a symbol of life? In an old sacred Ojibwe origin teaching it is told how the ancients found their Center when Makwa, the bear, pushed a green cedar tree up through the four layers of the earth as simultaneously, Migizi, the eagle, broke through the four sky layers to come down to the Center to meet the bear. This is where the people were and Makwa and Migizi brought on-going life to them, and in the process the cedar tree became the Ojibwes' sacred tree, actually their axis mundi. It stands in the Center of their world. I like that imagery—in fact, I like it a lot. It is a teaching that comes from right here, not from a distant land overseas, and, when I stand beside my mother-in-law's plastic tree I pretend it represents that primal cedar tree brought by Makwa. After all these years it makes sense. It fits this Lake Superior Country.

There still are many different ways to celebrate this time of year when our hemisphere starts to tip back towards the sun and days start lengthening. Using a tree to symbolize this important time is alright with me. Those lofty Puritans did not like it but it suits me just fine. Call it a Christmas tree if you want, but at this time of year I see an Ever-green tree standing in the Center of my world, and it is beautiful.

The Calling of Coyotes

June 21, 2007

LAST SUNDAY NIGHT AFTER TURNING IN, the yipping of coyotes woke me. Almost immediately one of our neighbors' dogs that is chained out all night answered with a few soulful barks. I lay awake for several moments contemplating what had just occurred and this morning these coyote calls set me to thinking.

This was the first time I heard coyotes at my Bayfield home. I have listened to them out at the Red Cliff cabin but that is a few miles into the woods and isolated. Hearing coyotes calling on Eleventh Street in Bayfield is something different.

This week I asked friends and neighbors if the sounds of coyotes yipping in town are an old thing for them and some indicated that they hear them now and then. But, they seemed unconcerned, as if it happens quite regularly. They intimated that it was nothing new. I cannot put coyote calls in Bayfield aside as easily as these friends seem to do.

In western Native American communities the coyote is often understood as The Trickster, a spiritual being that helps teach the people about life in this world, but here in the Great Lakes, even though the Trickster can assume many different forms, at least to the Algonquian people, this spiritual character is usually associated with waabooz, the rabbit. *Waabooz*, or *Wenabozho*, as he is often called, is a prominent culture hero of the Ojibwe people, and I have been assured that as in the days of old, he still travels these northern woods and waters.

Hearing coyotes call while I lie in bed adds something to my world. I am aware that throughout some of the United States the coyote has been adapting to urban areas and sometimes is perceived as a nuisance, perhaps even a danger, especially to smaller animals and even young children. But, for now I prefer to let them be and share my neighborhood. If they become more numerous and present a problem it will be another matter.

I have checked out what are supposed to be coyote dens in the woods on the other side of town and friends on both the north and south sides say they hear and see the critters several times throughout the year, especially in winter.

There is a stretch of highway between Red Cliff and Cornucopia where I have spotted coyotes in bright daylight a few times over the past two or three years. Once I stopped the car and my companions and I watched one in the ditch beside us pounce upon what we took to be a mouse in the matted grass. That coyote seemed oblivious to us. More recently we saw another about thirty feet from the roadway in a clearing and when it saw us stop it stopped too. We sat there for several minutes studying each other. That coyote was large and quite attractive. It looked healthy, as if it was not missing any meals. Finally, it tired of us and turned to trot away into the nearby woods.

Many years ago I had a friend who, when attending college out west, took a job to trap and poison coyotes on open rangeland. He claimed he patrolled a large circuit with his pickup and a four-wheeler in summer and a snowmobile in winter, setting and checking traps baited with poisoned chicken.

This summer I have seen or heard Canada geese, loons, sea gulls, eagles, crows, ravens, owls, and the usual array of songbirds from this Bayfield hillside. A week ago a granddaughter and I saw a black bear cross Manypenny Avenue in the thick woods just above our place. Down the hill a bit another neighbor told of having bird feeders destroyed by bears. White tail deer are common—their tracks on a path I take on my morning walks—and I suspect fishers are in the neighborhood as well, but so far we have not seen any. I have come upon fishers in the Red Cliff woods and am impressed with their size. Several years ago after they were returned to northern Wisconsin it was not long before we started hearing stories of house cats that suddenly disappeared. I guess that still goes on. Maybe fishers are preying upon the feral cats that supposedly live throughout our northern woods. If so, the birds should be pleased.

Recently someone mentioned that with the return of wild turkeys the numbers of partridges have decreased. I come upon both wild turkeys and partridges in Bayfield County now and then, and it is always a pleasure to see them, but apparently turkey's relish eating partridge eggs. Sometimes it's said Nature has many sides, some of which we might try not to think about. Denial is still a human trait.

These woods and waters of our world are home to many different kinds of life. Coyotes are only one of them, and as is true with so many of these species, they are companions of ours that we rarely see.

Sometimes we humans might need to be reminded that we are not the only forms of life on this planet. Those coyotes that woke me a few nights ago helped me acknowledge that there are many others who walk these Bayfield hills. Somehow that reality brings comfort.

Winter's Busy Days

January 12, 2009

T HERE IS A MYTH ABOUT THE STRUGGLE those of us who live in this North-woods all year go through once the heart of our winter season hits. You have heard it from friends who winter-over in more southern climes. They ask us what we do all winter long once the cold and dark days really arrive. Sometimes I suspect they think we rarely go outdoors; that we might step out for an armful of firewood now and then but that might be it. They seem to think that about this time of year we will soon catch cabin fever, or as a brother of mine who winters in Arizona says, "shack sickness."

Well, it has been five years that my bride and I settled in on this Bayfield hillside and our winters have been anything but long and dark. In fact, last week instead of complaining about cabin fever, we both agreed that there is too much going on. Our weekly calendars are penciled in just like in the summertime. What's happening, anyway? This is supposed to be the quiet time—a time when we pull the rockers up to the fire and relax. I am beginning to think we might have to leave town to get some down time.

There is so much going on that yesterday I did not make it to another of those free lunches put on by the good folks from C.O.R.E., that organization of friends and neighbors working to help we oldsters stay in our homes instead of moving into assisted living arrangements, or even nursing homes. I was sure I would not miss one of those lunches but yesterday it happened. I just had too many other things that screamed for attention.

Last week we attended three funerals, and I don't care to go to another one for a long time. Three in a week is enough, thank you. I would not have missed any one of the three but when I was at the third I was ready to turn my face to the heavens and say, "Enough already!" The cold weather did not help any, either.

There is a definite seasonal rhythm to life in this town. The summer is given over to tourists and those businesspersons whose income depends on them. At that time I try not to complain about the lack of parking spots Down-town and the lines at the IGA. We need those visitors and are glad for them. Winter is really our time. There are visitors, who come to dine, ski, shop and just relax in this cold season but they are far fewer than in the warm months. In the winter we locals "have the town back," as some of us say. Parking spots abound and any lines in the grocery store are not only short, but are filled with friends. We get some serious visiting done in those winter grocery lines.

Things do not slow down in winter. You would think that when the plethora of harvest dinners right after Apple Festival are over that we would slip into a slower pace—one with plenty of afternoon naps—but no. Those harvest dinners signal the start of winter-long events, one after another that move quickly, almost like falling dominoes. Thanksgiving, and you know what comes right after that. Maggie Rice's dinner out at the Wild Rice is a must, as is the lutefisk feed at her restaurant here in town. These have become institutions and cannot be missed.

Several newer activities are the colorful events put on by our Bayfield Recreation Center and Pool. That place has regular "doin's" that seem to go on all yearlong. And virtually every community organization in town has a dinner or tea sometime after the dust of summer settles. They seem endless but we try to make them all. After all, these are events put on by friends, relatives, and neighbors, and we cannot miss them.

It does not help that we have four very busy grandchildren right here in town, and two others only an hour away. Once school starts for those kids it begins, and we do not want to miss a beat. What do people do without grandchildren?

How did that old myth about slow and quiet winters in the north woods begin, anyway? Even when I am out at the cabin my days and nights are filled with things to do. An axe might need a new edge, or handle—good projects done beside the woodburning stove by the light of oil lamps. And evenings in the cabin are excellent times to get that important reading done. Many evenings out there I sit by a few oil lamps, reading and writing late into the night.

And today I have two dinners to attend, at the same time. Yes, a sister-in-law at Red Cliff is celebrating a birthday with a spaghetti feed, and Lennie Erickson and Bill Deragon are putting on a fund-raising ham and turkey dinner at The Bayfield Inn for Red Cliff's Duwayne Soulier VFW Post. When these two friends do these famous dinners I volunteer to scrub pots and pans back in the kitchen. This is the way it goes in winter.

A long, dark, quiet time? Who said? Our Bayfield winters are anything but long, dark and quiet. Our drumbeat does not slow down in winter. In fact, it might even speed up a bit.

BLACKBERRIES!

August 15, 2006

LAST WEEK THE BLACKBERRIES STARTED to come in. Word of their ripening spread through town quietly and some folks reported picking a few pints for jam. "Freezer jam," they call it—the kind that is easy to make and that tastes so good, especially in the cold of winter. Yes, blackberries set me to thinking.

Blackberries are in the genus *Rubus*, part of the rose family of plants. They are brambles, meaning they are a shrub-like plant with prickly canes that are quick to catch on your clothing. When going amongst them it is best to be prepared, and that involves wearing long pants and shirts with long sleeves. Even then, you are sure to be scratched on the hands when you reach to pick the dark and sweet fruits. There is no other way—when picking blackberries you had better expect to pay a price.

A few wild blackberry plants grow along the trail into our Red Cliff cabin and invariably I stop along the way to pick them. These few gems go right into the mouth to be treasured as I slowly make my way along the narrow path. Sometimes the birds beat me to them and on occasion the quick little red squirrel—called *ajidamoo* in the Ojibwe language—gets them before me. And always there are those hungry black bears that take their share. I do not begrudge these animals eating the fruit since I like to think these berries really belong to those who live in the forest anyway. I just visit now and then. When at the cabin I am reminded that we humans are the ultimate invasive species.

Blackberries were not one of the common fruits of my childhood and youth. The countryside I grew up in had been cultivated to such an extent that there was little room for them. Wild blackberries thrive in woodlots that have been logged recently and where I lived there were few such places. Almost all land was given to cultivated fields and our woodlots served as grazing areas for cattle. Those cows nibbled and tore at practically anything that grew in our woods. Wild blackberry plants went elsewhere, and for my family, the blackberry represented wilderness, something we saw only in magazines or in movie theaters.

Here in Chequamegon Bay there is still enough open and undeveloped land to allow the wild blackberry to grow. For me, this is one of the little, quiet joys of living in this Ojibwe Country. There are wild blackberry patches within walking distance from my Bayfield home and neighbors keep their eye on them to watch when the time is right for picking. Sometimes I venture to them, but most often leave those berries for the others.

A few of Bayfield's fruit growers have put in patches of blackberries and yesterday I drove out to one of the farms to pick a bucket or two. It was the first time I had ever picked domestic blackberries and when moving along the straight row of loaded plants I contemplated how different it was to pick them compared to their wild cousins. The domestic variety had bigger fruits but I wondered if they tasted as good as the wild. Maybe they were just as sweet and juicy, but when sampling one I could not help think that something was missing. They just did not taste the same as the wild berries. I suspect it was I—wanting the wild ones to be better.

Last season I made a batch of wild blackberry cobbler, complete with the hard white sauce that my mother used to make. It was a surprise dessert that my wife and I enjoyed after one of my homemade dinners. I thought it was especially good but even though I was given a nod of approval there were few words uttered in its praise. I wonder if sometimes this woman who has lived with me for over forty-five years is a bit taken aback by my attempts to turn-to in the kitchen. She is the one who did the bulk of that work for all these years and now with my retirement it must be odd to have the old guy messing around with her pots and pans. My blackberry cobbler with white sauce is pretty good —but I still am an amateur when it comes to such things.

As was the case when our local strawberries, raspberries, and blueberries came in, the arrival of the blackberries happened quietly. We do not have a Blackberry Festival with loud parades, mayoral pronouncements, and vendors lining the streets. Blackberry season is celebrated differently. When in that patch yesterday I fantasized about our local black bears and how they might be having their own blackberry festival one of these days. That wonderful song about Uncle Walter dancing with bears came to mind as I envisioned someone's Uncle sneaking off to the woods in blackberry time to do such a thing. If he returned with a quiet smile and scratches on his hands and arms his family would know what he had been up to.

Well, it's blackberry time. There are still plenty of domestic blueberries to be harvested, and now the last of the local fruits is here. This must mean that summer is on the way out and that fall is heading our way.

THE BREWERS AND ME

September 5, 2008

IT STILL IS A MYSTERY TO ME but at the end of the day, after supper when things slow down, I enjoy plopping into an overstuffed swivel rocker to watch the Milwaukee Brewers play baseball. As much as I badmouthed professional sports over the years, you would think I would refuse to watch these games, but night after night there I am, glued to Channel 38, watching the Brew Crew play ball.

Perhaps it really is a function of my advancing age. Maybe I simply am exhausted at the end of the day and need to sit back, put my feet up, and nod off as the innings crawl on. Maybe I have become just another tired grandfather snoozing before the television set.

I have written about my penchant to watch these games before and have concluded that I must be a baseball fan, but for some reason I go on pondering what that means. Television is meaningless for me except for the evening news shows, a very few select public television shows, and the Brewers' ball games. Yes, I watched a little of the China Olympics but after a few evenings I could stand no more. Beach volleyball? What in the world was that about?

I watch little more than the news shows and the ball games, and lately I entertain thoughts of quitting the news shows. Yes, those folks with the big salaries who read the news to us are losing my attention. And I am not sure why baseball holds my interest when so much of that game should turn me off too. It is big business and I come from the other side of the tracks where big business never seems to go—except, perhaps, to grow even bigger.

It is becoming very difficult for someone like me to relate to a young man who signs a contract to receive several millions of dollars a year to play ball. Why do I pull for them when they are out on the diamond? These days many players move to different teams every few years so the old notion of allegiance to "my town" is mythical. Today's players are like hired guns. They are the modern day Hessians of our sports arenas.

Some theorists argue that we have an instinct to play, and consequently we innately react to the crack of a bat and the smack of leather as the ball hits the mitt. And the deep joy of running—such a simple, natural act—captures us as well. Maybe these things appeal to us because they are, at base, physical. Yes, maybe the pretense at being the big-brained ones—the rational species as some like to say—takes second place to our prime underlying characteristic. Maybe more important than our yearnings to be intelligent and sophisticated beings, is a desire to get back to basics: to be physical. That might be the deep, underlying attraction a game like baseball has to us.

Or, in my case at least, I might be attracted to it because it was a game of my childhood, youth and young adulthood. Back in the 1940s my brothers and I played ball with neighborhood friends on many warm summer days. Then in high school I was in all our school's ballgames, either at first base or as a pitcher.

So perhaps when I watch the Brewers I am vicariously reliving those days so long ago when I was out on the diamond, wearing our school uniform, running, throwing and enjoying life. I was a baseball player. Now I can still be one as I relax in the overstuffed swivel rocker before the television set.

Fifty years ago I could name every player on every team in the majors. And that included all the second stringers and the entire bullpen. My brother and I kept scrapbooks for every team, filled with photos and starting lineups clipped from the Milwaukee Sentinel sports page. We talked about the players and how a few were our favorites, fellows like Alvin Dark, Stan Musial, Richie Ashburn, Charlie Keller, and Nick Etten.

Today I can name the Brewers players but little more. There are too many to learn and with the multitude of similar Hispanic names I easily get confused. No, I am a baseball fan but not one who thrives on trivia. It is enough just to watch the televised evening games and to occasionally glance at a box score in the morning paper. But all the time I wonder why I do such things. Baseball? After all these years I still follow it? Sometimes the reality of that seems very strange to me.

I will not drive to Milwaukee or the Twin Cities to watch a game. No, in fact I have yet to drive up the hill here in Bayfield to watch one of our local high school games. And I have at least one nephew on the local team, so I suppose I should be there cheering him on. But, I know that fine young lad does not need this uncle in the stands. He can do well without me hanging around the ball diamond, watching practices and yelling at every home game. No, the occasional Brewer game in the quietude of my living room is enough for me. I don't know why, but I watch those millionaires play ball.

THE APRIL BLIZZARD

April 12, 2008

THE TELEVISION AND RADIO PEOPLE told of the approaching storm so we were ready. It was to hit Thursday night and run through Friday with twelve to eighteen inches of snow, so this was no little matter. A foot to a foot and a half of new snow is something to reckon with, even in Northern Wisconsin.

Then, Thursday evening my dad phoned from Milwaukee. Just touching base, he had seen the television weather maps and told me of the red and yellow colors bearing down on us. "Be prepared for a big one," he said. I listen to my dad. I heed his admonitions. At age ninety-one he has seen more than I. This time he remarked, "When a kid, I liked blizzards." He was born in 1916, and his blizzards came down dirt roads and roared through his fields.

This time our April blizzard was not a disappointment. It disrupted electrical power all around, but for some reason our hillside was spared. Schools were cancelled the night before so those good people who drive the big yellow buses would not face the struggle of keeping those machines out of snow-filled ditches.

And our local grandkids were pleased to have a snow day. Those kids work hard too, and deserve a day off now and then. It was good for them just to kick back and relax—to get outside and romp in the storm.

What is it about an old-fashioned snowstorm that appeals to us? The gusty snow-laden winds that can blind us? The fact that when out in their fury we need to turn away from them to catch our breath?

An April snowstorm is a last hurrah. It is a gala farewell before the serious matter of spring takes over. This is part of what makes them so enjoyable. We know their fury will be followed by sunshine and birdsong.

But all of this is old hat. We are familiar with April snowstorms so perhaps I need not say more. Nostalgia is fine, if not overdone. Some readers might say, enough already, let's get to more important things; tell us something we don't know.

But what are these more important things? The economy? Our wars to end all wars? Our over-wrought presidential election campaign, or perhaps well-meant admonitions to refrain from poking fun at our short-timer leader?

Enough already. Sometimes I think we need a late April snowstorm to jerk us back into a more important reality. They remind us that we live in a huge world, and one that is always there even when we seem not to notice. When we ignore nature we miss the biggest show in town.

April snowstorms call us back to where we need to be. Our "property" with its carefully measured boundaries becomes an artificial construction that can easily be blown away by an April storm, leaving us where we always were—facing the winds, the earth and waters. Facing the natural world. All else is transient.

Sometimes we humans need to set aside our humanness, and an April snowstorm can help us do that. It blows through our self-imposed importance and says we can never match the wind's fury. We need to remember that we can be stopped in our tracks by a late spring storm.

A few mornings before the storm I was wakened at dawn by songbirds that just pulled into town. I had not heard them since last year when they shut the music off after a loud spring. Always one of the most important events of the year, these first songs never grow old. It is especially meaningful to be pulled from sleep by them. There is something about them that lifts my spirits spring after spring. For most of Friday I watched the birds come to the feeder just outside my office window under the roof overhang where it is protected a bit from the buffeting winds. The small birds struggled to grip the feeder's rung as they furtively shoveled seeds into their crops.

I have been watching and listening to songbirds for over seventy years and they still hold my attention. They are like these late storms—fresh and vital.

But today is Saturday and in early afternoon the winds and cloud cover moved elsewhere. Now we have sunshine and the snow on our neighbor's roof just down the hill from my windows is melting. In a day or so we should have very little snow left. The fury of our storm will be history and we will go back to admiring the early flowers peaking through last year's duff covering the front yard's beds. Flowers will take over where the storm left off. Another season is arriving.

So we have had our April snowstorm. Now we can move on. It is time to begin thinking about yards, gardens, and putting the snow shovels away. But my thoughts of April's loud storm linger. I still feel that wind and the bits of snow hitting my cheeks when on my morning walk. The storm told me I had made it to another April. And as the wind pushed against my slowly moving form I felt good about being out there, still upright, still walking into the wind.

Like my dad, I too, liked a good blizzard as a kid. And for what it's worth, I still do.

Wild Leeks and Marsh Marigolds

May 9, 2007

ONE OF THE REAL BENEFITS OF LIVING in this wonderful Northland is the abundance of colorful wild spring flowers and other plants that never fail to thrill us. This year they came again, and once more I marveled at their arrival, and as usual, these wild gems came without any effort on our part. As soon as the snow leaves and the ground begins to warm they go about their business, and it sets me to thinking.

A day or two ago, when on my morning walk through these Bayfield hills I enjoyed the perfume of apple blossoms, but it was not from the orchards up over the hill to the west, no, this perfume came from untended trees on vacant lots right here in town. These trees are not pruned to meet human expectations of what an apple tree should look like. Instead, they are domestic apple trees gone wild. Perhaps few human hands will pick their fruit, most of it falling to rot in the untended grass. Back in the mid-nineteenth century Henry David Thoreau sang the praises of wild apples.

And how about those marsh marigolds? A few of them can be found in town as well, and no one tends them either, but here they are again! Buttercups, my wife calls them. Some decades ago when I was on a wild food kick I would harvest their new leaves before the blossoms set and opened, and boil them up like spinach. Delicious, they were enjoyed by the family at dinnertime. If I remember correctly, they hold high amounts of vitamin A. But, it is their simple beauty that enthralls me. No fan of light hues, these wild flowers prefer deep, dark tones. Yellow and green, their petals and leaves almost drip with these bright colors.

And what about the leeks? Their pungent perfume might not be considered in the same class as that of wild apple blossoms, but each spring it is just as welcome. I have my secret places to gather these overlooked treasures and with a little effort a few wild leeks find their way to our dinner table. Just a handful is all I take. It has become a spring ritual for me.

Rhubarb is another of these old-fashioned treasures. So far I have had two batches of sauce and hopefully, soon I will find a large rhubarb-custard pie cooling on our kitchen counter. My wife excels at making these gems. She does not make many, but the few that turn up are eaten with joy.

When the bulbs of crinkled deep-green rhubarb leaves begin to poke through the garden's rich soil and turn their faces to the warm sun I am taken back to my youth when my maternal grandmother would be the one to make the pies. This woman was born in 1876 and knew the value of rhubarb. She kept a few plants in her kitchen garden beside her farmhouse and we youngsters were schooled in the wonders of this ancient plant. I still recall trips to the barnyard to get the dried cow pies that lay there. We brought these to the garden and after breaking them into smaller pieces, they were carefully placed beneath the large spreading leaves. My grandmother knew the benefits of side dressing with organic fertilizer. This woman also prepared at least a few spring salads from the new dandelion leaves that dotted our lawn.

Thirty or more years ago Euell Gibbons extolled the benefits of stalking the wild asparagus. Because of him I too, set out in search of this delectable wild plant. With asparagus in mind, there are a few sites at Red Cliff and elsewhere in the town of Russell that I frequent this time of year. This treasure is handled with special care as I trim and wash each tender stalk, then, ever so gently sauté them in a splash of light olive oil. Always served as a side to a main entrée, wild asparagus adds a bit of class to a main dish at suppertime.

The first wild mushrooms are also hunted. Morels and shaggy manes are the most sought after prizes. Making early spring forays into our woodlots for mushrooms was my mother's task. She would return with a small wicker basket holding these gems, then, after cleaning would incorporate them into the evening meal.

Beside the flavors, textures, colors, and other delightful features of these simple foods, there is something more that they bring to our table. Surely, it has to do with my past when such foods graced our suppers with regularity. My immediate forebears knew the struggle of the 1929 Depression, but the older ones went back much further than that. They were inveterate food gatherers who combed farm woodlots, country roadside ditches and railroad right-of-ways for wild treasures that were soon eaten or else put-up in glass Mason jars. These relatives had learned this from their elders, and they from theirs. We were Germanic peasants and in the Old Country our ancestors must have scavenged for the same foods. This is a welcome legacy that stays with me.

Frugal living. This morning's aroma of wild apple blossoms, like the allure of marsh marigolds and wild leeks, spoke to me of days long gone.

PART
V

PREFACE TO PART V

THIS FINAL SHORT COLLECTION OF ESSAYS sums up the previous four sections of this book by reminding the reader that those of us who have chosen to spend our lives here beside this big lake, and who truly enjoy the daily pleasures of this relatively undeveloped land, understand that we are still part of the rest of the world. A weekend spent at a lakeside log cabin isolated deep within the Red Cliff woods is always followed by a return to a faster-paced life distant from that idyllic setting. Like all of the planet's residents we have a responsibility to be stewards of our place, and we do not take this charge lightly. We—both Ojibwe and others—love this land and are grateful for the luxury of living here and we readily call to mind the fact that we do not merely live off the land, but live with it. It is the only way.

As the last essay attempts to point out, in the daily immediacy of our personal lives it perhaps is easy to lose sight of where we came from, what we are doing here, and where we are going, but if we simply pause to look around us we might, at last, capture a small glimpse of the preciousness, and precariousness, of our place and time.

HOME GROWN

October 21, 2009

LAST WEEK WHEN PREPARING A PAN of squash for baking I noticed a flores-cent orange stickie shouting at me with a loud block-lettered voice saying it was HOME GROWN. These eye-catching paper tabs have been showing up lately on some of the vegetables we find in our local grocery stores and today they set me to thinking.

The intent, of course, is to get shoppers to purchase the squash with such a tag instead of the many others beside it that, presumably, are not home grown. The tag says, "Buy me because I am better for you."

But, as I peeled the bright tag off my young blue Hubbard squash I won-dered about whose home it was grown at. Was it someone here in the Red Cliff area? Was it an Ashland or Washburn farmer, or was it from a home in Mexico?

It seems these stickies are a response to our national concern about things like energy use, transportation costs, world economics, corporation farming, mindless eating, and other related issues. Michael Pollan might even be the force behind their sudden appearance in our local produce aisles.

There was a time in my life when such stickies did not exist. I recall when some retail items might be emblazoned with a label that shouted, IMPORTED at the shopper. And if my memory is correct, my family was one of many that felt imported was better. It was like fine china, or chocolate from Switzerland. Hershey's chocolate was good, but Switzerland's was preferred. Back then we thought the better things came from far away places.

And we can remember when the word NEW! (the exclamation point was important) would be printed across the product's box or wrapper. I always felt that word was part of our western penchant to like what we called progress. Our way of life had to keep moving forward, as if staying put was akin to being in a rut, or worse yet, backward. These marketing ploys come and go, and maybe HOME GROWN stickies are just the latest in a long line of merchandising techniques we shoppers are confronted with.

In years past this readiness to prefer the new and imported was a function of the social class system in America. My family of immigrants wanted to climb up that social ladder as quickly as possible and in the process, like others, we desired to show our success. We wanted neighbors to know we were making it. In those days bigger was better, and new and imported was prized.

This is what seems to be so important about these HOME GROWN stickies. They just might be a harbinger of things to come. They're not unrelated to an assembly bill Representative Gary Sherman has that would allow for foods, canned and otherwise preserved at home, to be sold out of the home or at local outlets like farmers' markets as long as a person made no more than $5,000.00 a year from such sales. The cap on sales is interesting, but perhaps a line had to be drawn somewhere. I suspect our state health inspectors would still be involved in these small business ventures, with their requirements for stainless steel kitchens and whatnot, so there would be significant costs involved in these startups. I like Sherman's bill.

Could it be possible we might be witnessing a new, and serious, movement of the national ethic that smaller is better into the entire matter of our food production? Or has that movement been underway for several years, and is my orange stickie just part of its latest efforts?

Think of the ramifications of such a change in our values. Might we begin to appreciate, in new ways, the place we are at? Could we see a change in other behaviors, like our desires to travel to all corners of the globe? Or—is this just an old man espousing more out-of-step retrograde thinking?

That squash I baked was delicious and even though I did not know if it was organically grown or submitted to all sorts of chemicals during its growth I still enjoyed eating it and I enjoyed watching our dinner guests dig in. Those two pans of baked squash were gone in no time. But, most of the eaters at our table that evening were Native Americans, and I call squash a Native American soul food. Those folks relish it.

Squash is one of those foods that is good for us, and although when a youngster I could not stand it, I love it now.

So. That stickie raises lots of questions, but most of all it left me with the suggestion that in some way our culture might be coming full circle. We might be rediscovering the value of using products that derive from and are produced in our home regions. There is a term for this—that escapes me now—so this is nothing new. But lately, it seems we are hearing more and more of this issue. We might be witnessing a major change quietly going on right in our midst without realizing it, and my textbooks say this is precisely how many major cultural changes occur.

If homegrown squash is good for us, what else is out there that might be good for us, too?

HIGH SCHOOL GRADUATION

June 15, 2009

A FEW WEEKS AGO I WAS REMINDED of the deep importance of ritual and ceremony in our lives when the annual spate of invitations to local high school graduations and the open houses that follow arrived. Obvious rites of passage, these social gatherings help graduates—and the rest of us—adjust to their new identity.

For some graduates the ceremonies might be a doorway through which they rush to a new freedom, but I suspect many will walk through that portal with a degree of trepidation. Their adolescence is over—at least for most—and now their future stares them in the face. In this sense, high school graduation might be a scary turn of events, because now the graduates are expected to actually get out there and become self-sufficient, in other words, to be taxpayers. Some graduates will forestall this transition by enrolling in college, but in time they too must march to the drumbeat of the world of work.

Rites of passage in American culture can be very subtle, like the first appearance of chin whiskers and the following quiet purchase of a razor and can of shaving cream, or they can be explicitly obvious. With high school graduation exercises we are treated to a formal recognition of a process of change that has been going on for a few years. The caps and gowns, VIPs, and pompous music, together present a colorful use of ritual and ceremony. It does not take an astute observer to note what is going on. We are celebrating the completion of at least twelve years of continual schooling for these youngsters, and now the rest is up to them.

From the point of view of our social structure, rites of passage are standardized ways of moving from one social position to another. Conception, birth, the onset of puberty, marriage, and death are sometimes said to be the major examples, but in today's United States, high school graduation is right up there with them. Rites of passage have been studied well. Some good social science literature, like that of the famous European anthropologist, Arnold van Gennep, is well known.

Ritual has been defined as a standardized behavior that supports cultural values, and ceremony can be understood as a complex of related rituals. Looked at in this textbook fashion, high school graduation exercises can be broken down and analyzed as important events in the maintenance of a society. They are inherently conservative, and among others, one of their functions is to cause us to stop seeing the graduates as youngsters and to start relating to them as adults with requisite rights and responsibilities.

Another aspect of spring graduation time is the plethora of Open Houses held by the graduates' families. This time around my wife and I were invited to attend a handful of these food-fests, and as usual, we could not make them all. A card with a check dropped into the mail ahead of time has become a discreet way to pass our best wishes on to the graduates without actually being there.

Over fifty years ago in northeastern Wisconsin when I bid my high school years farewell there were none of these Open Houses, but they have proliferated at Red Cliff these past several years, so what is going on? Any serious student of human behavior would be quick to notice the patterned nature of these social events and how predictable the adherence to their rules is. It is as if a committee has determined proper procedures and that we are under orders to follow them. Has a decree come down from the front office that obligates us to hold Open Houses? An Open House protocol is clearly evident and once again as I took part I noted our conventionality. As I watched other guests arrive and how they were received, I quickly saw what was expected. We all knew what we were doing without any prompting. There was a clear pattern and we followed the rules. Each Open House was like a blueprint of the previous one.

Who wrote these rigid rules? This year I was intrigued enough to check this question out by surfing the internet and I found a site that provided a list of nine things to be carried out to ensure a properly held Open House.

Banners, balloons and table decorations can be found at these events but the centerpiece is the food. Why do we humans celebrate by sharing food with others? And, what does celebrate mean, anyway? It is an interesting word, and one that, I suspect, most of us do not ponder. When it comes to celebration we just jump in and enjoy. Maybe we are genetically hardwired to do this. Maybe it is simply part of being here.

Sometimes it might be better to turn the thinking off and just enjoy, but at this year's Open Houses I could not do that. As we moved from household to household I was reminded how similar we humans are. Our days and nights are patterned and we move through them in a near mindless fashion. We pride ourselves in being the big-brained species—the rational one—yet at times it seems we follow the drumbeat of our community's life like ducks in a row.

ON CANNED MUSHROOMS

December 28, 2009

NOT MANY YEARS AGO WHEN I TOOK a regular turn at preparing the evening meals in our house I used canned mushrooms in a number of my dishes, and there seemed always to be a stash of such small metal cans in our kitchen's pantry. They would be used in soups, omelets, stir-fry recipes, salads, and piled a-top the occasional grilled beefsteaks I served to the family. We enjoyed them, and maybe I even felt we were eating "pretty high" because when I was a youngster, mushrooms in any form seldom came to my mother's dinner table. We simply did not eat many mushrooms and except for the rare wild varieties my mother gleaned from our woodlot, the fresh ones were simply unavailable. The only mushrooms we consistently knew came from metal cans.

Mushrooms were an "extra," and when fresh ones did show up they were talked about and we were careful to assure that everyone who wanted a taste had an opportunity to take some.

But, times change, and today fresh mushrooms are generally available at our grocery stores, and not just those nearly white buttons we usually purchase. No, today we can choose from a handful of fresh mushroom varieties. I do not buy mushrooms in a can anymore, preferring the fresh by a long shot.

Today I am thinking about mushrooms because they were often included in the great piles of food placed before me during our recent holidays, and they bring to mind a story that came my way last summer in which one of our town's visitors told how disappointed he was with a meal served him the night before. That restaurant meal did not meet his standards, and to top off his dismay he said the dish included canned mushrooms, not fresh ones. He thought that was terrible.

This little story reminds me that these days we not only prefer fresh mushrooms, but we have come to expect them. We have altered our behavior—added a new custom—and I must ponder this change. What has happened to us when we turn our nose up at something as innocuous as canned mushrooms?

I suspect there was a time in the past life of this fellow who complained of his dinner, when, like me, he may also have relished canned mushrooms. But now that fresh mushrooms are available almost every day of the year, he, like me, not only prefers them, he has come to expect them. We get "hooked" on things like fresh mushrooms, and if we have the discretionary cash, we buy them.

This incident reminds me of another remark a good friend made to me sometime last winter. We were in a popular local breakfast spot, one that offers a nice selection of crusty, homemade breads, when we expressed our appreciation for such culinary treats. My friend said he did not like the kind of bread that comes to town in big trucks anymore, but the look on his face told me he was a bit puzzled with such a turn of events. His look implied that our fresh crusty homemade bread is a bit pricy and now he spends more of his precious monthly budget on bread than he really should. Like the rest of us, this friend has come to prefer the "homemade" bread and, perhaps, now he expects it on a regular basis.

Times must be pretty good when we can have fresh mushrooms whenever we want. Never mind where they might have been grown, how they were grown, the expense of getting them to our dinner plate and all the rest. If we can afford fresh mushrooms and if we like them we probably will buy them. And if we like Australian wines, and have the cash, or credit, we probably will buy them, too.

This is the way it is now. We have the option to purchase fresh foods almost every day and if the money is in our pocket we might just reach for our wallet.

It seems to me we Americans are expecting a bit too much. I still hold memories of a grandmother bent over a kitchen workbench busily trimming thick layers of fat from a newly slaughtered pig for making her homemade bars of soap. And images of glass mason jars on basement fruit cellar shelves, lined up like a marching band waiting for the signal to begin the parade, are easily recalled. These jars held preserved—not fresh—fruits and vegetables that we relished all winter long.

In those long-ago days we thought such "canned" foods were just fine, but I wonder how we would feel about them today. Like our town's summer visitor, would we turn up our noses if they appeared on our dinner table? Or might we be a bit contemplative and consider what is really involved when we enjoy fresh foods at almost every meal set before us?

We relish fresh foods and since they usually are good for our health we should eat them as often as we can. But when we come to expect them it becomes another matter. This little story about a man who took offense at being served canned mushrooms might be saying something about the way we all have come to live.

Janus and the Maw of Winter

January 6, 2010

Today there can be no denying that we are heading into the heart of winter. Those weather mongers on radio, television, the Internet, and now on the trendy small hand-held techno-devices the kids have, keep cranking out the statistics showing our cold temperatures and depths of snow, and sometimes I think their job is to tell us what is obvious: there is no turning back. Winter is here. We are well into the month of January.

This cold month takes its name from the Roman god, Janus, who is said to have had two faces, one directed toward the future and the other toward the past. Among other things Janus was a guardian of gates and entranceways— really of boundaries—and was called upon at the onset of new undertakings like marriages and long, dangerous sojourns. The unknown future was put into his hands in hopes he would work to make it pleasurable. And as for the past, Janus reminded his followers that although they were entering a new year with a slate still unmarked, their deeds of the past year were being contemplated. Past behaviors did not simply vanish with the New Year.

Thoughts of Janus with his two faces come to mind these mornings now that the joyous warmth of Christmas and New Years is over. We have celebrated, and the reality of winter in Lake Superior Country sits before us, like a big hungry dog waiting to be fed. January in northern Wisconsin is a time to pay attention. These are not the carefree days of summer.

For the last several weeks each morning after rising and coming out into the dark kitchen I step into the living room to plug-in the Christmas tree's lights. Then I pause to take a look at that beautiful tree, and for just a moment I consider the sacrifice it made. In early December a friend and I kneeled down beside it out in John Hauser's tree lot to use a small and very sharp hand saw to cut it down. Now it stands in our house without its roots, and I ponder the ancient European custom of using a dead tree as a symbol of life; a symbol related to what is happening each morning this time of year as the vertical axis of the earth corrects itself.

Those ancient Romans knew what they were doing. They were in touch with their natural world as it moved through its annual cycle of changes. Yesterday when I saw a young lad exit his school after another busy day I noted that he was wearing shorts. He had a heavy winter coat, a hefty cap of some sort and large boots, but his legs were bare from his knees down. When I was in grade school my parents would never have left me out of the house dressed like that in January. What has happened to we moderns? What would the early Romans have said?

It might seem odd that January is the month situated at the heart of winter even though each of its days brings just a little more sunlight. January is about the cold of winter but also about the promising warmth of spring. Like its namesake, it looks backward and forward all at once.

When trying to understand this I am a bit befuddled. How did Janus do it? How did he contemplate the notions of past and future simultaneously? Perhaps it is best to turn to mathematics and remember that opposites cancel each other out, so in the case of January, where we stand at the threshold of both the year just over and the year just beginning, we are left to consider our location. We are in a truly nebulous space. The old year is still very fresh in our memories, while the new year eagerly beckons us on. We are betwixt and between. We are caught in the moment.

Maybe that is the key to January. After all is said and done, it is simply a time unto itself and we might take that realization as a cue to pause and take stock of its wonder. In January maybe the best is to refuse to contemplate what is behind and ahead–maybe we should just accept what is here now.

Yesterday's energetic young man exiting his school after spending another day with his friends might have figured it out. He was in the moment. His bare legs had to have felt the cold but he kept them moving and hopefully, he soon would be back indoors where it was warm. Maybe it is just the old men who think about things like automobiles slipping into ditches leaving their occupants stranded out in the cold. Maybe it is just old men who layer-up each morn before stepping outdoors. Besides, if something happened that young barelegged Janus-like lad could touch-in a number on his cell phone and help would soon be on its way.

I like that old Roman god Janus. Sometimes his two faces must have been bothersome, but I prefer to consider the positive. Janus was a synthesizer. He saw polarities—opposites, really—and he collapsed them into the here and now. He balanced things out, and gained the insight of the present. I think he would have enjoyed winter in Lake Superior Country.

On the Farmers' Market

August 9, 2009

FOR THE PAST FEW WEEKS HERE IN Red Cliff and Bayfield we have been enjoying our Saturday morning farmers' market. After a cold spring and early summer things are in full swing and the vendors' tables are filled with eye-catching fruits, vegetables, homemade baked items, fresh cut flowers and more. Last Saturday I was caused to ponder what I was witnessing when visiting the loaded tables and chatting with the people behind them. Most of the vendors were friends who I always enjoy seeing and sharing tidbits of news with, and when such conversations are carried out over a table of fresh, locally grown produce their value is doubled. Obviously, there is a psychology at work here, but I do not care if I am manipulated at these times. These are friends doing the manipulating, and what would we do without them?

There is so much to say about a well-stocked farmers' market and most of it might be old-hat, but last Saturday the setting was almost idyllic. The weather was cooperating—cool, but not demanding a sweater or sweatshirt—so we were comfortable and took our time selecting our purchases. A day like that probably helps customers loosen their purse strings and cause them to carry more produce back to their automobiles than they intended to. It was an unusually special day since for the first time in a long time my wife was free from her weekend job at the grocery store and we met at the market to make a few purchases. Good produce, good friends and a few moments with your bride of almost fifty years? How can a mix like that be anything but good?

When driving home with our prizes we pondered what it is like in societies where, in season, folks do most of their food buying at such open-air markets. In those cases all items they bring home are fresh, and hopefully, actually good for you, unlike when we purchase the familiar packaged and processed foods we often do.

For the first time this season Saturday's market held an abundance of onions. I love onions, especially scallions—what some of we older folk also know as "table onions"—and last week I was troubled with finding two of my friends offering these gems. I struggled with making a decision on which I should buy. So, trying not to show favorites, I purchased a bunch or two from both. This week I have been gorging on table onions. They are as mild as can be and are regulars at lunchtime when enjoying a sandwich out on our windy and cool deck. I think I have it pretty good.

Another item it is difficult to pass up are fresh greens. Last time I settled for a large handful of collard greens, that, when sliced into strips and sautéed in just a bit of olive oil turned out to be very good. These, with a side of brown rice and a serving of boiled fresh beets can not only fill your plate but your stomach, too. At such times, who needs the flesh of animals?

Fresh greens have become a favorite of mine. In fact, this summer I go to our backyard grape arbor, select a handful of large leaves, bring them into the kitchen and after washing and slicing pop them into the blender along with a bit of water and any fruit we have on hand. Yesterday along with two overripe bananas, an aging avocado went in as well. Such smoothies are like drinking green gold and make for a good lunch all by themselves.

The subject of eating fresh greens takes me back to my youth when about the only greens we ate on a regular basis were the tight heads of iceberg lettuce shipped in from California. We thought iceberg lettuce was the cat's pajamas. We usually got a small crop of leaf lettuce from our kitchen gardens in spring and early summer, but our lettuce often bolted, and my parents rarely tried growing spinach or other greens. Lettuce was not so important to us, and to be honest, back then eating greens on a daily basis was unheard of for my family. Mashed potatoes and a chunk of meat yes; greens, no. Maybe we associated eating greens with poor folk. Maybe we wanted to see ourselves living in the Big House rather than the small cabin out back.

Spinach was served now and then but it came from a can and it took me years to develop a taste for it. I grew up with Popeye and he made it seem that eating your spinach was akin to taking your cod liver oil. Popeye's serious promotion of spinach was a clear signal saying that it really was pretty awful stuff to get down, and I suspect that in those times he really was doing it a disservice. It took me years to accept spinach as a really tasty and good food. (And how about Wimpy? He was the fellow addicted to eating hamburgers. Such a cartoon character must have been good for the beef industry.)

Our local farmers' markets are an important part of life in these north woods. We are fortunate to have them and, of course, to have those farmers too!

OUR CANADA

March 1, 2009

YESTERDAY WHEN OUT AT THE Northern Great Lakes Visitor Center I was introduced to another sojourner of the paper trail we westerners leave behind us. This gentleman was tracking down some illusive forebears who happened to reside in these parts a hundred and fifty or more years ago, and he was a fount of information on matters of the British and Canadian power structures of that time. His articulateness and love of detail as well as his natural inquisitiveness and willingness to share set me to thinking.

He was Canadian, conversant in both English and French, and he knew what appeared to be tons about Canadian history, and, I soon learned, American and British as well. I know few Canadians and when I meet one I am interested in what they have to say, and yesterday's visitor was like a sudden ray of sunlight that unexpectedly breaks through the clouds, and for just an instant or two, illuminates your world. He had a quest, and his passionate pursuit was infectious. He claimed he recently came upon Hamilton Ross's early book on the history of Madeline Island in a used bookstore way out in British Columbia and it led him here. He wanted to see Madeline and what it could tell him about his ancestors.

What intrigues me this morning is how we here in the Northland live so close to Canada, but know so little about it. Except for a very brief introduction to world geography in grammar school that included the big country just to our north where the Eskimos lived, I learned nothing more of substance about the place. When in high school Canada was barely mentioned, and in college I took no courses on it. Its geology, geography, history, peoples, current issues, and art and literature remained practically unknown to me. In my later years there were some exceptions, of course, when I studied anthropology and when in a course or two we took a brief look at Canada's indigenous people and their struggles to meaningfully relate to Canadian authorities, but for the most part information on our northern neighbor simply was not stressed in my American education. Certainly in my earlier years I learned Canada was not a country I needed to study. It was up there all right, the globe showed us that, but it was rarely in the news.

We northern Wisconsinites are oriented to the south. Our important matters of commerce, politics, and whatnot generally emanate from that direction and maybe it is true that for most of us our really important things come to us—as older folks at Red Cliff used to tell me—from "down the line" not "up the line."

Perhaps this is what makes my encounter with the recent Canadian visitor so interesting. He was a stranger; he spoke with a slight accent, and he pronounced some words differently than I do. And of course he had a perspective on things that was just a little new to me. All of that piqued my interest and made me want to know more.

Last summer I had a similar experience when working in Stephen Dunker's Bayfield bookstore. One day a couple came in who were true book people and it was not long before they engaged me in a conversation about the history and current issues concerning Lake Superior and its southern shores. This couple was from Thunder Bay and it was good to converse with them. Among other things they reminded me that I must not put off my desire to take the Circle Tour around the big lake; that time really is "a-wastin'," like Snuffy Smith, the cartoon character, used to say. Interestingly, before they left the shop we exchanged cards and I agreed to accept their invitation to phone them when in their city so we could have a cup of tea.

Over this past year I have been exchanging emails with a few other Canadians about matters we are writing about, and hopefully, before too much time passes we also can get together in person to talk further. I want to learn more about Canada, and these good people are willing to share. Besides, I have in-laws who live up there, and it has been nearly fifty years since my wife and I paid them a visit. If we do not do it now, it might never get done.

What this recent Canadian visitor reminded me of was how insular we in the United States can be when it comes to people outside our borders, unless they have something we want, or they cause us to be troubled in some other way.

Canada is a foreign country that is very close to us, and its peaceful demeanor might have lulled us into complacency about it. Some of my friends go there to ski, or just to see its natural wonders, and a few go to fill their prescriptions, but not many of them get to know Canadians. I am the same. That fellow at the Visitor Center reminded me of this. He knew more about my land than I of his.

Well, maybe this summer I can head north of the border, place a few phone calls and make some connections. Maybe I can visit a few friends and have a cup of tea.

Chilean Pears

July 18, 2009

THIS WEEK A SMALL BOWL OF THOSE dark golden brown pears we purchase now and then appeared on our kitchen counter-top. These were Bosc pears, the slender type with flesh that can be as crisp as a Braeburn apple—and whose flavor resembles these popular apples. In my thinking the flavor of a Bosc pear does not meet the high standards of a Bartlett or more familiar variety, although it still is quite good. Yesterday when picking one up and looking it over before washing and eating it, I took time to read the stickie prominently appended to its swollen bottom. The little paper tab said the pear was from Chile. Yes, that long, thin country of the Mapuche Indians down on the far southwestern coast of South America. Surely, that Chilean pear set me to thinking.

An understanding of today's international economics is not my strong suit, but I had to ask myself why we were importing pears from a country so far away? I guessed it had to do with things like production costs, and that apparently according to someone's thinking it made sense to purchase these pears instead of more locally grown varieties. I have no knowledge about the specifics of the production of these golden brown pears, of insecticides and herbicides used, of the history of indigenous peoples' land loss regarding the fields in which they grew, of wages paid to persons who did the heavy lifting of their production and harvesting, nor of the jet fuel burned to get them here. Let's be candid—when I bit into that pear I was doing what some folks call "mindless eating." In other words I was simply letting my need for nourishment take precedence over other motivations for my behavior.

We humans are an adaptable species, and some say this ability to adjust to a myriad of situations is what has kept us here for the million or so years we have been on this planet. After all, we are the species that thinks our way along life's path rather than instinctively reacting to things and situations.

But sometimes I suspect a good degree of our behavior is carried out without much thought. Bosc pears from Chile? Don't our fruit growers produce Bosc pears right here in North America? What are the ramifications of me purchasing

Chilean Bosc pears in far northern Wisconsin in August? Am I really so thoroughly enmeshed in a worldwide system of commerce that I must simply continue to involve myself even further? Is it good for me to purchase these Chilean pears?

These are not questions I usually raise because they could open a virtual Pandora's box of complexities that might befuddle me. Gasoline, oil, food, clothing, plastics, steel, lumber—perhaps all commodities coming to my house from some distant place. And perhaps someone with more astuteness regarding our current state of world economics would say, yes, they do come from distant places, and that's why it is so important I use them. I might be told that as a citizen of the world it is my responsibility to take part in its system of international commerce.

Well, be that as it may, I still must ask why I eat pears that come from the tip of South America when I live way up in North America? And as long as we are speaking of stickies, only this week I noticed a clutch of nice looking tomatoes with stickies saying they came from Canada. Canada? Tomatoes from Canada?

My coffee comes from Meso-America, I think my tea comes from somewhere across an ocean, and although I try to purchase only local honey I suspect some of the honey I use comes from China. Several years ago after purchasing what I thought was an American-made automobile and driving it for a few years I happened to pay attention to another stickie. This was a paper label appended to one of its inside door jambs where I had not noticed it before. I was taken aback when upon reading its fine print I learned that a large part of my car's parts came from places outside the continental United States. My automobile was assembled in America but many of its components were manufactured elsewhere.

About thirty years ago some of us who taught social science classes liked to have our students read a popular essay that told of this person who rose most mornings to do his bathroom ablutions and after using all sorts of things that were either made or first invented "overseas," he looked into his medicine cabinet's mirror and soberly gave thanks for being one hundred percent American. His naiveté was meant to be both humorous and thought provoking to our students.

Well, Bosc pears, coffee, tomatoes from north of our other border, tea, the foreign parts to my "American" car—these and more tell us something important about how we live today. There was a time in America when we took pride in being able to purchase and use valued products that came from another part of the world. But there are voices that ask us to think about what this penchant to purchase the "imported" has done to us, and to our planet earth. So I wonder: do we need Bosc pears from Chile?

Remembering Bill Holm

March 16, 2009

Bill Holm passed away on 25 February 2009, in Sioux Falls, South Dakota, after returning from Patagonia. He was sixty-five and about a year ago retired from a long term of teaching English at the university in Marshall, Minnesota. His death is said to have been due to complications from pneumonia.

Notice of Bill's exit might have been published in one of our local newspapers, but if so, I missed it. Who was Bill Holm—and why does news of his passing stop me in my tracks this bright, sunny mid-March morning on this snow covered Bayfield hillside? Today I have a writing deadline shouting at me, a chocolate Labrador patiently waiting for me to take her out to Orchard Country for our daily walk, and my bride's list of other pressing chores desperately needing to be done—but how can I push Bill Holm's death aside until I have time to accept it later today? No, I will take time for Bill and his wonderfully ebullient life right now.

Bill was a writer of poetry and prose, a musician, a singer of life. He was a seeker of what is right in this often not-so-right world. He must have snorted at the sadness of Bernie Madoff and his cadre of tower-top wealth-seekers and all of the other nonsense we have recently read and heard about in America. Bill once said that when he began writing years ago as a young man his pieces were so harshly political that he finally tossed them aside and decided to write about what really held his interest; what he really knew, and loved. That is when he returned to Mineota, Minnesota, his small southwestern Minnesota town, and that is when success came his way. Perhaps we could say he wrote about little things, maybe even common things, but as he must have known all along, these are the really big things, after all.

To know Bill Holm was to catch your breath, stand back, and try to take all of him in. Those of us who were just outside that circle of really close friends stood by to watch. But there would be times when we could get up close, and then we welcomed the fresh air from his voice, the essential wisdom from his prose. Bill had a presence that could fill a room, and he would not abide a fool.

Perhaps in northern Wisconsin only the local literati knew of him. After all, we have our own favorites and passions right here in our woodsy backyard. But, it interests me how so few local people I know confess never to have heard of him. It's a big world and we cannot take it all in.

For those of us who notice such things and love to hold forth about them, Bill was part of that category of persons who somehow escaped the mainstream of economic and political this-n-that which consumes the bulk of time for many of us. Right from the start, he chose not be strive to be one of the conventional leaders in his society, instead siding-up to those who were pushed to the periphery by the whirlwind of commerce these leaders are fascinated with. He chose to get to know, and appreciate, those quieter folks who often go unnoticed by the fast walkers and fast talkers. His forte was to cozy up to the man who mopped the bank's lobby instead of to the man who lived his life in the obviously oversized rear office.

It is endlessly interesting how we humans choose to spend our lives on this planet earth. Most of us buy the package thrust at us when we begin learning The Three R's, and we go on to wear our harnesses well. We get the work of society done; even fight its wars when called upon. When it is time to pick up a pen and vote, we do so, and every several days we show up at our holy sites with the others and give thanks to our god. We are virtually completely system oriented, and we seem to love it. But there are others who live amongst us—those friends and acquaintances that may even labor right beside us—who remain distant from it all.

These persons are just as essential as those who show up at their workstations on time day after day, and do a fairly good job of paying their bills when due. These poets, or bards, can cause us to pause and take stock of our lives in important ways.

A friend once told me the prairie of far southwestern Minnesota was a wasteland. "There is nothing there," she insisted. I listened and marveled how some people can be so different, and still be friends. Bill Holm was one of those fortunate persons who went home and grew to love the place in which he was born. In the early years of his writing career he once remarked, "Writing in America is like dropping a handful of feathers into the Grand Canyon and waiting to hear them hit bottom." Bill went home and after time began to hear the thunderous sounds of his "feathers" hitting the Grand Canyon's floor. Those "feathers" can be found in the many books, articles, and other forms of his work.

DUMPING IT IN THE WOODS

May 4, 2009

NOW THAT OUR SNOWCOVER HAS LEFT US and the true greenup is only getting underway we are in that in-between time after the end of winter and the rich, green onrush of spring. It is a special time, a window of only a week or two before the grasses grow long enough to once again shield our eyes from the detritus, or fallout, of our annual cold time. I am speaking, of course, of roadside litter and how each year at this time we are reminded how some of us still reside in a place where we seem to say "out of sight—out of mind." As much as I feel we Americans have genuinely become aware of the importance of what is called our stewardship of the land, and as much as I enjoy reading environmental literature I must accept the reality that not all of my neighbors feel as I do about such things.

It is easy to recall a time when I, too, threw all sorts of refuse out a speeding automobile's window, but that was years and years ago and much has changed regarding our understanding of our place in this world. Now we know of the connectedness of things—of the systemic nature of our existence. We no longer see ourselves as unattached from other forms of life in the ways we did in the past.

Last week I did some roadside pick-up on my morning walk. It is easy to do and it allows me to feel that in this little gesture I am doing some good. At the end of my journey my plastic bag was full of aluminum beer and pop cans, plastic pop bottles, and a few other items. As I had noticed last summer, someone who travels that stretch of road likes his (or her) vodka. The empty, small, pocket-sized clear plastic bottles I discovered last season have returned, discarded into the ditch after being gulped down by someone, I presume, driving that road.

The beer and pop cans might seem innocuous compared to the vodka bottles. A very good friend of mine—a helicopter side-door machine gunner in Vietnam—drank himself to death with vodka, so when I bend down to pick up these emptied small bottles I see him—and relive that last phone call he placed to me the night before he died. My friend was still at war, and I wonder if the person who tossed these small bottles is fighting a battle, too. In some cases we do not really know our neighbors.

Roadside litter could be part of all sorts of stories. Most, I suspect, would tell of youthful exuberance and its joyful experimentation with life, and if correct, this roadside dumping will soon pass. I don't mind picking up after such youngsters, because they likely will soon go on to other, more productive things. I will cut them some slack.

But, just last week while out on my morning romp I spotted a spent rubber tire, tossed into the woods beside the roadway. A bit further on, beside a small trickling creek that is active only during the time of the spring runoff, lay more household debris. Then I noticed a child's heavy, metal swing set, lying on its side, discarded into the ditch, and I recalled how last summer I came upon a spent automobile oil filter canister and five empty plastic quart oil cans. After changing his (or her) vehicle's oil the person had taken the time to drive to an isolated, wooded stretch of roadway and carefully placed these items just on the far side of the ditch, into the woods.

The fact that some of us see the forest, or woods, as a place where we can safely discard such unwanted items tells us something about our perception of the world. In Northern Wisconsin woods surround us, and to some of us the woods might still be that diffuse and distant place "out there." It could be a place few people enter, and therefore it is outside our usual, important, and safe place. In this way, the woods might still be that dark place of myth and legend where witches and all sorts of unwelcome figures reside. Early European literature depicts the woods, or forest, as the shadow of civilization, meaning it is the dark side of our existence. In this case, the woods is a place representing our discontents, and more. It is for wild animals—like bears and wolves—and a place to which criminals might retreat. As such it is a lawless place that stands like a dark wall around our farms and villages, threatening our civilized existence.

Whoa! This is a far cry from mere roadside litter. Besides, a few beer and pop cans are minor when we call to mind the tall chimneys in China belching out toxic smoke and steam, and our own industrial and energy producing plants that still contaminate our air, water and earth. The obscenity of the Exxon oil spill up in Alaska is fading in our memories, but it still comes to mind, and our state's regular issuance of fish advisories is another reminder that we are still trashing our surrounding countryside.

Well, it is a good time of year even if these days we are forced to witness the litter of our lives.

ON GROWING OLD

April 27, 2010

FOR SOME REASON THIS SPRING I THINK a lot about growing old. Maybe it is the spate of funerals of older friends and acquaintances we have been having lately, or maybe it is the new aches and pains that have been visiting me with more regularity these last few months. Whatever is going on, being one of our town's elderly is on my mind.

There is comfort in growing old, and there are realities, the obvious one being that there is no option to aging, so I must make the best of it. But I am speaking of something else, something almost ineffable—that is, something about the innermost nature of growing old and the opportunities it avails. Perhaps older readers will know what I am trying to say. What is it about growing old that makes it different from anything else?

It is a bit humbling to realize you are often the oldest person at a social gathering, and without any obvious prompt, you are given a chair before others, and sometimes even waited upon. At Red Cliff, when the call for Elders to step up to the head of the food line is made, I find some people quietly looking at me as they wait to fall in behind. A few years ago when that happened the first time I was taken aback, but now have grown accustomed to this new deference, and accept it quietly. What else can one do but accept it? We should show grace in our growing old.

This morning when out with my two four-legged furry companions on our daily walk I had time to reflect on this. It was sunny, and that downright chilly breeze from our big lake we have felt so much this month was reaching up the hill we were walking on when I realized I no longer walk the way I used to. Now I move deliberately, mindful of where I place each foot. And, lately I have been using a new walking stick, compliments of a caring Red Cliff sister-in-law. As I moved along with those two dogs I wondered if the new, attractive stick added a bit of style to my walking, but quickly pushed such thoughts out of mind. Who cares about things like style at my age? I was just glad to be out there.

When I think about the elders I knew as a youngster, different sorts of people come to mind. Some seemed not to notice we kids at the fringes of extended family gatherings, but some seemed unable not to notice us. These latter folks were openly embracing, like one of my grandmothers who sought my brothers and me out when it was time for us to go home—time to leave the crowd that had come for dinner. She invariably had hugs and warm parting words for us, and in the process slipped homemade treats into our side pockets. She knew what she was doing, and after these seventy plus years I remember her still. How can you not love a grandmother like that?

In some interesting ways, it is a wonderful ride to be growing old. No longer faced with the responsibilities of rising five days a week and going off to perform some job or set of tasks for others, now I am free and usually have the whole day to myself. I don't need to perform for anyone anymore. Since retiring I earn my living another way. Now I work at growing old.

But just what is it I am working at? What is that inner quality of becoming an elder? Is it something as simple as The Golden Rule? Is it just the old admonition to be good to others? Struggling with this question, this morning I decided to see what my thirteen-year-old granddaughter thought about it. This beautiful girl is excited about her life as she embarks on the journey of her teenage years, so when driving her to school after telling her what I was trying to discover about growing old, I asked, "If the young live for the moment, what do the old live for?" Without batting an eye, she replied, "Maybe the moment lives for them."

That remark stopped me, and I quietly marveled at this girl's insightfulness. She had turned my question on its head, and after arriving at her school her challenging wisdom stayed with me as I drove the few miles home. Could it be that "the moment" lives for we old-timers? What did that girl mean?

Growing old can be debilitative, a process during which something is lost. But I choose to see it as a process wherein something is added. We elders are like crescent moons—always getting larger until the circle is completely filled in. It is then—when we are full-circle—that we really can shine. In other words, aging is a crescive process. It is a taking-on of something valuable. And now my granddaughter has caused me to ponder how my constant surroundings— "the moment"—is allowing me to be all I can be.

Well, be that as it may. Growing old is something to think about. And today one of my granddaughters reminded me that I am a lucky man. Today I will focus on the pleasure of being alive in this time and place—in this moment.